DAWN POWELL

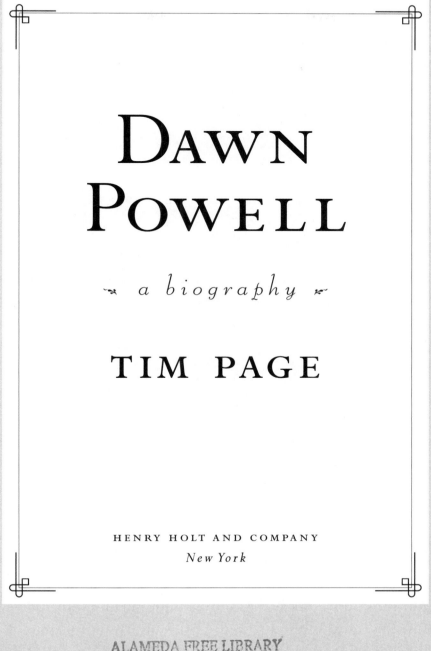

DAWN POWELL

a biography

TIM PAGE

HENRY HOLT AND COMPANY
New York

Henry Holt and Company, Inc.
Publishers since 1866
115 West 18th Street
New York, New York 10011

Henry Holt® is a registered trademark of
Henry Holt and Company, Inc.

Library of Congress Cataloging-in-Publication Data
Page, Tim, 1954–
Dawn Powell : a biography / Tim Page.
Includes bibliographical references and index.
ISBN 0-8050-5068-X (HB : acid-free paper)
1. Powell, Dawn—Biography.   2. Women authors,
American—20th century—Biography.   I. Title.
PS3531.0936Z46   1998
813'.52—dc21   98-19907
[B]   CIP

First Edition 1998

Designed by Ellen Cipriano

Printed in the United States of America
All first editions are printed on acid-free paper.∞

1   3   5   7   9   10   8   6   4   2

For Jack Sherman, with love and gratitude —

❧

and for the cherished memory of G. Christopher Fish

Wits are never happy people. The anguish that
has scraped their nerves and left them raw to every
flicker of life is the base of wit — for the raw nerve
reacts at once without any agent, the reaction direct
with no integumentary obstacles. Wit is
the cry of pain, the true word that pierces the heart.
If it does not pierce, then it is not true wit.
True wit should break a good man's heart.

DAWN POWELL, 1939

❧

It is the soul's highest duty to be of good cheer.

RALPH WALDO EMERSON

❧ CONTENTS ❧

Hart Island——1998

∾⁂∾

Blessed are the poor
In spirit   for theirs is
The kingdom of heaven

My child
Peace I leave to you
My peace I give to you

The Almighty
Has His own purposes
He must have loved them
He made so many of them

Cry not for us
For we are with the Father
No longer do we cast shadows
On the ground as you do
We are at peace

These words——an idiosyncratic combination of phrases adapted from Scripture and from folk wisdom——are carved into a dark granite monument at New York City Cemetery, on Hart Island. The 101-

acre island, unknown to most New Yorkers and accessible only by a restricted ferry from the upper reaches of the Bronx, serves as the city's potter's field, a public burial ground for the unknown and impoverished. Since its first interment—the body of a young orphan, Louisa Van Slyke, who died at Manhattan's Charity Hospital in 1869—Hart Island has provided a final resting place for some three quarters of a million souls, many of them unidentified, all of them lying in mass, unmarked graves.

Between two and three thousand fresh burials take place on Hart Island annually. These are accomplished using inmate labor from the municipal prison on Riker's Island, with teams of volunteers receiving thirty-five cents an hour for their work. Adults are buried 150 bodies deep, while the coffins of infants and children are stacked a thousand high. Hart Island is a remote and haunted place; only the occasional buzz of jets flying to and from nearby La Guardia Airport and the distant skyline of Manhattan will remind the cemetery's rare visitors (it is not generally open to the public) that they are well within the boundaries of the largest metropolis in the United States.

The people buried on Hart Island would seem to have had one thing in common: bad luck. Here are the lost vagrants pulled frozen from their sleeping bags, the city's miscarried babies, the corpses dredged up from the Hudson River every spring, eroded beyond recognition. Finally, here are countless unfortunate New Yorkers who simply outlived their families, their friends, and their funds.

Now and again there will be a burial "by mistake" on Hart Island; shortly thereafter, a family member or old friend will usually appear, file some papers, and arrange for removal. There are about a hundred such disinterments annually, "but almost all of those take place within a few months of the burial," according to a spokesman for the New York City Department of Correction, which oversees the cemetery. "Because our burials are so simple—plain pine caskets stacked on top of one another deeply into the ground—after a few years you really can't tell one person from the next."

The remains of Dawn Powell were buried on Hart Island in the springtime of 1970, almost five years after her death. She is believed to be the only "celebrity" in the cemetery. The strange way in which one of America's great writers—a brilliant wit, a friend to many wealthy and influential people, a woman blessed with a large and loving extended family that would have cared for her—came to this place is just one of many implausible stories to be told in this book.

The author herself would likely have been grimly amused by such a turn of events. It might have made for a particularly bleak witticism, perhaps even a scene in one of her satirical novels. At the very least, she could have consoled herself that she was now forever a part of her beloved New York; indeed, her adopted city had even paid for the funeral.

Powell came to New York in 1918, at the age of twenty-one, a gifted and ambitious young woman from small-town Ohio. There she would live for the next forty-seven years, most of the time in Greenwich Village, that first and most fabled of American bohemias. Yet she would never affect the blasé ennui of the "seen-it-all" New Yorker; throughout her life she would refer to herself as a "permanent visitor," and exalt the multiplicity and sheer sensory overload of her Manhattan.

She wanted to write, and write she did: dozens of poems, hundreds of short stories and articles, at least ten plays, magnificent diaries that span three and a half decades, and—the accomplishment that meant the most to her—a number of dizzying and inventive novels. Absolutely unsentimental about mortality, she would have been far more concerned about what happened to her work than about what became of her exhausted body. As a character in Powell's first acknowledged novel puts it, shyly allowing a new friend to read her writing, "This—well, this is *me*."

When Powell died, in 1965, virtually all of her books were out of print. Not a single historical survey of American literature mentioned her, even in passing. Among the best-known critics, only Powell's friend Edmund Wilson had examined her work with anything like the seriousness it deserved. She seemed destined to be forgotten— or, to phrase it more exactly, never to be remembered.

Instead, more than thirty years after her death, Powell's work is now more popular than ever. It was Henry James who so memorably predicted a day when his books would all kick off their headstones, one after another; something similar has happened to Dawn Powell in the last decade of the twentieth century. As I write this, eleven of her fifteen novels are once again available, and the publication of her diaries in 1995 was hailed on the front page of the *New York Times Book Review* as bringing to light "one of the outstanding literary finds of the past quarter-century."

Such a large-scale revival is decidedly out of the ordinary. To find a parallel in American writing, we must go back to the 1950s and the great posthumous recognition of Nathanael West (the resurrection of F. Scott Fitzgerald was a different matter, for he had once been enormously popular). In most cases, writers who are undervalued during their lifetimes are forgotten after their deaths. Contrary to one of the many legends that have sprung up in recent years, Powell was not entirely an unknown—as one friend recalled, she was "generally considered a good novelist of the second class"—but at least in part because she was so amusing and enjoyable to read, she was rarely taken for the exacting artist that she was.

Reading through the notices Powell received during her more than forty years as a novelist and playwright, one comes to the conclusion that her reputation also suffered through her blunt, plainspoken honesty and her determined resistance to any form of Utopian idealism. She displeased social conservatives with characters who drank, slept around, and behaved foolishly and without discernible moral scruples, yet who still managed not only to get by but to *enjoy* themselves in the world, with no threat of impending damnation. For critics on the left, one suspects that Powell's satire wasn't quite angry enough. She had fun; she never suggested that any revolution, past or present, could change fundamental human nature; she drew her millionaires with as much affection and acerbity as her workers, finding them equally inane, deluded, transparent, and—despite it all—rather likable. As Gore Vidal, who did much to revive Powell's work, wrote in 1987, "She saw life with a bright Petronian neutrality, and every host at life's feast was a potential Trimalchio to be sent up."

Powell was mystified when readers found her characters cold and unfeeling. "The artist who really loves people loves them so well the way they are he sees no need to disguise their characteristics," she noted in her diary. "He loves them whole, without retouching. Yet the word always used for this unqualifying affection is 'cynicism.' "

Her great subject was the secular Pilgrim's Progress of small-town boys and girls who (like their author) come to the Big City to prove their worth—and, not so incidentally, have a grand old time in its barrooms and bedrooms along the way. In her Ohio novels, her favorite characters are usually striving to uproot themselves and run away, most often to Manhattan; in her New York novels, her dubious heroes are caught up in new lives within the urban maelstrom but seared by memories of their early years in provincial small towns. All of this makes Powell sound like a "one-book novelist," and there is a certain validity to the charge. Unlike most such writers, however, Powell succeeded in varying her theme in each new book, and almost all of those variations are worth reading.

Powell lived a restless and troubled life. Her youth was a ghastly one, a long series of deaths, disruptions, and petty cruelties. Her only son was born mentally and emotionally impaired, and her husband became a chronic alcoholic. She drank too much herself and suffered from mysterious health problems for most of her days. Her mood swings were drastic and sometimes incapacitating. In her mid-sixties, she was desperately poor and, indeed, essentially homeless for a time.

Throughout it all, she persevered—and now, with the reissue of her life's work, she has triumphed. That is part of the story, too, a story that has been too long delayed.

DAWN POWELL

❧

CHAPTER ONE

Story of a Country Girl

~≫≪~

All of Ohio is simply infested with my family,
the Powells and the Shermans, and at a distance
I get quite sentimental about them.

DAWN POWELL, 1928

THE TOWN OF MOUNT GILEAD lies amid the gold and
verdant farmlands of central Ohio, some forty miles north of
Columbus and a world away from New York City. Settled by 1817, it
was incorporated in 1824; since 1848, when Morrow County was
fashioned from portions of the four adjoining counties of Richland,
Knox, Marion, and Delaware, Mount Gilead has served as the
county seat.

Whetstone Creek provided power for grist and saw mills, and
the town prospered. By the late nineteenth century, Mount Gilead
was a community of some twelve hundred people, linked to the
rest of the country through the New York Central train line. In addition to the small businesses—groceries, pharmacies, law offices, and

undertakers—that flanked Main and Marion Streets, there was a medium-size factory, the Hydraulic Press Manufacturing Company, which, at various times in its history, employed more than an eighth of the population. Grand Victorian mansions with expansive lawns, porches, and gingerbread gazebos were built on the hilly outskirts, with smaller, more utilitarian clapboard houses nearer the village square. The town boasted an established hotel, the Globe, and a disproportionately large opera house, Levering Hall, which could seat almost a thousand people and accommodated visiting musicians and lecturers, vaudeville shows, and high school commencements.

Mount Gilead was soon recognized as a classic American small town—as late as 1940, the *WPA Ohio Guide* could praise its "unusually handsome residences and public buildings"—and there remain long, unpeopled vistas of fields and farmhouses on the state roads outlying the town center that are virtually unchanged from the day Elroy Powell and Hattie Blanche Sherman were married: September 12, 1894.

Nobody who is alive today is certain how or when they met. Roy, as he was always called, was born in Morrow County on August 24, 1869,* the son of Samuel Powell and Henrietta Walker Powell. The Powell family, of Welsh-Irish descent and mostly millers or merchants, had come to the area in 1848 from Loudoun County, Virginia.

Only a few photographs of Roy Powell have survived, and most of them date from his final years, when, though only in his midfifties, he was bald, paunchy, and prematurely aged. The one known picture from his youth presents a good-looking, well-groomed man with a dapper mustache. Around 1890, he assumed the middle name King to go along with Elroy (which he sometimes spelled "El Roy"). He seems to have been possessed of an immediate and considerable charm,

---

*Both Roy Powell's and Hattie Sherman Powell's headstones give incorrect dates—1868 for Roy's birth, 1902 for Hattie's death. In both cases, town records, obituaries, and family documents confirm the subsequent years.

but he was also rakish and irresponsible and had difficulty holding on to jobs. He worked in several mills in and around Morrow County and served a brief stint as the night manager of the Globe Hotel. But he was happiest as a salesman, meandering through Ohio, Michigan, Pennsylvania, and the surrounding states, reportedly purveying (among other things) perfume, bedding, cherries, cookies, and coffins.

Hattie Sherman's family had roots in Morrow County dating back the better part of a century. In 1810, Amasa Shaerman, a farmer from Washington County, New York, had moved to an area called Bethel, a few miles to the southwest of Mount Gilead. Bethel was neither junction nor town but rather a vast expanse of farm country (in the early nineteenth century, it was possible to buy prime Ohio land for two dollars an acre, with up to five years to pay it off). There the Shaermans built a large house that was passed on from generation to generation until about 1900; the family's dead were buried across the road in the Bethel Cemetery.

Judd Sherman, Hattie's father, was born in the farmhouse in 1828. He was the grandson of Amasa Shaerman and the only son of Delano and Catherine Chapman Sherman (who had by then modified the spelling of the family name). Judd divided his time between working as a trainman and conductor on the B & O and Big Four railroad lines and farming his land. He was married twice, first to Louisa Miller, who died shortly thereafter, leaving one son, Ross Sherman. In 1863, Judd wed nineteen-year-old Julia Ann Miller (no relation to his first wife), who bore him eight more children, seven of whom lived to adulthood.

Julia Miller Sherman prided herself upon being descended from one of the first nineteen families in Cardington, another small town in Morrow County ("It never seemed to me there were many more than that there even 100 years later," her granddaughter would observe wryly in 1933). Miller legend had it that their heritage included Cherokee Indian blood thanks to the kidnapping and impregnation of a daughter sometime in the eighteenth century; it was also believed that the historical "Johnny Appleseed," John Chapman, was a direct ancestor.

Hattie Sherman, born on March 24, 1872, was the third child of Judd and Julia Sherman; like her father and siblings, she was delivered in the Bethel farmhouse. Family tales of Hattie suggest a woman who was both gentle and strong, and her sole existing photographic portrait supports such an impression. Hattie was said to be quick-witted, expert with horses, an aficionado of midwestern thunderstorms. By all reports, she was devoted to the footloose and improvident Roy Powell—and, later, to their children.

In the course of their nine-year marriage, Roy and Hattie Sherman had three daughters: Mabel (born July 11, 1895), Dawn (November 28, 1896), and Phyllis (December 29, 1899). The older girls were born at 53 West North Street (now demolished and replaced), in the center of Mount Gilead; in early 1899, the family moved a few hundred feet away, to a tiny house that still stands at 115 Cherry Street, where Phyllis was born. Sometime during the 1920s, Dawn apparently decided to drop a year from her age and thereafter gave her birth date as November 28, 1897, the day that has since been stated as fact in almost everything published about her. However, each and every primary source before 1925 (including the U.S. Censuses for 1900, 1910, and 1920, her records from high school, her transcript from Lake Erie College, her marriage license, and other documents) has served to confirm the earlier date.

From the beginning, the slight, dark-haired, ruddy-cheeked Dawn was phenomenally bright and, like many prodigies, well aware of her gifts. Within the family, her memory was renowned; she even claimed to remember being taken to the Bethel farmhouse as an infant. She was reading before she was five; by the age of nine, she had made her way through the complete works of Alexandre Dumas. Dawn also invented elaborate stories for the enjoyment of little Phyllis, who was regularly left in her care, and delighted in creating impromptu plays with friends and relatives. In the eyes of her father, Dawn was the "clever one," as opposed to Mabel, whom he called the "pretty one," and Phyllis, the beloved baby and perpetual plaything.

Despite numerous promises to give up the road and settle down in Mount Gilead, Roy Powell soon returned to his itinerant rounds of hotels and night trains, leaving Hattie to cope as best she could with their three small children. Many in the Sherman family would later shun him for this behavior, but Dawn, however disappointed she may have been at the time, always defended her father and seems to have identified closely with him from an early age. In her autobiographical novel *My Home Is Far Away*, she describes Marcia Willard, the character modeled on herself, as feeling "light-headed and gay, the way Papa did when he was going away from home. She thought she must be like Papa, the kind of person who was always glad going away instead of coming home." Dawn would look upon traditional home life with distrust: "Any barroom brawl is better than the persistent pinpricks of the happy little family," she wrote in 1936.

Dawn's childhood was ruptured, rudely and irrevocably, on December 6, 1903, when Hattie Powell died in Shelby, Ohio, at the age of thirty-one. The official cause of death was given as pneumonia. However, two surviving daughters of Dawn's sisters recall their respective mothers' telling them repeatedly that Hattie had in fact died as a result of a botched abortion—an operation that was then, of course, illegal and often either self-administered or performed under hurried and unsanitary conditions.

As Hattie Powell's body lay on a flowered bier, Roy lifted his daughters to say a final good-bye. Then three years old, Phyllis later remembered that Hattie's face was covered with red blotches, and throughout her remaining eighty-two years of life, she would never again be able to tolerate the smell of carnations. The young mother was buried in Shelby's Oakland Cemetery.

There followed a nomadic period for Dawn, Mabel, and Phyllis. "Since the father traveled, the three small daughters were dispatched from one relative to another, from a year of farm life with this or that aunt, to village life, life in small-town boarding houses, life with very prim strict relatives, to rougher life in the middle of little factory towns," Dawn wrote in a 1942 biographical entry she supplied for the reference book *Twentieth-Century Authors.*

These towns included Galion, Shelby, Crestline, and Cardington, as well as the somewhat larger city of Mansfield, all within a fifty-mile radius of Mount Gilead. In Mansfield, Powell was for a semester a classmate of Louis Bromfield, a near-exact contemporary who also attended Marion Street School and later became a bestselling novelist. It is doubtful that the two were ever friends, but in any event, Powell would heartily dislike Bromfield's work and resent his success.

In August 1907, Roy Powell remarried. As so often in most matters throughout his life, he made the wrong choice. His bride, Sabra Stearns Powell, thirty years old, hailed from one of the founding families of North Olmsted, Ohio, then a hamlet just to the southwest of Cleveland. Her grandfather Elijah Stearns had settled there in 1815 on a thousand acres of two-dollar land abutting the Butternut Ridge Road, an important east-west thoroughfare. Asher and Emily Stearns, her father and mother, lived and farmed on a parcel of the original Stearns farm; Sabra, the older of their two daughters, had worked as a schoolteacher and a cashier.

No one knows what drew Roy to Sabra, who was a tense, anxious woman with a perennially pinched expression. But Roy's three daughters believed it might have been the promise of some inherited wealth—the main chance. Shortly after the marriage, Roy gathered his scattered clan back together again, and they all moved into a spacious farmhouse in North Olmsted, which was several times larger and infinitely grander than any place they had lived in before.

Then, as was his custom, Roy immediately took to the road and abandoned Mabel, Dawn, and Phyllis to Sabra's care.

Standards of discipline were stricter in the first decades of the twentieth century than they are today. But even so, and even if some of the stories told about Sabra Stearns Powell are exaggerated or false, enough evidence remains to convict her as a genuinely wicked stepmother, unbelievably vicious and sadistic. She beat the three girls regularly, almost, it seems, as a form of physical exercise, and behaved, on occasion, so bizarrely that a latter-day chronicler must question her sanity.

A particularly ghastly example: in 1914, Sabra gave birth to a premature baby, Emily Helen Powell, who lived only five days. After Sabra recovered consciousness and her convalescence ended, she was furious to learn that her first child had already been buried in what she considered to be less than proper clothing. And so, with her husband and fourteen-year-old Phyllis in tow, she insisted upon traveling to the cemetery, where they dug up the tiny corpse and reburied it in the dress of the one and only doll Phyllis was permitted to own.

This is the stuff of Gothic horror; the day-to-day torments were more along the line of constant, petty humiliation. The children were not allowed to enter by the front door, to sit in the living room, to play the piano, or to touch any of the books in the house, which were kept under lock and key. (This last proscription was especially galling to Dawn, who was already a voracious reader.) A kindly neighbor taught little Phyllis how to crochet and gave her a hook and yarn to work with on her own; Sabra took the gifts away because she said they made the girl "nervous." When the desperately interested child tried to resume her new hobby, practicing with the poor substitutes of hairpins and string, Sabra banished those, too.

"Stepmother's greatest joy was in making us go downtown on errands, with no hems in our ragged calico skirts (and forbidden needle and thread to sew them as Waste) so our schoolmates would sneer," Dawn recalled in a 1941 diary entry. "Another sadistic treat for her was to make us come out on [the] porch on Monday morning and run wringer or washboard in worn-out Sunday dress (instead of cute bungalow aprons like other girls) in full view of the children playing so they could mock us."

Such treatment cemented a firm, if sometimes uneasy, bond among the three sisters, who united in a conscious struggle to live through Sabra's abuse. Dawn was closer to Phyllis; a certain resentment on her part toward Mabel (the "pretty one") had probably begun even before their mother's death. Surviving family members unanimously remember Mabel Powell (later Pocock) as a warm, generous, gallant woman, but Dawn would never dedicate any of her books to her older sister, corresponded with her only rarely, and painted a far from flattering portrait of her in *My Home Is Far Away*, the novel based so directly on the early lives of Mabel, Dawn, and Phyllis that in early drafts the characters were sometimes identified by their true names.

"My mother was beautiful and contented," Dorothy Pocock Chapman, Mabel's daughter, said in 1994. "She was married very young and very happily to a successful businessman. They lived well, in a big house in a beautiful neighborhood, and they raised three healthy children. When I think of all the struggles Aunt Dawn went through—all of her life, really—I can understand why the relative ease of my mother's life might have bothered her."

Phyllis Powell's middle daughter, Phyllis Poccia, offered an alternative explanation for the schism: "Aunt Mabel and my mother were interested in material possessions, in collecting things, owning things," she said. "Aunt Dawn wasn't interested in that at all. She had her possessions—lots of them—but they were in her mind."

Dawn and Mabel would become closer to one another in later life; for several years in the 1930s and 1940s, the three sisters and their families would gather every summer at a cottage that Dawn rented on Long Island. "They loved to laugh," Carol Warstler, Phyllis Poccia's older sister, recalled of those visits. "They'd get together and close the door and laugh so hard that we'd think something was wrong with them. We weren't invited in—and husbands weren't especially welcome, either. They'd go off by themselves and just laugh and laugh—probably to keep from crying, I don't know."

Their harrowing upbringing scarred the three sisters. "I realize more and more how instinctively pessimistic I am of all human kindness—since I am always so bowled over by it—and am never surprised by injustice, malice or personal attack," Powell wrote in 1933. Each of the daughters eventually ran away from home; only Phyllis subsequently returned, and then just for a little while. Still, Phyllis and Mabel finally made an uneasy peace with their step-mother, and Phyllis remained in touch with her until Sabra died, in 1956. Consequently, several of Sabra's step-granddaughters knew her quite well.

"There was something really wrong with Sabra," Phyllis Poccia said in 1995. "I think she was cruel because of some kind of disease rather than by intention. She was very sour, always looking as if she'd swallowed a lemon. And she was obsessive about tidiness, with an unbelievable hatred of any clutter, anything out of place. My mother used to say that Sabra spent her life chasing a piece of dust.

"All three girls responded differently to her," Poccia continued. "My mother was forgiving, but she was haunted by the memory of her childhood. Mabel was just plain angry. And Dawn dealt with her early life in another way—she wrote about it."

By the time Powell was ten years old, she had determined to become an author and was passionately devoted to what she already knew was her life's work. The happiest moments of her childhood were those idyllic times when she was hidden away by herself, in treetops, thickets, or attic rooms, pencil in hand, observing people, places, and events and recording everything in her notebooks. Before she entered her teens, Powell sometimes wrote for more than seven hours a day. Writing, far more than any personal relationship, would be the constant anchor of her life. This mysterious, redemptive gift for words, stories, and conveying impressions was something that was entirely *hers;* within an anarchic universe, it was something tangible that she could bring under her control.

Besides Dumas, the young Powell's most revered literary heroes were Victor Hugo and Charles Dickens (*David Copperfield* would remain one of her favorite books throughout her life). But she also devoured everything else she could find, from the popular nineteenth-century novels of Mrs. E.D.E.N. Southworth to encyclopedias to the ancient classics to women's magazines. She was interested in philosophy early on and particularly inspired by the beliefs of Emile Coué, the French psychotherapist who believed in self-help through autosuggestion (summarized in the slogan "Day by day, in every way, I am getting better and better"). Serving as a countermeasure were the works of Arthur Schopenhauer, which fortified her intrinsic pessimism.

Several factors precipitated Dawn Powell's decision to run away from home in the late summer of 1910, when she was thirteen. The explanation she routinely gave was that Sabra had discovered some germinal stories and drawings in a hidden notebook and burned them all—"Trash, she called them," Powell would recall some thirty years after the fact, still furious.

This bonfire may have provided the immediate impetus for her flight, but it was not the only reason. Powell had found out that her education would soon come to an end if she stayed with her father and Sabra. She had graduated from the eighth grade in a one-room schoolhouse in Cardington before the family moved north, but because North Olmsted had no high school (only about a hundred thousand students a year graduated from American high schools then), she would have had to commute nine miles by trolley, horsecart, or foot to Elyria every day to continue her schooling. Moreover, there was no money to pay the tuition that might be due from an out-of-town student.

And so Dawn Powell gathered her few possessions and fled. Decades later, she wrote about it in an aching, elegiac six-page memoir that was published as "What Are You Doing in My Dreams?": "What you have to do is walk right on down the street, keeping your eyes straight ahead, pretending you're on your way someplace a lot better. And that's the way it turns out, too; wherever you land is sure to be better than the place you left."

Powell claimed that she had taken money earned picking berries (sometimes remembering the amount as thirty cents and sometimes as ninety cents) and gone spontaneously to the small city of Shelby, about an hour away by train. In fact, however, the endeavor was carefully planned. Dawn had run away at least once before, probably in about 1909, but had been forced to return. This time she took no chances and arranged for financial and logistical help from Mabel, who had already escaped to Shelby and now traveled to North Olmsted on the train to pay her sister's fare.

Shelby had an established high school dating back to 1876, open to any resident of Richland County. There Powell would live with Orpha May Sherman Steinbrueck, Hattie Powell's oldest sister and an unconventional and altogether remarkable woman.

Orpha May—the cherished "Auntie May" to the several nieces and nephews she raised as her own children—was born in the Sherman family farmhouse in Bethel on September 27, 1869. In 1891, she married Otto Steinbrueck, a recent German immigrant who had come to America to avoid military conscription. They moved to Archbold, Ohio, where Steinbrueck became a pharmacist, and had one daughter, Gretchen.

"Aunt May became unhappy in her marriage, divorced Otto and came to Shelby with Gretchen," recalled John Franklin Sherman, Dawn Powell's favorite cousin and another family member who was raised by Orpha May, in a 1997 letter. "She purchased a lot about 1896, and she had a home built on it, the address of which became 121 North Broadway. She chose this location because it was a short walk to the Shelby Junction railway station, which was at least a mile from downtown Shelby.

"It was a very busy railroad stop," Sherman continued.

> In order for passengers to get downtown in those years, they had to order a horse drawn carriage from the livery service, or wait for an Interurban street car that stopped at the depot at specific times. Knowing all of this, Aunt May decided to have her home built in the near vicinity of the depot. . . . She was a superb cook, and became known for serving excellent meals. Her home was a haven for children and other family members in need of help, as well as lucky hoboes riding the rails of the hundreds of freight trains passing through Shelby.

The cries of passing locomotives, promising escape to a better life, entranced Powell, and they are a recurring motif in her fiction. *Angels on Toast* and *A Time to Be Born* both begin on trains, and *My Home Is Far Away* ends on one; *Dance Night* concludes with the hero's decision to board for an unspecified city, while "What Are You Doing in My Dreams?" includes a depiction of an overnight ride from New York to Ohio. (*The Happy Island* is unique among Powell's books in that it begins on a *bus*—yet the bus has come, once again, from Ohio, and one of the passengers muses on the strangeness of a New York arrival anywhere but Grand Central Terminal.)

Powell enrolled in Shelby High School in September 1910, but her most important education came from her aunt. The emancipated, self-reliant Orpha May, who did as she pleased, followed her own moral code, and insisted upon being treated as an equal among men, provided Dawn with her greatest role model. It was well known within the family—and considered scandalous by some—that Orpha May had at least one significant romantic relationship, with a Cleveland businessman named Charles Lahm, who regularly stayed with her at 121 North Broadway. Her freethinking also manifested itself in her decision to permit a black employee and his new wife to spend the night at her house, in an era when a local ordinance forbade anybody of African-American descent to remain within Shelby's city limits after sundown.

And yet despite their genuine, profound, and lifelong independence, neither Orpha May Steinbrueck nor Powell herself could ever have been mistaken for any traditional version of a feminist activist. Both had little sympathy for popular mass movements of any sort; both were fundamentally Republican in their political beliefs (Powell's enchantment with Adlai Stevenson in 1952 notwithstanding); both believed that genuine emancipation had to be won, inevitably at a cost, by a determined individual, and that very few women would ever care enough to make that effort. Indeed, both were quite comfortable with the status quo—that is, so long as they themselves were allowed to circumvent it. "Progress is so personal," Powell reflected in her diary in 1936. " 'They' couldn't do that in those days. Yet George Sand seems to have been able to hang around the cafés of Paris in 1830."

Today Shelby is a quiet, modestly affluent bedroom community for neighboring Mansfield. But at the turn of the century, it was a very different place, an industrial town with three large factories: the Ohio Steel Tube Company (known as the Tuby), the Shelby Cycle Company, and the Shelby Mills. Not far from 121 North Broadway (which still stands, albeit sadly altered), a good number of recent immigrants lived in what was then considered a somewhat rough area, nicknamed Irish Town and crowded with cheap, company-sponsored housing. On the other end of the spectrum, a wide, spacious street called Grand Boulevard was the most fashionable address; it was here that Shelby's doctors, company presidents, and more reputable lawyers lived. In short, Shelby was a vibrant and variegated town that provided the young author with a wealth of material. Powell would make good use of her experiences there in novel after novel.

Orpha May was not the only member of the Sherman family in Shelby: Grandmother Julia Sherman, who had been widowed in 1903, operated a large boardinghouse in the center of town (she would eventually marry a second time, at the age of seventy, and close up shop). Until a few years earlier, the woman for whom Dawn had been named—Hattie Powell's youngest sister, Dawn Sherman Gates—had also lived in Shelby. But Dawn Gates had died mysteriously in 1906, at the age of twenty. The *Shelby Globe* attributed her death to acute heart failure and yellow jaundice and did its best to quash a curious town rumor that had her being poisoned by eating oyster sandwiches.

In fact, according to Sherman lore, Dawn Gates, too, had died from the complications of a disastrous abortion. Her namesake had adored this merry, high-spirited young aunt and was agonized by her death. A central character in *My Home Is Far Away*, Bonnie Purdy, is modeled on her. "It is grievous to know you will be forgotten but more to know you will forget," Powell wrote on a scrap of paper later found among her effects. "When I was ten and Aunt Dawn died, I swore I at least would always remember. I did."

Late in life, Powell addressed the subject of abortion in an undated notebook: "Women get jobs, get the vote, have their freedom, but there's one thing that never changes—a single girl who finds she's pregnant is still a girl in a jam. The price of abortions is up—and who can tell you where to go, what can you do, unless you are professional and know all the angles?" Even in an era of space missiles, Powell mused, there was "still no cure for the common child."

The mature Dawn Powell's unconventionally matter-of-fact approach toward sex had its genesis in Shelby. By the time the young writer reached puberty, her mother was years dead, her father was roaming wild on his out-of-town trips, and her guardian had divorced her husband and was living part-time with another man, whom she was unlikely to marry. Moreover, Dawn herself had already been able to observe a panoply of human behavior, in her grandmother's boardinghouse, at her own home, and at the Shelby Junction train station, just across the street.

As a result, she was unusually worldly at an early age. "Saturday a lady came for dinner and I was alone," she wrote in her first surviving letter, which dates from about September 1913 and is addressed to Orpha May, then away visiting relatives in Middletown, Ohio. "She remarked that I seemed awfully young to be running a boarding house. I told her I *was* awfully young."

"Some people seem to 'never grow up'—they do not take personal or emotional responsibilities," she would write many years later.

> The fact is they are in reverse—they were forced to be adults as children, to understand and be part of extremely adult problems—financial, professional, amorous, domestic, psychological—and they cannot get to a certain other plane without some period (the equivalent of an ideal childhood) of security, love, money, being cared for and cherished. Many of us continue seeking this childhood of which we were deprived and will not surrender until we have had our share.

If Aunt May couldn't give Dawn that "ideal childhood," she nonetheless ensured that her charge's teenage years would be an improvement on what had come before. She talked with her about any subject Dawn chose, gave her straight answers to her myriad questions, and encouraged her reading, her independence, and her creativity. Although Orpha May lived in a small Ohio town, she subscribed to the *Smart Set*, the sophisticated, iconoclastic magazine edited by H. L. Mencken and George Jean Nathan, considered highbrow even in New York, and passed along issues to her niece. She worked as a local buyer for the most prestigious department store in the state, Halle Brothers in Cleveland, and took Dawn with her on business trips into what was then a booming city of almost six hundred thousand people. In Cleveland she introduced her niece to cosmopolitan friends, elevated conversation, good hotels, sumptuous restaurants, and what must have seemed a very high life indeed. Orpha May believed in the brilliant and unbowed young woman and supported her in every way she could.

"There was Auntie May, laughing, handsome, understanding, wholly sympathetic Auntie May," Dawn wrote in her first known diary, from the summer of 1915. "She gave me music lessons and thought I had genius and when I wrote crude little poems and stories she cherished them, positive that I was another Jean Webster or Ella Wheeler Wilcox." In the opinion of Dawn's sister Phyllis, Orpha May deserved "most of the credit" for her success. Certainly, the right mentor at the right time can transform a life, and it is difficult to imagine what might have become of Dawn *without* Auntie May.

Powell worked hard at Shelby High School, got respectable grades, and graduated with the class of 1914. While there, she edited the school newspaper and, in her senior year, served as editor of the yearbook. Like most such endeavors, especially in that era, the yearbook was fundamentally a solemn and sentimental affair but it contained a number of playful Powell touches, notably a pair of pictures of the editorial staff. In the first of these, purportedly taken in the autumn, all the young men and women look bright, alert, and well scrubbed; the second, from the spring, finds the exhausted group sprawled out asleep in various awkward positions, Dawn with her head down on the table.

After her graduation from high school, Powell made up her mind to attend Lake Erie College for Women, a patrician academy in Painesville, Ohio, modeled on Mount Holyoke College in Massachusetts.

It was a surprising decision, in several ways. Very few American women attended college in those days; in the 1909–10 academic year, the nearest for which reliable data exist, only 8,437 baccalaureates were awarded to women across the country. Considering Dawn's fierce resolve to further her education, one might have assumed she would prefer—and more likely be accepted by—Oberlin College, a more distinguished school, more broad-minded in outlook, and closer to Shelby. But Oberlin was out: Roy and Sabra Powell had recently moved to 237 East College Street there, and Dawn never wanted to see her stepmother again.

And so, according to Eleanor Farnham, a classmate who would become a lifelong friend, Dawn wrote a pleading letter to Vivian Small, the president of Lake Erie College from 1909 to 1941. The document itself has disappeared, but Farnham remembered that it said something to the effect of "I'd like to come to your school and will do anything to work my way through, from scrubbing back stairs to understudying your job."

Opinions of the woman universally known as Miss Small were mixed; people seem to have taken to her either strongly or not at all. "She was a very proper, Episcopalian, Victorian lady," recalled Olive Hoover Ernst, who was two classes behind Powell at Lake Erie. "I was truly afraid of her."

Still, the autocratic president believed in educational opportunity for students of little means. "Poverty should not be a barrier to education," she proclaimed in her regal manner. "We see our best nature about the girls who find it necessary to earn their way through college." True to her philosophy, Small found a place for the penniless Dawn Powell among the refined daughters of Ohio and Pennsylvania millionaires who composed much of the student body.

Dawn was accepted as a member of the class of 1918, her expenses paid partially by Orpha May (whom she listed in the school records as her sole "parent"), partially by a Shelby attorney named G. M. Skiles, who was close to Orpha May, and partially through help from the college itself, including a personal loan from Small. As late as 1952, Lake Erie had yet to be reimbursed for some outstanding tuition, and given the author's financial problems in the final years of her life, it is unlikely that the debt was ever repaid. But in her way, Powell did what she could for the college, donating some of her own books (as well as signed first editions by friends Lloyd Frankenberg and Charles Norman) to the school library and returning on several occasions to lecture to and meet with the students.

"I arrived at Lake Erie College in September of 1914 with a delirious sensation of having been shot from a cannon into a strange wonderful planet," Powell wrote in an article she contributed to a campus publication, *Nota Bene*, in 1958:

> The world of girls seemed mysterious and infinitely fascinating after my town full of factory-men. It is a rich, illuminating experience to discover the thousand different ways girls can be girls and still be nothing like yourself. There were girls who cried from homesickness for a hometown twelve miles away, there were girls who sat up after hours fiercely arguing about the prophet Moses, girls who borrowed each other's Housman or Leacock or Shaw to take on hikes, girls who fitted each other out for fine parties with sublime selflessness, a girl who wrote poetry brooding over her childhood memories of the bayous, a beaming happy girl who loved Bach and played the pipe organ in chapel.

Almost seventy-five years after Powell graduated from Lake Erie, her classmate Antoinette Burton Akers still recalled her vividly. "She was short—only about five feet or so—she had brown hair and she was always saying something funny, clever or sarcastic," Akers said. "We knew she had grown up on the wrong side of the tracks— that her aunt or her grandmother had run a boardinghouse right on the railroad. She had a very different background from most of us at

Lake Erie, where a lot of the girls had their own horses. But everybody loved her."

For her part, Ernst remembered Dawn as "just a little pixie, an elf, a delightful character. She was like Topsy—she just growed, all by herself." Powell's eyes especially captivated her: "They were not large but they were like two beads. She was a pretty little thing—not a beauty, but she reminded you of a fairy dancing."

Every student was assigned certain chores. Powell's principal duty was to operate the elevator in the main building, which even in 1914 was the subject of much complaint. In 1997, it was still there, creaking slowly up and down the five floors of the spookily handsome Victorian structure, but by then it at least had a motor. In the early part of the century, it ran hydraulically, and it was Powell's lot to pull some heavy ropes up and down, a task that built up her strength but caused her considerable back pain.

Lake Erie was a tiny school (Dawn's class had a mere nineteen graduates) and very strict. Vesper services were held each morning, and students had to attend classes six days a week. It was forbidden to go to lunch or dinner with a male friend unless a chaperone was present. There were two big dances every year, for which "we had to import boyfriends from Kenyon or Case—usually somebody's brother," Akers remembered with a wry expression on her face.

Cleveland was the great escape, a forty-five-minute trip on the Cleveland-Painesville-Ashtabula Interurban, carried along in what Akers remembered as "dark, wine-red cars."

> One got dressed up for the excursion—hats and gloves and suits—and we'd go to Halle's Department Store and have the time of our lives. We might come in for an event—I remember a violin recital by Mischa Elman and a visit from the Ballets Russes—or just to have fun. It was a beautiful city then, clean and safe. A few of us would occasionally have a drink at the Hollenden Hotel and feel very daring about it.

Powell was as active at Lake Erie as she had been at Shelby High School. She joined an organization called the Philologia Literary Society and presented a paper on Gogol (*Dead Souls* would always be one of her favorite books). A lecture about the modern theater by the New York–based editor and drama critic Barrett Clark made a lasting impression, inspiring her to try her hand at writing her own play; the result was *I Am Looking for a Lady*, which she wrote, directed, and appeared in with Charlotte Johnson, a friend from Vincennes, Indiana. She also played Miss Prism in a Drama Club presentation of *The Importance of Being Earnest*, and, in a bit of inspired casting, Puck in an outdoor production of *A Midsummer Night's Dream* (several vibrant and charming photographs survive from this interpretation; it is almost impossible to believe they were taken more than eighty years ago).

In October 1915, Dawn and two friends, Eleanor Farnham and Dorothy Worthington, put together a newspaper parody called the *Sheet*, complete with news, gossip, advice, and satirical reviews. Copied on a duplicating machine after midnight and distributed anonymously on campus, the *Sheet* was greeted by much hilarity among the students. "No one knew who printed it or where it came from," Powell wrote home to her aunt Orpha May. "It was just like throwing a bomb. Everyone's wild over it and we've cleared five dollars already and everyone wants extra copies. Dort and I both have been accused of editing it but we absolutely deny it. They say our stuff sticks out like an apple on a pear tree."

Along more conventional lines, Powell became a contributor, then a literary editor, and finally the editor in chief of the *Lake Erie Record*, the campus quarterly. It was in the *Record* that she published her first fiction, a little sketch called "Phyllis Takes Care of the Children." It appeared in the March 1915 issue, and though even Powell herself knew it was a frivolous piece—"I'd send a copy to you but it's so punk," she wrote in a letter to Orpha May—it has some biographical interest and is worth reprinting here in full:

99 little girls out of a hundred have an instinctive love for children younger than themselves, and are never so happy as when they can take care of someone's baby. But the hundredth little girl is a fanciful, rather sarcastic little creature, who treats all babies as inanimate beings and refers to another little girl's doll as an "it." Phyllis was one of the latter class. She hated all children—or if she didn't hate them, she considered them entirely unnecessary to her world. Because of her attitude toward the little people, she was rarely asked to take care of her little cousins. But one night her Aunt Margaret wished to see "Twelfth Night" and after some coaxing prevailed upon Phyllis to take care of her five little children.

"But of course if you'd be afraid —" hesitated Aunt Margaret. It was a fortunate remark, for Phyllis prided herself upon not being silly like other little girls, and not being afraid in the dark.

"Me, afraid!" she exclaimed scornfully, "Why I'm not afraid of *anything!*"

So it happened that a little while later Phyllis found herself alone with her five little protégés.

"Well, what are we goin' to play?," pleasantly asked Billy, his face glowing from the strenuous scrubbing his mother had given him before she left.

"Play!," exclaimed Phyllis disdainfully. "I'm too old to play. I'm almost ten years old! You children will have to amuse yourselves because I shall read my book." She settled back comfortably in her chair and began to read, occasionally lowering her book to scowl blackly at her discontented charges.

"Wish'd you'd tell us a story," wistfully observed Billy, after a long, unhappy silence on the part of the children. The others clamored loudly for a story. Phyllis paid no heed to them until a brilliant and malicious idea occurred to her, and then she laid down her book and with her eyes fixed dreamily on space, began:

"Well, once upon a time there was a great big, black man —"

"Is this going to be a bad story?" inquired Billy. "Because Ellen always cries when it's a bad story."

"Oh mercy no," Phyllis deceitfully assured them. "Just a lovely, long story about a nice, big, wicked black man who comes around every night to see little boys and girls about your size." She proceeded to tell them at great length and with much gusto about this unpleasant person, delighted at the way the children squirmed and cast apprehensive glances at the window.

"Is he dead yet?" asked Lucy with wide eyes.

"Oh no," answered Phyllis. "He goes around even yet peeking in people's windows and knocking on their doors!"

A shiver went through the children. All eyes, even Phyllis', were drawn toward the window. At that instant a loud crash was heard, as though someone had broken in the front door.

The guest chamber opened into the living room and it was into this that the children rushed with a shuddering cry. In a trice the five of them had leaped onto the bed and covered themselves up to the eyes with blankets. It was at this moment that Aunt Margaret walked in. The children scrambled out of bed and excitedly told her about the noise.

"We thought it prob'ly was the big black man," said Billy.

"No, no!" laughed Aunt Margaret. "I heard it as I came up the walk. It was only that you left your big sled standing on the front porch, and the wind blew it over so that it fell down the steps."

The children drew a simultaneous breath of relief.

"And were you scared, too, Phyllis?" exclaimed Aunt Margaret, catching sight of Phyllis for the first time.

"Oh no," cheerfully lied that young person. But her five little cousins, who had been watching her eagerly, then broke out in accusing chorus:

"Then what were you doing under the bed?"

Setting aside the reflexive racism endemic to its time and place, "Phyllis Takes Care of the Children" presents a portrait of a startlingly self-aware young author—outside the norm, "fanciful," "rather sarcastic," defiantly uninterested in family life, impatient to get on with her reading, possessed of a pointed and slightly cruel sense of humor. What redeems this last quality is the fact that Powell does not exempt herself from criticism—she acknowledges that her character's unafraid exterior is nothing but a mask, and ultimately, Phyllis/Powell is made the butt of her own joke.

When she became the editor in chief of the *Record*, Powell decided to leave campus politics and editorial sermonizing to other students. Instead, she wrote prose poems and little philosophical tracts, most often (though not inevitably) shot through with humor. Her last contribution, printed in the May 1918 issue, is heavily influenced by Finley Peter Dunne and his "Mr. Dooley" stories, but the message is pure Powell: "Plague take those old philosophers. Let them fuss and fume and heatedly discourse whether Being is or Being ain't, but as for me, of one thing I am sure—I KNOW I BE."

The rest of her stories for the *Lake Erie Record* are light and playful as they go by, yet some are also unusually skeptical and antiromantic for a young woman of that era. Already there are signs that Powell foresaw her future—and that she did not believe in happy endings.

Take, for example, "The Rut," a much longer and more ambitious story than "Phyllis Takes Care of the Children," which appeared in the May 1916 *Record*. It tells of two friends, Anne Gregory and Marjorie Bliss, who have grown up together in Cardington and are now taking courses in stenography there. Anne announces her intention one day to leave town, and Marjorie is shocked: "It had never occurred to Marjorie that her friend had any other plans after business school than to get work in Cardington as every one else did and after a few years marry."

Far from it: Anne tells Marjorie that she "loathes" Cardington.

"I am going to get away and do something different and even if I don't make a success, I'll at least be out of the rut—this miserable, deadly rut!"

The girls go their own ways; six years pass before they are finally reunited in Cardington. Anne has been hardened by her move to a large town called Richmond ("the restless dissatisfaction of former years was still in her eyes and there was a trace of bitterness in the downward droop of her lips"), while Marjorie, married with two children, is "a little more plump but as pretty as ever, with a placid contentment in her face that Anne envied."

Marjorie asks Anne whether she, too, is happy, now that she has wriggled her way out of "the rut."

> Anne thought of the years of struggling behind her, the lifetime of hard work before her. "No, I am not what you would call happy," she said slowly, adding with assumed lightness, "I believe it is the people in the rut who are happiest after all. Once they get resigned, they make the most out of it and things are so much easier. Ambition seems to be the obstacle to overcome on the road to happiness."

But Anne is aware of her destiny, and she will not—*cannot*—return to Cardington. "At least I want to make my own rut," she tells her friend. The story closes with an ambiguous self-proclamation:

> As she walked home, Anne thought of the rut that would lead her to happiness. Suddenly a thought came to her that made her stand still and laugh aloud.
>
> "Silly!," she said to herself. "It isn't happiness I'm after, at all. If I had wanted this mild content Marjorie calls happiness I should have stayed in Cardington. What I want is work. And as soon as I find myself making a dent in the road that may develop into a rut for myself in Richmond, I'll start all over again!"

In fact, Powell had been in her own emotional "rut" during the 1915–16 academic year. During another depressive period in 1932, she reflected on this time: "Since sophomore college days I don't remember ever being in such a feeble nervous state, ready to weep over a blot, a lost pencil sharpener, a pound gained."

Fortunately for us, she kept a detailed diary in the summer of 1915, while she was working as a maid and waitress at a Lake Erie resort in Painesville, called the Shore Club. This was the first, and in some ways the most intimate, of the many diaries she would keep throughout her life. Much of it is a chronicle of dread, woe, and disappointment, but it is leavened by some witty caricatures—Powell was a shrewd and perceptive amateur cartoonist—and humorous essays on tennis and swimming.

As a whole, the epistolary diary is addressed to an imaginary friend named Mr. Woggs, but sporadic comments are also directed to a distant biographer, as if Powell innately knew that one would eventually come her way:

> I wouldn't have come down here at all to earn my expenses for next year at college if I hadn't have had the sneaking idea that someday my biographers would write it and the world would admire and praise and I would only laugh then and say— "Really, it was just heaps of fun."

Other visions of the future, however, were less sanguine:

> I must make myself strong for the knocks that are to come, for no matter what you tell me—"You've had enough knocks, you'll have happiness the rest of your life"—something in me says that life for me holds more knocks than joys, and the blows will leave me crushed, stunned, wild-eyed and ready to die, while the joys will make me deliriously, wildly, gloriously

happy. It's the way I'm made, that Irish strain in me, perhaps. Yet better for one of my nature to have it that way than to have life a peaceful, placid flow of quiet containment. I must have days of rushing excitement.

In cheerful moods, she listed things she would have in her imagined "palmy future," including a "perfectly stunning street suit, perfectly stunning evening clothes, perfectly stunning everything," a "Steinway grand," a mandolin, an "electric limousine," a maid to keep her clothes and dresser in order, and a town house. Some of her desires were more altruistic: she wanted to "send Phyllis to school for a year, take Auntie May for a winter in the Isle of Pines," and "raise foundlings." Finally, she wished for a "perfectly stunning man." But all of that remained fantasy: for much of this period she felt lonely, underappreciated and exploited in her menial job, homesick for Shelby, and remorseful about having run away and abandoned Phyllis to Sabra's care.

Armchair psychiatry is a dubious practice at best, but it seems safe to say that Powell's sense of self-worth fluctuated dramatically from day to day and that, then as later, she was never able to reach any reasonable perspective in her self-opinion. She simply could not envision her good times during her bad ones—and the bad times were dreadful:

Woggsie, I'm sorry I talked so blue to you a while ago. I mustn't let myself do that anymore, right at the beginning of the battle—time enough at the end. But it does seem one of life's tragedies that I should have been born at all. Why couldn't my soul have been put into some pretty and wealthy girl? Oh well, no use moralizing or philosophizing. My nose is all red and my eyes too and I have a headache. I'm tired. Perhaps I'll learn to swim and drown.

And yet there were occasions that summer when she enjoyed herself. She developed several casual crushes and became an adept flirt, a habit that annoyed her friends and inspired some paragraphs of self-defense:

Can't I have a little fun? I know I shouldn't but I can't help it when my hand accidentally brushes his arm, or my cheek either—or if my shoulder should touch his when we both stoop to pick up a card. And if I should glance up at him and find him looking at me, why should I drop my eyes at once, instead of returning his look—oh, for the briefest possible second and then sort of drag my eyes away? . . . [I'm] insincere and fickle and I am afraid that after all it isn't nice to flirt and I suppose that is all I do when I act that way. But I can't help it and don't want to.

I was dreamily prophesying my future the other day for the girls. "In ten years from now," Katherine said, "you'll be left. You get all the men you can on a string and make them unhappy and pretty soon when you want a man you'll be left. You are too flip altogether." "Yes, I'll be left," I said slowly and with overwhelming conviction. "Ten years from now I will still be Dawn Sherman Powell—but girls, that name will be famous then. Ten years from now, I will have arrived." And Woggs, I know it will be true. I never entertain the slightest fear of an obscure future. I'll be before the public eye in some way and you know it, too.

At the end of the season, she concluded her diary with a prescient farewell to "Mr. Woggs":

At times I grow a bit weary of these tremendous jumps and bumps in my life but I suppose—I *know*—that if life for me

were a placid, smoothly-running path, I would die of the tire-
someness of it. Well, Woggs, we are destined for a hard ride in
life, with many bumps and jumps, but it will be a swift, breathless ride and we will arrive all the sooner. So we may as well
pull down our hats, button up our coats and hang on to our
seats, instead of pausing to speculate. . . . We've had a fine
summer together—almost ideal—but it's time now to worry
about money and college. I did think I would borrow some but
I guess I won't. I'll get it someway. You'll hear great things of
me, someday. Goodbye, Woggs.

When America entered World War I, in 1917, Lake Erie College threw itself behind the cause. "Dawn would write little skits,"
Olive Ernst explained, "and we would put together a cast and go up
on each floor. We'd charge only a nickel or something but we'd have
an audience in each corridor. We raised more than a few nickels that
way, all of which we donated to the war effort." On other occasions,
Powell would put on solo shows to earn enough money for train fare
and admission to a concert or play in Cleveland.

The closest friends Powell made at Lake Erie had ambitions
similar to hers and would go on to have distinguished careers of their
own. Cornelia Wolfe became a published poet and later worked in
Hollywood at the Walt Disney Studios. Eleanor Farnham, who lived
to be almost a hundred (1896–1995), was one of the first woman
reporters employed by the *Cleveland Plain Dealer* and eventually
founded a successful publicity agency. Charlotte Johnson became an
editor of *Ladies' Home Journal*, a position she would hold for many
years. A few years before she died, in 1958, Johnson returned a
dozen letters Dawn had written to her four decades earlier; these
allow us a privileged glimpse into Powell's first days in New York.

Powell also had a shadowy but fairly steady relationship with a
boy whose name has come down to us only as "Ben." He is men-

tioned, with varying degrees of fondness, in her letters from 1916 until late 1918, after which time he seems to have vanished from her life forever. In early 1917, Ben enlisted in the armed forces, and for security reasons, his letters to her had to be passed by the censor. Thus edited, "they aren't nearly so interesting," Dawn complained.

Powell's grades at Lake Erie were only fair; she was too wrapped up in her many extracurricular activities to concentrate on her academic studies, and she graduated without honors in the spring of 1918. "At commencement time, she held up the procession because she couldn't find her cap," Ernst remembered. "It was found eventually, under a pile of something in her room, but only after holding up this very solemn, distinguished procession. She was very disorganized. I was never in her room, but it was *famous.*"

Immediately following graduation, Dawn moved almost five hundred miles east, to the small town of Pomfret, Connecticut, where she stayed on a farm suggested to her by a college friend. Her classmate thought she needed a "summer in *artistic atmosphere* where I could develop my *genius*," she told her sister Mabel with exaggerated irony. Fox Hall Farm, owned by a family named Matthewson, seems to have been a retreat for wealthy and talented people of a liberal persuasion; her time there probably represented Powell's first sustained experience with any sort of bohemia, however rural and elite. "There are usually several rather famous people—artists, writers, etc.—and Miss Matthewson herself is so clever and interesting!" she noted.

In the mornings, Powell worked on the farm ("hoeing, etc."), but her afternoons were theoretically consecrated to writing. "To keep myself from getting bored with myself, I've taken up suffrage," she wrote to Mabel. "Thus far, I haven't broken any windows or beaten up any policemen, nor do I expect to go on any hunger strike—Lord forbid!"

She elaborated on her activities to Orpha May:

A lot of [the suffrage work] has been among the Irish and I've had a perfect circus. If they look as though their husbands drank, I tell them they want to vote to get the saloons out and they say, "Sure, then, I'm a suffragette." And if they look as though they liked a nice nip themselves now and then, I use the soft pedal on my prohibition line and say that the pope is all for suffrage and there's some talk of there being a lady pope. So then they say, "Sure, I'm a suffragette!"

Powell was never deeply committed to politics; it was altogether typical of her to be more attracted to the "perfect circus" she found in the recruitment experience than devoted in some self-sacrificial manner to an important cause. In any event, she was already plotting her next escape: "I reckon I won't be here very long so they can't get me," she informed Orpha May.

"New York's a big city. . . ."

CHAPTER TWO

New York:
Joe, Jojo, and Jack

❧

There is really one city for everyone just as there is one major love. New York is my city because I have an investment I can always draw on—a bottomless investment of twenty-one years (I count the day I was born) of building up an idea of New York—so no matter what happens here I have the rock of my dreams of it that nothing can destroy.

DAWN POWELL, 1953

POWELL LEFT THE BENIGN WILDERNESS of Pomfret for New York City on Labor Day, 1918, bolstered by a few letters of recommendation, fourteen dollars in cash, and a friend's promise to stake her to two weeks' rent. "I love the farm but there comes a time when the sight of a flock of Jerseys grazing on a patch of poison ivy fails to thrill and one yearns to go someplace where the band plays all the time and life is not so simple," she had written to Orpha May the week before her departure. "God knows the thought of five feet of me struggling along in the heart of the wicked city occasionally gives me an empty sensation around the lung and just below the stomach but 'tis written that I go to New York—so why try to fool with the gods?"

It must have been a wonderful place then: the largest city in the Western Hemisphere, perhaps the largest city in the world, a chaotic hive of activity. Manhattan alone had some 2.3 million people— close to its peak population—living amid the towers and tunnels of what Powell would later call the Happy Island. Subways and street- cars carried people uptown and downtown, to the woodsy recesses of the Bronx and out to the sun and fun of Coney Island, for five cents a trip; they were clean and efficient and ran all night. It was considered safe to walk anywhere in New York: Powell had no qualms about attending parties in Harlem or wandering dimly lit stretches of the Lower East Side.

There were more than fifty daily newspapers, 250 weeklies, and 450 monthly journals and magazines published in New York then, including dailies in French, German, Italian, Bohemian, Croatian, Ser- bian, Arabic, Yiddish, Ukrainian, and at least a dozen other languages. Political views were reflected on the right by the *Globe*, the *Mail*, and the *Tribune* (the last of which was shortly to merge with the *Herald* to create one of America's greatest newspapers), and in the middle by the *Times*, the *World*, and the *Sun*. The *Evening Post*, to which Powell would sporadically contribute for forty years, represented enlight- ened liberal opinion, while the tenets of socialism were advanced by the *Call* (the legendary *Masses* had just folded).

The sixty-story Woolworth Building was the tallest skyscraper in the world, though others were already climbing to rival its pri- macy. The fanciest shops had by now moved uptown to Fifth Avenue, where ladies donned hats and gloves for the promenade. Fourth Avenue was dotted with secondhand bookshops, and pocket theaters were to be found throughout lower Manhattan, offering vaudeville "two-a-days" as well as plays in English, Italian, Yiddish, and other languages. The Provincetown Players were staging the early works of

Eugene O'Neill in a rented theater on Macdougal Street, while near Times Square, Ziegfeld's Follies "glorified the American Girl" with a succession of titillating songs and dances in a different production every year. Admission to Broadway shows ran from fifty cents to two dollars per ticket, ranging up to four dollars for the most fashionable musical hits. With silent films less expensive to present than live theater, movie houses were suddenly everywhere.

Then as now, New York markets and restaurants offered delicacies from around the world, at widely varying prices. Hotels proliferated throughout the city, with even those of the second rank usually providing a comfortable and secure stay for about a dollar and a half a night.

These were the last days for more than a decade that one would be able legally to purchase alcoholic beverages. Prohibition would take effect in mid-1919, but the constitutional amendment would be a flop from the first, and by the end of the 1920s, it would be estimated that the city had twice as many speakeasies as it had once had bars.

As always, New York was supremely indifferent to the lives of its inhabitants, but its aloof, perennial laissez-faire could also, in the right circumstances and for the right person, be spectacularly liberating. The exuberant, blunt, aggressive city gave no quarter; it was fundamentally amoral and often shockingly unfair. But there was an unrivaled concentration of genius in New York, and those whom the city did reward were rewarded handsomely.

Into this whirligig, in early September 1918, stepped a slight, impoverished, and wide-eyed woman of twenty-one armed only with her brilliance—a woman who had never before lived in a city of more than thirty thousand people and had spent most of her time in markedly smaller towns. She lodged in a boardinghouse for women at 353 West Eighty-fifth Street and was roomed with a young writer named Katherine Vedder, who became first a nurse and then a successful real-estate agent and would remain her friend for life.

Unlike most of Powell's early addresses on the Upper West

Side, 353 West Eighty-fifth Street still stands, an unprepossessing
tan-and-brick apartment structure that now seems somewhat shabby
by comparison to the rest of what has become its affluent neighborhood. By chance, Powell had immersed herself in an artistic milieu:
the building's thirty women residents were all "players, artists,
dancers, etc., of the nicest kind," and Broadway, just a few steps
away, offered a rich and cosmopolitan night life. She would use her
first New York apartment as the setting for one of her strongest
plays, *Walking down Broadway.*

Promptly and somewhat improbably, she found work as an
"assistant efficiency manager" with the Butterick Company, a leading
publisher of dress patterns and magazines such as the *Delineator* and
Women's. "Only the fact that I was a college grad and had done library
work—and wanted to know how a magazine was made—got me the
job," she wrote to her Lake Erie friend and roommate Charlotte
Johnson. Her salary was twenty dollars a week; she budgeted thirteen cents per day for lunch.

After only five weeks, Powell abruptly quit Butterick and
joined the U.S. Navy, enlisting for four years. World War I had not
yet ended; though women would not be permitted on active duty
until 1942, the administrative post of "Yeoman-Female" had been
open since 1916, and by the conclusion of the war, 11,275 so-called
Yeomanettes would be on the government payroll. Powell was put to
work as a typist at the New York Naval Headquarters, downtown at
44 Whitehall Street, where she received a substantial raise: she now
made thirty-five dollars a week.

This new career was soon interrupted. Immediately after Powell's
acceptance into the navy, a routine medical examination revealed
that she was suffering from Spanish influenza, a virus that would kill
some twenty million people worldwide that year, with half a million
deaths in the United States alone. Powell was admitted to the hospital, where she enjoyed the servile attentions of the staff, developed
crushes on the young doctors, and wrote what she termed "sad,

beautiful poetry." In an odd twist of fate, she was released on Armistice Day—November 11, 1918. "Dancing in the streets— everybody singing—French sailors carried on the shoulders of American sailors down Fifth Avenue," she relayed back to Charlotte Johnson.

Johnson was Dawn's principal correspondent during this period, and thanks to her fortunate decision to preserve many of her friend's early letters, we can have a fairly good idea of what that thrilling first year in the city must have been like:

> Do you know I've lived about twenty years since Septem-ber 2—the date of my arrival in New York? Everything whirls around you all the time . . . and you grab what you want and then let it revolve again. It makes me dizzy to think of all the warm friendships and Passionate Affairs I've been through in three months. The funny part of it all is that you have to come to New York to appreciate the virtues of a small town just as you have to go to college to learn how easily you can do with-out a B.A. And all the men say "I love you" and look at you with long wistful "I-surely-am-hit-now" gaze and you kiss them and say this is the first time I've ever cared like this and then you never see each other again. And on the subway in the mornings you suddenly find yourself talking to a man or girl who is a gen-uine soul-mate. They get out at Times Square and you see them looking back at you through the windows and both of you know you'll never meet again. Somehow there's nothing tragic in it, though. You recognize and love it all as Life—the World— Humanity—whatever it is.

Powell's description of her initiation into Greenwich Village life is particularly amusing. Her evolving response to this quarter of town was not dissimilar to the reaction a newcomer might have seventy-five years later:

There are three stages you go through in regard to the Village. First and foremost "Oh-so-this-is-Bohemia!! My dear! Don't you just *love* it all? Everything is so—well, so absolutely *spontaneous,* don't you know!!! Bohemia—oh thrills!"

Stage No. II—you begin to realize that all the biyes and goils from back home think Bohemia's great, so you begin to see it with jaded eyes. Everyone tries to be a freak—wants to be noticed—does everything for effect and down in his heart is worse than ordinary—is in fact a ten-cent rube like yourself. Bah! Village theatricals! Bah! Bah! Bah!

Stage No. III—you combine and condense and admire and sift—and after all the Village is the Village when all's said and done.

Powell was not always so ebullient. She went through a phase of screaming in her sleep, so loudly that her landlady was forced to come in and wake her on at least two separate occasions. "The boarders are sort of touchy about it," she admitted. The problem does not seem to have become chronic; it was never mentioned again. But Powell regularly complained of her solitude and embarked on a crusade to bring Johnson, herself a talented poet, to New York. Unfortunately for biographers, Johnson eventually succumbed to her pleas, and the letters stopped, to be replaced by ephemeral conversation and companionship.

With the resolution of the war, Powell's navy work lost its urgency. She stayed on until July 31, 1919 (when all "Yeomanettes" were released from active service with a twelve-dollar monthly retainer until the end of their enlistment), but in those last months she suddenly found she had a lot of free time on her hands. And so she attended a goodly number of films and plays, went out to bars and restaurants (where she quickly and avidly learned to drink), and visited the Village for sport while remaining, for the moment, a convinced West Sider. She would always consider Riverside Drive the most beautiful street in Manhattan.

In late 1919, Powell appeared as an extra in a silent film, *Foot-lights and Shadows*, produced by the Selznick Pictures Corporation. It starred the ethereally lovely Olive Thomas, best remembered for her mysterious suicide (or accidental overdose) in a Paris hotel room the following year. Only a minuscule percentage of silent films have survived; there is no known print of *Footlights and Shadows*, nor does one seem likely to turn up. But Powell left a vivid reminiscence of her initial three-day labor in the newly "glamorous" world of motion pictures:

> I worked all day Monday over at the Universal Studio at Fort Lee, all day Tuesday and Wednesday from 8:30 in the morning till 7 o'clock Thursday morning! . . . Along about 3 A.M. we all lined up for coffee and sandwiches and staggered home Thursday morning—simply dead. It's supposed to be a big cabaret fire—there's a panic scene in which one of the poor extras got her nose smashed and another got her dress torn out. Believe me, this movie life is no cinch.

"I never saw such a group of absolute moral degenerates in my life as these movie extras," she concluded.

Her most important activity remained her writing—articles, sketches, stories—which was now beginning to sell. Someday, some courageous and enterprising scholar must undertake a complete bio-bibliography of Dawn Powell. It will be a difficult task (the present writer gave up the effort, overwhelmed by the bulk and variety of her freelance work). Powell seems to have published just about everywhere, sometimes under a pseudonym or a variant of her given name (such as the genderless "D. Sherman Powell") and sometimes with no byline at all.

She wrote for such disparate publications as *American Agriculturist*, *Southern Ruralist*, *Fashion Art*, and the *New York Evening Sun*, which printed the halfhearted suffragist's "Impressions of a First Voter" on November 8, 1919 ("They had told me that we women ought to oust Tammany and I felt that I might even do it personally"). She wrote articles about current celebrities, even though "I hated the people I had to interview," she later said. "I felt like we were a couple of strange dogs circling around each other wondering where to bite first." She reported on Mesopotamian oil wells for the *Oil and Gas Journal*, on Boy Scouts in China for *Boy's Life*, on Burmese music for *Musical Monitor*, on what she called "Pekinese poodles" for *Dogdom*, and on Japanese labor unions for Samuel Gompers's *American Federationist*. Gompers responded with a personal letter, saying her article "was one of the most interesting he had read on that subject and he would use any further articles sent him," she proudly informed Orpha May.

Powell had visited her family in Ohio just prior to her demobilization and found herself news: women in uniform were then a rarity, especially in the Midwest. When a Cleveland newspaper published a few trivial facts about her work, she worried that she might have breached government security by discussing American wheat sales to Sweden. After leaving the navy, she joined the publicity department of the Red Cross and worked on famine relief for Armenia.

In the middle of 1919, she moved to 411 West End Avenue. This was her grandest residence to date (one of her fellow tenants was the great soprano Emmy Destinn), but she did not stay there very long. By early 1920, she had settled into an apartment up the street at 569 West End Avenue (now demolished) with her friend Helen Kessel, a tall, shy, gifted young woman from Iowa who was studying piano in New York. The flat cost $165 a month and included a living room, bedroom, kitchenette, and bath—"all new and furnished exquisitely by an interior decorator."

It was, Powell acknowledged, a great deal to pay for a place to live, but handsome apartments were one of the creature comforts she would permit herself whenever possible throughout her life. "I would rather live here than in a $7 or $8 a week lousy room on the East Side someplace and since I expect to stay in New York I think I might as well have a home of my own," she wrote to Orpha May. She was delighted with Kessel's Steinway and spent many hours playing it, in the process refining what was already an adept amateur pianism.

Dissatisfied with the thirty-five dollars the Red Cross was pay-ing her weekly for intensive and exhausting work, she switched to a publicity job for the Interchurch World Movement. There she met a slim, courtly, poetic-looking twenty-nine-year-old man named Joseph Gousha. The friendship apparently began with an invitation to take a ferry ride. In the last piece she published during her lifetime—a sentimental valentine called "Staten Island, I Love You," which ran in the October 1965 issue of *Esquire*—Powell, by then desperately ill and still in mourning for the recently dead Gousha, wrote lyrically about that initial outing:

> What I love about Staten Island is that in the year 1920, fresh sprung from Ohio, conquering New York and knowing every-thing as I never have since, I was asked by a fair young man in the office next to mine if I would care to go walking Saturday on Staten Island.
>
> "I've always wanted to," I cried, never having heard of the place.
>
> I would have agreed just as eagerly to go mushing over the moon's crust, since I had already decided to marry the man and had not even caught the young man's name which (we might as well get these happy endings over right at the start) later would be mine.

Of French and German extraction, Joseph Roebuck Gousha had been born in Philadelphia on August 2, 1890, the son of Harry and Laura Mathias Gousha. The family name had originally been Gouget, but allegedly irked by being called "Gouge-it" in the small Pennsylvania towns where they lived, Gousha's parents had changed it to a marginally more phonetic spelling (the name is pronounced "Goo-SHAY").

Joe had attended school in Pottstown, Norristown, and Oil City, Pennsylvania, and moved to Pittsburgh in about 1915 to become a drama and music critic on the *Sun*. When preparing Joe's obituary in 1962, Powell would name him as one of those who had exposed the "Spectra" hoax, a sort of artsy-craftsy parody of Amy Lowell's "Imagism" perpetrated by Witter Bynner and Arthur Davison Ficke, who published their amusing and incomprehensible verse under the names Emanuel Morgan and Anne Knish. The only history of the spoof, however, does not mention Gousha.

Gousha himself had only recently moved to New York, and so the city was a fresh adventure for both of them. The walk on Staten Island was soon followed by Dawn and Joe's first formal date: a luncheon at the Claremont Inn, a stately, pillared, Mount Vernon–like structure on Riverside Drive, just north of Grant's Tomb. Until its demolition in 1951, this was a popular spot for excursions and special celebrations, offering a panoramic view of the Hudson River and the New Jersey Palisades and dining al fresco in the warmer months. It is doubtful that the young couple ate outside on that first date— on February 28, 1920—but Joe presented Dawn with a dozen red roses, a romantic flourish she would never forget.*

The friendship quickly became passionate. Dawn and Joe attended the theater, supped frequently at the Bretton Hall Hotel at Eighty-sixth Street and Broadway, drank at some of the embryonic speakeasies that were springing up in Greenwich Village, and took

*In the years remaining to her after her husband's death, Powell regularly bought herself roses every February 28, a wistful and uncharacteristically sentimental gesture that she believed brought her good luck.

leisurely hansom cab rides through Central Park. It must have been a joyful spring; by May, Dawn was telling Orpha May of her love for Joe, whom she called her "Most Adorable." Eleanor Farnham has left us an account of his first visit to Dawn's apartment:

> Operating on the theory that a man would run a mile from a brainy woman, Dawn sat at the piano one evening, hammering out what was then known as ragtime. Joe, meanwhile, picked up from the table a copy of Schopenhauer's *Essays in Pessimism*. "Why, Dawn," he said, "are you reading *this*?" Glancing nervously across her shoulder, she replied, "Oh, somebody left that here." "But your name is on the flyleaf," persisted an astonished Joe.
>
> So the secret was out and, as Joe told me after their marriage, it was a delightful surprise to find that the girl who so appealed to him physically could also be his mental companion. Indeed, as he came to discover what she was, he felt that his role was to foster Dawn's genius.

On November 20, 1920, Joseph R. Gousha and Dawn Powell were married at the Church of the Transfiguration (better known as the Little Church around the Corner) in New York. They spent their honeymoon in the city, staying at the Hotel Pennsylvania, opposite Penn Station on Seventh Avenue and Thirty-second Street. Orpha May came in from Ohio for the intimate ceremony; the official witnesses were Joe's boyhood friend Harry Lissfelt and Powell's roommate Helen Kessel, who themselves would marry shortly thereafter.

The profiles of Joseph Gousha published to date have been unflattering. He has been portrayed as a drunkard, a spendthrift, and a negligent husband whose transgressions dragged down his talented wife; by some traditional standards, Joe might be described as a cuckold as well. At best, he has been treated as a shadow figure passing gravely through what was otherwise a spirited, devil-may-care revel. Powell herself reinforced some of these impressions in her diaries, during periods of unhappiness.

In Gousha's defense, it should be pointed out that he married a decidedly unconventional woman in decidedly conventional times, that he accepted and loved her for what she was, and that he supported her in good style (except for those fleeting, flush times when Powell made most of the family money and briefly—and rather grudgingly—supported *him*). Their married life was often trying, and it was interrupted by a number of separations, some of them amicable, some not. For years at a time, they lived what were essentially separate lives, and both enjoyed a succession of lovers on the side. But their affection for one another persisted, and Dawn was bereft when Joe died; indeed, she never really recovered. For all her extramarital sexual activity (from the better part of a decade into their union), Powell was also, in her own way, a fiercely committed wife, and her fundamental devotion to her husband never wavered.

In 1972, Charles Norman, a poet, novelist, and biographer who was a friend of the Goushas' for more than four decades, recalled the young Joe, with his "very blond hair, very blue eyes and charming old world manners":

> When he greeted you at the door the greeting was princely; even when he did not actually bow, a bow seemed to hover between his guest and himself. He had been a newspaperman and wanted to become a writer. "But I married a girl with more talent than I have," he told me, "and I think she should have the chance to develop it." During the thirty-five years that I knew him he worked in an advertising agency. Time and his sedentary occupation, together with drinking, bloated his figure, but his princely manner never left him.

Still, this was, from the outset, an unusual marriage, and it began with an incident that brought the couple national publicity.

After the honeymoon, for whatever reason (and several contrasting explanations would be offered), Joe returned to live with his mother, brother, and sisters at 540 Eighty-first Street in Brooklyn, while Dawn went back to living with Helen Kessel on West End Avenue.

Powell would later say that they had been inspired by the example of novelist Fannie Hurst and her husband, Jacques Danielson, who maintained separate establishments while admitting to "breakfasting regularly" together. Intrigued by this arrangement, Dawn and Joe apparently thought it might work for them, particularly since they were having difficulty finding a home they both deemed suitable.

Somehow the press got hold of this (the fact that the central players were both professional publicists probably didn't hurt matters). Newspapers in places as far away as Chicago ran long, bemused stories about these two young New York poets (as Dawn and Joe described themselves, though both held steady, and fairly traditional, day jobs) and their newfangled notions about old institutions.

The story broke only after the experiment was over. On January 4, 1921, the *New York Evening Journal*'s headline blared, "NEWLY-WEDS HUNT FLAT AFTER TRIAL OF FANNIE HURST'S PLAN." "Nothing in This Latter-Day Idea of Married Folk Living Apart, Declares Poetess Bride and Poet Husband as They Prepare to Start Housekeeping Together," read the subhead.

"We thought the idea great at first but soon found that it did not appeal to us as much as a modest apartment in common would," Powell supposedly told the reporter. "If two people truly love each other and have tastes and a profession in common, it is my contention they will be happy only when living together, where their ideas may be an aid to mutual happiness and advancement."

The press, only too eager to debunk any implication that a marriage could be conducted in such scandalous manner, played up the "happy ending"—that is, the eccentric but fundamentally wholesome young bohemian couple's coming to its senses. A few papers even treated the whole episode as something imposed on Dawn and Joe by a housing shortage in Manhattan. "Cable dispatches recently said this sort of predicament was common in Vienna," the *Journal* tutted. "The case of the Goushas is the first reported in New York but undoubtedly there are others."

What was the real story? Nobody knows; not a single diary entry or personal letter has survived that might illuminate the issue. Was it a mutual decision to live apart, or did one partner push for it against the other's will? What ended the experiment? Was it all a publicity stunt? (Extant news clips, with their detailed interviews and photographs of the Goushas, suggest the two were more than helpful to journalists.) The answers to these questions would obviously help to trace the trajectory of the Gousha-Powell marriage. We can only speculate; however, given the independent manner in which Dawn and Joe would later choose to live, it seems improbable that New York's chronic housing shortage was the only impetus for their plan.

Dawn and Joe eventually found an apartment together at 31 Riverside Drive—"just an attic but so lovely"—and settled into the most traditionally domestic period of Powell's life. She gloried in her new status as a wife, priding herself on her sewing, her pies, and the comfortable home she was making for Joe, who had taken a job in advertising, a field in which he would become quite successful. But she never adopted the Gousha name, except on legal documents. Dawn Powell would remain Dawn Powell.

At the start, Joe seems to have been an attentive husband. Dawn confessed that they had some financial troubles (they would pale in comparison to what was to come). "But it's silly to worry yourself unhappy about money when you have everything else," she wrote to Mabel, "— the man you want, first and foremost. Furthermore, after being left to shift for ourselves ever since we were infants, don't you think it's wonderful to have someone finally spoil us—just like we should have been spoiled when we were kids?"

A tiny two-and-a-half-by-three-inch notebook, which Powell called "The Book of Joe," reflects her contentment. On June 23, 1921, pregnant with her only child, Powell wrote:

> I want so much for my lover. At night when our beds are drawn close together I waken and see his dear yellow head on the pillow—sometimes his arm thrown over my bed—and I kiss his hand, very softly so that it will not waken him. He is happier now that he is writing a play. I know he will succeed with it. I think we will have a boy baby and he will be born on the 20th of August. Everyone else has a girl baby and at times I don't believe I should mind having a little Phyllis Dawn but Dearest wants a boy and I do. Besides, it must be a boy—the little golden-haired boy in the blue rompers.

Joseph Roebuck Gousha Jr. was born in New York's St. Luke's Hospital on August 21, 1921, a day after Dawn predicted and almost exactly nine months after his parents were married. Literally from the moment he came into the world, his life would prove to be one long series of disasters.

Powell was in the hospital for three weeks following the delivery. On September 3, the doctors allowed her to sit up for half an hour and lifted her out of bed into a chair. There, gazing out over the chasm of Morningside Park, she drafted a detailed, gloomy letter to her sisters:

> I feel pretty good but won't be able to leave for another week—both on my own account and on the baby's.
>
> You see, I didn't know till two days afterward that they didn't think the baby was going to live. I had a terrible time and it was just as hard on the baby. He is awfully husky but being born was a tough business for him and just before he came out his heart went bad. Doctor said I should have had my babies five

or six years ago. That would have been awkward, as I would have had some difficulty in explaining them about that time. I didn't dilate at all. Poor little lamb had a clot on his brain that caused a sort of convulsive paralysis besides several bad bruises from the forceps. Joe didn't tell me but the doctors let it leak out to me by saying that it looked as if the baby had a chance after all. We had to have a special nurse for him night and day for a week ($12 a day besides the $6 a day for me) and consulting infant specialists were called in. On Friday he began to perk up and now he is entirely out of danger and is raising the dickens in general although his external bruises haven't quite healed up yet. The clot is all absorbed and he is O.K. He was able to recover so quickly I suppose because he had such a swell appetite and general constitution to fall back on. He has coal black hair and big blue eyes and a tiny little nose and a beautiful mouth and one ear flat and the other sticks out. He is unusually tall. Got that from me. He has a fat little face—looks just like a Chinese mandarin but very very beautiful.

By mid-September, Dawn and Jojo (as the boy would be called throughout his life) returned to 31 Riverside Drive, the trauma of his birth seemingly behind them both. Jojo suffered from infant eczema and grew only haltingly during his first year, but he weighed in at a hearty twenty-four pounds at his eighteen-month checkup ("The correct weight is 23 and ¼ so he's more than made up for his early backwardness," Dawn observed proudly).

"He pulls himself up in his bathtub now by hanging on to the faucets and turns around a dozen times," she wrote in a letter to Orpha May in the fall of 1922. "He gets all excited trying to catch the water from the faucet. He gets saucier and saucier every day and has a rather disturbing trick of catching your finger and biting it. Guess he thinks he might as well teethe on that as anything else."

By the age of two, Jojo was speaking in complete sentences, shouting "Kick the ball!" to older children he saw playing in Riverside Park. "He wears three-year-old clothes," Dawn noted. "He dances and sings to the Victrola and reads 'Cinderella' and calls me 'Mother, dear.'" Before he turned four, Jojo was already reading at a precocious level and had developed an early passion for the music of Richard Wagner. Dawn bought shellac 78 rpm recordings of his favorite pieces, which inevitably were broken, after which she would provide replacements. Jojo distorted the question "What seems to be the trouble?" into "What string beans the trouble?" which so amused his parents that they took up the phrase between themselves. He was, in most respects, a brilliant, original, and attractive child.

But it soon became clear that something was terribly wrong. Jojo was subject to howling, inconsolable tantrums that lasted all night. He could not be toilet-trained. He was constantly trying dangerous stunts and often ran off, heedless and at full speed, into the city streets. There were times when he seemed detached from reality altogether, babbling reiterative gibberish at the top of his lungs. He demanded the closest attention at all times.

Jojo's doctors, at a loss to explain his behavior, pronounced him "retarded"—an absurd diagnosis. Whatever else he may have been, the boy was extraordinarily intelligent, and his capacity for memorizing facts and figures was on the genius level. Within his extended family, Jojo was merely considered "strange"—something of an "idiot savant," as his cousin Phyllis Poccia remembered in 1995. "When he was just a little boy, he was enormously sensitive to music," she said. "He'd just sit there, listening and crying. He could read, and he knew all of his multiplication tables by the age of three or four. He had these *enormous* gifts. He just didn't have any of the other skills we take for granted."

Over the years, schizophrenia and cerebral palsy were also blamed for Jojo's condition, and one or both of those may indeed have played some part in what would prove a lifelong incapacity. However, it is more likely that Jojo, had he been born today, would have been quickly diagnosed as suffering from autism, an uncommon (and, to the outsider, eternally fascinating) mental illness that wasn't even identified until the early 1940s.

Autism is a rare, profound, and debilitating form of obsessive self-absorption (the name is derived from the Greek word for "self") that occurs in roughly 4.5 children per ten thousand live births, afflicting boys at least three times as often as it does girls. Most autistic children are of normal appearance and physique—a disproportionate number are actually quite beautiful—but 80 percent of them are mentally retarded, and the remainder are given to bizarre and uncontrollable behavior. Usually apparent within the first three years of life, autism is almost surely of biological origin, though scientists continue to be puzzled as to exactly what causes it. Nor have they been able to explain why some individuals, after decades of institutionalization or home care, manage to break through and begin to recover.

Almost half of all autistic patients are mute; those who are able to speak tend to do so in an abnormal manner, slurring their words or using language that is stilted and artificially formal. Many autistic people share certain characteristics, including an exceptional memory, a fanatical need for unchanged environments and unbroken routines, and an obsession with—and talent for—art, music, and mechanical objects.

None of this was known, let alone understood, when Jojo was born. The Goushas had absolutely no idea what to do with their son. It seemed impossible that such a beloved, astonishingly smart little boy couldn't learn to dress himself, control his temper, or use the toilet. Were his tantrums sheer exercises in will, to be countered by the imposition of greater strength and authority? Or should he be indulged and coddled until he outgrew them? There were no answers; the most that Dawn and Joe could do was try to regulate their household and hope that Jojo would eventually grow out of his blatant and alarming disturbances.

In the meantime, Powell hired a day nurse, Louise Lee, who would remain with the family until she was incapacitated by a stroke in 1954. Of African-American and American Indian descent, Louise had been born in about 1890 and raised in Boston; she was "proud of her New England background but not above occasional hard work," as Dawn told one of Jojo's doctors. Still, she had her own ideas about what was best for the boy:

> While we were trying to teach him to do things for himself, she was determinedly trying to make him completely dependent upon her. It was impossible to persuade her that, if she loved him, she would not handicap him, since her own security lay in his helplessness. She always felt that anything the family did together without her was bad for him (since it was bad for her) and redoubled her cosseting. . . . Outside of her excessive piety and babying, she was a good sensible woman and gave him a great deal of love and devotion, which members of her own family had managed to wriggle out of.

Dignified, handsome, and authoritative, Lee was devoted to her young charge; years after she died, even a fleeting thought of the lost "Deesie" could send Jojo into a dangerous depression. During two separate periods of financial difficulty for the Goushas, she refused to be fired and came in to work every day without remuneration, an act of unselfishness that Dawn and Joe viewed with mixed emotions ("We were in the position of keeping on a sort of mother-in-law . . . who could not be put out like an ordinary employee," Powell explained).

Whatever complaints could be harbored about Louise Lee, her very presence enabled Dawn to escape from maternal chores and begin writing again. She became a regular contributor to *Snappy Stories* and *College Humor*, among other magazines, and started her first published novel, *Whither*, in October 1922. Her two favorite places to work were Central Park and the children's section of the New York Public Library. The writer and educator Hope Hale Davis has left us a sharp picture of Dawn hunkered down in the latter:

> Every day during its empty school hours she sat in a child-size chair at a child-size table concocting her comic tales of non-conformist love life for *Snappy Stories,* the odd article and interview, meanwhile working on serious fiction that revealed the kind of midwestern lives I would have thought she'd be glad to leave behind her forever.

"Bent over a book," Davis continued, "Dawn looked like a child herself, with her round face, dark curls and fleeting dimples that suggested a highly subversive secret." Davis was always tempted to talk with her, "but usually I resisted; I knew Dawn had to make every undisturbed moment count."

After a day's work, Powell would be more sociable. Davis recalled that she looked "oddly demure as she sipped her fourth martini":

> Her dimples appearing and disappearing, she would quietly add to someone's risqué story a postscript subtly more shocking than anything that had come before. Yet while I laughed I think even then we heard overtones of mockery at her own comedy, at her obligatory pretense that all was merry in her life. But when we marveled at her ability to exceed the high standard of alcohol consumption then in style, I'm not sure any of us realized that we were witnessing in desperate reality that cliché about drowning sorrows.

Powell's consumption increased markedly after Jojo was born; she would be a heavy drinker for the rest of her life, by some criteria certainly qualifying as an alcoholic. She drank almost every day, she drank quickly and eagerly, and, more often than not, she drank to get drunk. She preferred hard liquor, mostly whiskey or gin; she never cared much for wine or champagne and became a beer enthusiast only in her final months. She liked the effects of alcohol, the tingling sense of *permission* it gave, the enhanced conviviality, the diminution of self-consciousness and temporary immunity from personal demons that it provided. On occasion, she even found hangovers inspirational.

"Yes, he was tight now and he thought what a splendid word it was," she wrote in her book *The Happy Island:*

> "Tight"—the moment when your words and deeds swell up to fit your sagging personality, leaving not a chink for reason to probe, not a crease where dignity can hide; now you are tight, neat, exactly as big as you are small and small as you are big; now the lens of the mind magnifies to include only the immediate object, this cigarette, this match flame, this forefinger.

The writer and editor Matthew Josephson, who knew her for forty years, said that Powell "drank copiously for the joy of living, but seldom appeared overborne by drink even in the small morning hours." Compared to her husband, however, Powell was downright temperate. Taking advantage of the expense accounts allotted to senior advertising executives, Joe indulged in daily three-martini lunches in the speakeasies near his office on Lexington Avenue; after work, he would regularly drink into the night until he passed out.

By 1925, the fifth year of the marriage, theirs was a disquieted and unstable household. Jojo's condition was no less mysterious, and he was getting no better. Joe and Dawn were both frustrated with the progress of their writing (Joe would eventually give up the effort altogether), and their drinking binges often resulted in savage quarrels.

A spare, solemn poem that Powell submitted to the *Independent Poetry Review 1925* gives some sense of her desolation. It is entitled "Dead Things":

> *Tears, tears for dead things:*
> *For stifled songs—*
> *They hurt me with their beauty;*
> *For dreams I quenched*
> *Lest they might possess me;*
> *For loves I slew*
> *That they might not destroy me;*
> *For faith I trampled on*
> *Lest, one day, it betray me.*

In mid-June 1925, Dawn and Joe decided to separate—perhaps temporarily, possibly for good. Joe stayed in New York while Dawn went out to Ohio with three-year-old Jojo to visit her sisters and Auntie May.

Four terrible letters to Joe chronicle that journey. Dawn immediately recognized that a complete break was not at all what she wanted; the first of the letters is a curious mixture of apology (for her perceived "selfishness") and passive aggression (expressed in gently barbed references to Jojo's misery at being away from his father). One morning shortly after their arrival in Cleveland, Dawn took the boy along on a grueling taxi ride out to Painesville for a Lake Erie College class day. Homesick and confused, Jojo had a tantrum in the cab. "It took two hours to calm him down and by that time I did not look like the rich New York alumnae at *all*," she reported to Joe. "He had sat all the pleats out of my dress and left in their place a large wet blue stain. I arrived like that at college, a hat on one ear, my dirty child under one arm, my face gray—sort of a *leberwurst* color—and all my friends telling me how crushed my verve was and how awful I look."

Throughout much of their stay in Ohio, Jojo was "totally un-manageable." He smeared cold cream over Mabel's recently redeco-rated walls, and every morning woke up the whole household (including Mabel and Edgar Pocock's three young children) three hours before the appointed time. He wet the bed twice ("in spite of a hearty spanking," Dawn said). And he had "never cried so much or so inopportunely in his life."

The pressures and embarrassment were enormous. On June 30, Powell exploded in the most shocking outburst preserved in any of her letters:

> I have just spent two hours trying to beat my son into some sense of obedience but I haven't enough brute strength behind me. I have worked up a slow furious hate for him and believe I'd better come home as these dizzy rages are too murderous for either my good or his. . . . I'm afraid this trip has cured me completely of even any liking for him. I'd like to tie him up and beat him to a pulp.

Eventually, her fury passed. "I'm very fond of him again," Dawn wrote home a week later. "We are used to sleeping with each other now and really it comforts me to come to bed and get squeezed tightly by two little arms and have him breathe into my neck and occasionally drench my nightie with holy water. He is constantly astonished and pleased to wake up and find me there."

Mother and child returned to New York in mid-July. Whatever resolutions Joe and Dawn had made during their time away from each other would seem to have saved their marriage; but something had changed, and from this point their lives would increasingly diverge. An undated sketch by Powell posits a

> married couple—like Joe and me—who really know little about each other's friends, triumphs and, above all, defeats. . . .

He tells me little because the people are important in his profession but little to me beyond his connection. If anyone were
to write a biography of me—asking him to check whether I
knew these people—went here or there—had this or that ca-
tastrophe—he would know no more about it than someone
who never saw me.

Clearly, this was not the sort of marriage that would have satisfied many couples—and there were undoubtedly times when both
Dawn and Joe were deeply unhappy with whatever arrangement,
spoken or unspoken, they had made for themselves. Yet there is no
bitterness in the passage quoted above, only recognition and acceptance. The bond between husband and wife persisted throughout dal-
liances and travails that would have driven many others to a quick
divorce. It would be presumptuous to "judge" the Gousha marriage;
on some level, it clearly *worked* for both participants, and the mere
fact that it lasted for forty-two years speaks for itself.

It was around this time that Powell began to take trips away
from New York in order to write; a favorite destination was the
Hotel Traymore in Atlantic City, where she worked on her second
and third novels, *She Walks in Beauty* and *The Bride's House*. The process
was effective but lonely, particularly at the start. "It's funny writing
away from you—like shouting in a tunnel and getting no echo," she
said in a letter she sent to Joe from the Traymore in March 1926.

Even in town, however, the two had begun to move in different
circles. Joe was spending his spare time with buddies from the advertising world, and frequenting midtown spots such as the Blue
Ribbon, a German restaurant, and Tony's, a speakeasy. Dawn, meanwhile, was immersing herself in a cosmopolitan milieu of poets,
playwrights, and novelists, with some actors, directors, artists, and
musicians thrown into the mix.

Such company had become easier to cultivate after 1924, when
the Goushas moved to 46 West Ninth Street, in Greenwich Village.

Even then, it was said that the Village's great days were over, with the quarter's having already become a popular tourist destination. A restaurant guidebook published in 1925 entitled its chapter on the Village "Eating Among the Artists": "The Village is something not to be captured in a moment," readers were assured. "It has great beauty, but it is hidden. It is a collective charm, made up of many experiences, of glimpses of odd angles of architecture and queer corners of human hearts, of rousing parties in low-ceilinged rooms, deep arguments with wild-eyed enthusiasts and contemplative hours, alone, in a green garden."

Local landlords, in an effort to cash in on this "collective charm," had dutifully sliced up old town houses and tenements into tiny apartments to be let for the highest possible prices. By 1925, Greenwich Village was already a "golden garret," which meant that genuinely starving artists had to live elsewhere. (Luxury high-rise residences with pretentious names such as The Cézanne and The Van Gogh would come later.)

And yet having taken her own advice and combined and condensed and admired and sifted, Powell had decided that the Village really *was* still the Village after all. More poets and writers lived there than in any other neighborhood in America. Theaters, bookshops, nightclubs, restaurants, and coffeehouses were peppered throughout the narrow, tree-lined streets. Speakeasies were plentiful if you knew where to look, and finding out where to look was not very difficult.

The talk therein might be of Marx, Nietzsche, Ibsen, Henry Adams, the "Soviet Experiment" abroad (and the "inevitable" revolution in the United States), the underlying seriousness of the films of Charlie Chaplin, or the current issue of the *New Republic* (published on Fifteenth Street, just north of the Village border); equally, it might be merely some new tidbit about the area's most famous poet, Edna St. Vincent Millay, and her dramatic love life. The Village was a center for sexual varietism, where Puritanism was affronted every day by thought, word, and deed. A woman might take a lover, or a series of lovers, and have no fear of being shunned by her neighbors—a privilege hitherto reserved only for men. Finally, the Village had a substantial (and, for its time, astonishingly "out") gay population.

The names Powell drops in the diaristic appointment books she began keeping in 1925 are tantalizing: Conrad Aiken, Sherwood Anderson, Maxwell Bodenheim, e. e. cummings, Floyd Dell, Theodore Dreiser, Michael Gold, Genevieve Taggard, and many others. She met Ernest Hemingway one night that same year, when his hosts for the evening, the novelists Josephine Herbst and John Herrmann, simply happened by, tapped at the West Ninth Street window, and brought her out for a bender. Several other people who would become lifetime friends or acquaintances—such as Matthew Josephson, Charles Norman, the writer and editor Malcolm Cowley, and the poet and novelist Evelyn Scott—were among her neighbors.

Her choice companions included a charming, bibulous poet named Canby Chambers and his longtime love, Esther Andrews, a handsome, financially independent writer and editor who had been an intimate friend to D. H. Lawrence in England. In the late twenties, the two would move to Florida, where Chambers would spend the remainder of his life writing hundreds of mildly erotic stories for men's magazines. Of necessity, Powell kept in touch with Chambers and Andrews mostly by mail in later years, but the friendship was never broken off, and Andrews left her a handsome bequest upon her death in 1962.

Both Dawn and Joe were close to the Jolas brothers—Jacques, a distinguished pianist, and Eugene, a journalist and editor who founded the prescient literary magazine *transition* and published much of James Joyce's "Work in Progress" (later to become *Finnegans Wake*). Eugene had moved to France in the early twenties, but Powell saw him whenever he returned to New York, and she would spend several evenings with him and his family during her stay in Paris in late 1950.

Another early friend, Jacques LeClercq, was a poet, writer, and translator (his rendition of the complete works of Rabelais was available from the Modern Library for many years) whose own book *Showcases* presents a set of engaging, pseudoautobiographical short stories about some of the unconventional folks encountered over the course of his travels. His daughter Tanaquil LeClercq, whom Powell knew from her earliest childhood, would one day become well known as a ballet dancer.

The artist Niles Spencer quickly became one of Dawn's favorite companions. Associated with the Whitney Museum of American Art, Spencer was considered a member of the "Precisionist" school; his paintings often resembled architectural studies. A heavy and exuberant drinker, he managed, during one particularly well lubricated cocktail party at the Whitney, to push a Vanderbilt scion into a chocolate cake. This was not only bad manners but bad politics—the museum had been built with Vanderbilt money.

Yet another new friend, Dwight Fiske, embodied a certain stereotype of the witty, sophisticated, self-deprecating homosexual, a type that was viewed as both daring and fundamentally "safe" in the years between the world wars. A pianist and entertainer who sang arch, bawdy stories in a knowing and deliberately campy style, Fiske was a great hit in nightclubs and society circles.

Powell often worked with Fiske on his song-stories and was the dedicatee of his book *Without Music* (1933). "For Dawn Powell," the inscription reads, "through whose inspiration many of these stories came to be." Well put: Powell claimed to have contributed substantially to thirteen of the twenty-five skits, and she resented *Without Music*'s success ("Book reviewers who have ignored my hard-fought novels find whole columns to rave over this work by Dwight in which I helped so considerably," she remarked bitterly).

Powell also developed an especially close relationship with the writer John Dos Passos. He was already a celebrated novelist when they first met, in the early 1920s, through Esther Andrews; in his sadly abbreviated autobiography, *The Best Years*, Dos Passos calls Powell "one of the wittiest and most dashingly courageous women I ever knew." Indeed, she would be one of the few friends who would stand by him when, starting in the mid-1930s, he underwent a seismic political conversion that would eventually transform him from revolutionary Communist into conservative Republican.* Powell and Dos Passos never saw eye to eye politically—she would chide him for his communism in the 1930s and for his effusive praise of Barry Goldwater in 1964—but they never let such matters interfere with their long, serene, devoted, and rewarding friendship.

One person in particular dominated Powell's thinking during this period: the radical playwright and theorist John Howard Lawson. It is my own belief that the two had a passionate but highly secretive love affair between 1925 and 1929; at the very least, Lawson influenced Powell's life profoundly in those years, for good and for ill.

He had been born in New York on September 24, 1894, the son of wealthy second-generation Jewish immigrants (the family name was originally Levy). A precocious scholar, he was accepted into Williams College at the age of fifteen, and wrote his first play while still in Williamstown. The actor, songwriter, and producer George M. Cohan, then at the height of his career, took an option on another play, *Standards*, in 1915, but he ultimately fell out with the author and decided not to proceed.

When America entered the war in 1917, Lawson signed up for the ambulance corps; he met Dos Passos in France, and the two remained the best of friends for many years. After the war, Lawson returned to New York, where he lived in Patchin Place, a courtyard just off Sixth Avenue and Tenth Street in the Village (Djuna Barnes and e. e. cummings would also make their homes there). He became associated with the Washington Square Players, one of the many

---

*The Dos Passos archive at the University of Virginia is a fascinating collection that contains admiring letters from both longtime American Communist party leader Earl Browder and right-wing U.S. Vice President Spiro T. Agnew.

small experimental troupes then to be found throughout the neighborhood, and won his first acclaim with the Theatre Guild production of his *Processional*, a so-called "jazz symphony of American life" that was a critical success when it opened in January 1925.

"That play's combination of stock vaudeville characters and scenic techniques, jazz arrangements, dream symbolism, popular dances and expressionistic devices had been intended to forge, on a proletarian theme, a native dramatic idiom distinct from both realism and expressionism," Ira A. Levine has written in his book *Left-Wing Dramatic Theory in the American Theatre*. After *Processional* Lawson was deemed a visionary innovator within the tight-knit realm of the stage. In 1926, with his like-minded fellow writers Dos Passos, Michael Gold, Francis Faragoh, and Em Jo Basshe, he founded the New Playwrights Theatre, a proudly subversive organization that presented ideologically charged plays in working-class venues.

In the years when Powell was closest to him, Lawson was still an unaffiliated radical (albeit one with a deep admiration for Leon Trotsky). But after he became a screenwriter and moved to Hollywood, in 1929, he joined the Communist party and served as an intellectual leader in the Los Angeles chapter. As one of ten "unfriendly" witnesses who appeared before the House Committee on Un-American Activities to answer questions about their politics, Lawson would be blacklisted by the Hollywood establishment in 1947. Even among the so-called Hollywood Ten, he would stand out for his defiant Stalinism, and would be imprisoned from 1950 to 1951 for contempt of Congress.

All this was far in the future when Powell met Lawson in the early 1920s, probably around the same time she was introduced to Dos Passos. Lawson was then a charming, bright-eyed, driven young man, supremely self-assured. According to his biographer, Robert H. Hethmon, Lawson "adopted, or strove to adopt, the position of the learned man, the sage, the thinker, the supreme analyzer who recognized the complex nature of situations and saw through, beneath and behind them." In another era, he might have been described as a sort of guru, and he made an enormous impression on the distraught, insecure Dawn Powell, herself just beginning to write plays and delighted to be instructed by such an attractive and acknowledged master.

Two entries from the diaries of Cleveland-based editor Nathaniel Howard suggest that Dawn took her first extramarital lover sometime between the summers of 1925 and 1926. During her trial separation from Joe in 1925, while talking one evening with Howard and his wife, Marjorie, at their home in Ohio, she divulged that she had never been unfaithful to her husband. In September 1926, Howard visited New York and spent another evening with Dawn, during which they discussed their common domestic problems. "Dawn was very kind," he reported. "She has felt as badly as I did, only many times. She is hardened now."

Whatever may have happened over the course of that year, Lawson had become a mantric refrain in Powell's appointment book by late 1925:

> *October 13*—Tea with Jack Lawson. New things to think about. . . . *October 19*—Jack L. called up. I was flip. Lunch on Thursday. . . . *October 26*—Jack called up for Thursday luncheon date. . . . *October 27*—Wrote to Jack calling off all Thursday dates. . . . *January 23* [1926]—Breakfast with Jack. . . . *October 28* [1926]—Saw Jack Lawson. Never want to see him again.

And so on. Lawson's is far and away the most common name in Powell's diaries for 1925, 1926, and 1927 (she either lost, destroyed, or never began any journals for 1928 and 1929). Anyone who has ever kept a confidential diary under compromised circumstances knows how code words may be woven into a seemingly innocent surface narrative. What could the "new things to think about" reference have meant, for example, especially when followed by an entry that records, just as elliptically, "Joe and I decide to readjust our lives"? If Lawson was "only" a friend, why should Powell be in such a constant tizzy over him, alternately worshipful and on the brink of banishing him from her life?

Whatever its nature, her relationship with Lawson continued only during those few years, and should be discussed all of a piece. After Lawson married Sue Edmond in 1926, the new Mrs. Lawson began to appear in Powell's diaries as well. The two women evidently hated one another pretty much from the start, but Powell seems to have been half determined to stick it out and become the other's great friend. This made for some awkward moments over the years:

> *August 4, 1931*—Sue and I had a terrible fight—she said I was a God-damned fool for not realizing that Jack patronized me. I was knocked out by the crack, went up to bed, then suddenly rushed down and told her I hated her, she was terrible and all sorts of awful things. I was quite sick afterward and of course unable to do a bit of writing all week.
>
> *October 6, 1931*—I hold it against [Sue] that she is dulling Jack to her level, making a rather average person of a very extraordinary genius. A female advantage that keeps him from being desirable to better women than herself, of course, but a sad spectacle.
>
> *June 8, 1932*—Drove in with Lawsons and party at Esther's where Sue and I were great pals but in parting I socked her, also Jack.
>
> *October 21, 1933*—Sue was secretly mad at me and later at Sam's struck me, on pretense of something else. Funny the way we always start out so jollily and end up with the same old row.

For her part, Sue Lawson seems to have been aware of some romantic liaison between Powell and her husband. On July 17, 1928,

she wrote a letter to Lawson in California, telling him about a recent
Manhattan party:

> At this gathering, Dawn, being full of hooch, got in quite a state
> because she knew you were having affairs in Hollywood and
> knew I must be upset. I claimed I would do my best. The way
> that girl carries on about you is simply disgusting—she not
> only boasts that you influence her entire lit'ry career, which is
> the only thing that means anything to her now, she says, but she
> intimates that there is still quite a romance, aside from the
> affair you had when you had her to teas before Jeffrey [Sue and
> Jack's son] was born and told her you weren't living with any-
> one. All this was shouted in a most casual manner and I was so
> affable in my gin that I didn't know she was even trying to pull
> anything until the next day.

This is the only known direct reference to an affair between
Powell and Lawson. Indeed, aside from Powell's diaries, any other
record of the friendship is suspiciously lacking. She is never mentioned in his unpublished autobiography, despite the fact that they
saw each other almost every day for several years; and not one letter
has been found from her to him or from him to her, though both of
them saved their letters and we know from Powell's diaries that Lawson wrote to her often. This suggests a mass destruction—surely
something from their extensive correspondence would have turned
up unless both parties were determined that it wouldn't.

Looking back almost seventy years later, Jeffrey Lawson, an
author and photographer, believed an affair between Powell and his
father was "highly probable." "When we lived on Long Island, my
father was always taking the train in to New York and my mother was
quite upset about it," he said in 1997. "He was a real ladies' man,
combining a strong intellect with enormous vitality and animal

energy. As he grew older, he felt very guilty about all he had put my mother through. By then, due in part to Communist discipline, he had become almost mechanically moralistic."

The rupture came in the mid-1930s. Throughout 1932 and 1933, as Powell worked on her novel *The Story of a Country Boy*, she planned to dedicate it to Lawson. It was plotted along fairly stringent dialectical lines, inspired by literary and political ideas she said she had acquired from him. But when the book came out, in 1934, the dedication was in fact to Jacques LeClercq; by that time, Lawson had virtually disappeared from the pages of her diary and, it seems, from her life.

What finally occurred? A clue may lie in a diary entry Powell wrote in the early-morning hours of January 1, 1934:

> Such a dreadful nightmare has just happened to me—like nothing ever before in my life, and with it came such a quiet realization of facts that I do not believe anything like that can ever touch me again. I am erasing the picture from my mind and half of my own heart at the same time. From now on I will be absolutely free, no affections can touch me, nothing. It is sad to learn the final lesson—that the only way to avoid such stabs is to school yourself to a denial of feeling, both pleasurable and bad. This is such a queer physical sickness and I must control it—the cause and effect must go and, by God, *will*.

Half of my own heart . . . : Powell clearly ended an association with somebody dear to her in those terrible first hours of the new year. Whether or not that person was Lawson, Powell's subsequent references to him were few and dismissive.

In fact, whatever romantic relationship there was between them had probably been over for a while, and had perhaps been carried on in the last few years only as a doomed crush in Dawn's

unhappy mind. Certainly Sue Lawson thought the affair was long finished when she wrote about it in the summer of 1928.

My own guess is that Powell and Lawson's last meeting as lovers
may have taken place in early 1929, when he visited New York briefly
to prepare for Sue's impending move to Hollywood. A decade later,
on January 26, 1939, Powell, who observed many private anniversaries, wrote a cryptic sentence fragment—"End of ten years"—at
the top of the page in her diary and then commenced a solemn meditation:

> There is an overwhelming kind of love—not born of habit but
> a love of the person's nature, mind and very self (apart from a
> physical attraction which should be present)—that enables one
> to want the best for that person because they deserve it, to
> want it even at one's own expense. This is a truth not many
> people find out because it is hard to find a person one admires,
> enjoys, loves, likes and lusts for all simultaneously.

In John Howard Lawson, I believe that Dawn Powell found such
a person, though the evidence for that conclusion is maddeningly
skimpy. It would not be worth examining in such detail, however, if
it were only a casual affair; rather, Lawson was probably Powell's first
extramarital lover—and her last new love—and the impression he
made on her was obviously enormous. It is always dangerous to use
the works of any artist, even one so resolutely autobiographical as
Powell, to bolster theories about that artist's life. Still, for whatever
it is worth, Powell was writing *The Bride's House*, a strong, direct, and
seemingly very intimate book about a woman torn between affection
for her husband and passion for a dashing and mysterious stranger, in
late 1925 and early 1926, at just the time she was closest to Lawson.

Finally, in 1934, after Powell had "erased half of her heart," she
abruptly changed her prose style and launched into the acute,
unflinching satire of *Turn, Magic Wheel*. Whatever might lie in store

for her, she was determined to survive any personal dilemmas; her childhood had taught her that much. "I will be absolutely free, no affections can touch me, nothing," she swore—and she knew by now that it was her work, if anything, that would save her.

The Early Novels

❧

The novel is my lawful married mate.

DAWN POWELL, 1933

DESPITE THEIR MANY IMPERFECTIONS, Dawn Powell's first three books introduce and explore themes that would obsess her throughout her career. Because they were all finished during the same short period—within about eighteen months of each other—the novels are best discussed together.

Whither, begun in 1922, was completed in late 1924 and published in February 1925 by the Boston firm of Small, Maynard (soon to be absorbed by Dodd, Mead). Powell disavowed the book almost immediately, well before her second novel, *She Walks in Beauty*, was promoted as her debut in 1928. Thereafter, she refused even to acknowledge *Whither* in her official biography or in lists of her publications; she considered the book a genuine embarrassment and was quite put out when her young friend Hannah Green found a copy in a secondhand bookstore in the early 1960s. "Reading *Whither* I was horrified at how completely hopeless and devoid of promise it was— far worse than what I had written at thirteen," Powell observed in her diary on December 1, 1943.

She was right: *Whither* is not very good. Paradoxically, it is both cautiously formal in its structure and decidedly disorganized in its use of material, with an unbelievable happy ending that the reputedly "hard-boiled" author may actually herself have believed for a moment. Her profound aversion to the book may have had to do with her displeasure over its brazen incorporation of raw autobiographical material that she never went on to transform into polished fiction; *Whither* is not so much a novel as it is a proclamation, a statement of intent, a self-justification—almost a manifesto.

But if *Whither* is unarguably the poorest novel Powell ever published, it is nonetheless a source of uncommon fascination for anybody interested in her life. With the possible exception of Marcia Willard in *My Home Is Far Away*, Zoe Bourne, the heroine of *Whither*, is the character Powell based most completely on herself, at least externally. And unlike *My Home Is Far Away*, with its distant memory play, *Whither* is all present tense—a book *about* a New York woman writer in her twenties *by* a New York woman writer in her twenties— and therefore preserves a more or less contemporaneous self-portrait of Dawn Powell on the threshold of her professional life.

Zoe is modeled so closely on Powell's own early adulthood that the novel has a distinctly diaristic quality. Like the young Powell, Zoe ("around twenty-one or so and probably the clever sort!") has moved to Manhattan to live in a rooming house on the Upper West Side, just off the Hudson River, with several talented and eccentric friends.

She hails from a small town ("Albon," the ancestor of Lamptown, Lakeville, Lesterville, London Junction, Silver City, and other invented midwestern towns to come) and has escaped from a bickering father and stepmother. Described as a "girl who was breaking off with her family and all the stupidities which Albon represented, for a career in New York," she loves literature, classical music, and the theater, is seemingly well educated, and plans to be a writer (either plays or novels—but absolutely no screenwriting, please, no matter how well it might pay). For a while, she reluctantly takes a job in publicity, with an office on Madison Square, but eventually she starts to sell articles to a new magazine called *Vanity Box* (the original *Vanity Fair* was the hot magazine of the day) and embarks on what we can only assume will be a brilliant career.

Zoe gets drunk in speakeasies ("Truly, alcohol was a great leveler") and spends her evenings in Greenwich Village ("You should live down here," one of her male friends tells her during a visit to his Bank Street studio; Powell was planning her own move as she prepared *Whither* for publication). She is matter-of-fact about sex ("Perhaps she attracted him mentally and not at all physically!" she frets. "Ghastly thought!") but deeply romantic all the same. Cutting short a budding relationship with a "healthy, good looking but very stupid young man" and resisting the advances of a decadent theatrical producer who promises to "settle some stock" on her, Zoe remains pure, having lost her heart to a smart, kindly advertising executive named Christopher Kane (who is, unfortunately, already married— a complication that is cleared up all too tidily in the final chapters).

From here, Powell veers into fantasy. Kane loves Zoe back but, curiously, accepts a job in London so as not to interfere with her writing, telling her, "You're to work and write and become the great Zoe Bourne—just as you've always dreamed! And nothing is to come in your way. You mustn't let it! Stick to your dreams, Zoe, please. . . . I am so abominably selfish—so weak, Zoe, dear—that I couldn't let you work out your own brave little destiny."

This is awful—the stuff of the most flowery silent-film titles. But the two of them inevitably fall into each other's arms, and

Whither concludes with a short chapter in which Zoe bids farewell to her rooming-house friends and prepares to sail for England with Kane, whom she has suddenly married.

It is, of course, the sort of "happy ending" that Powell had envisioned for herself, and some remnants of that dream undoubtedly lingered. One has the sense, when reading *Whither*, that the novel was specifically intended to answer everybody who had ever doubted its author—her family, her peers, the small "town full of mediocre people, all in mediocre professions," that she so despised—and to forecast a glorious future in which she would "show" them all. Zoe has unshakable faith in her powers, her perceptions—in a word, her *importance*—and she will not let anything keep her down. She has escaped; she is in the middle of her journey; today is better than yesterday was, tomorrow must be brighter than today: the same Coué philosophy that so often sustained Powell herself. Life will be a grand adventure; Zoe Bourne/Dawn Powell simply won't have it any other way.

A central problem with *Whither* is that in it Powell rarely fleshes out these passions and convictions with enough detail to compel readers with different backgrounds, different experiences. Too often, she is content to sum up Zoe's excitement about her new home with the facile ejaculation "New York!" (there are probably more exclamation points in *Whither* than in all of Powell's other work combined), without giving us any real description of the city itself.

We are meant to feel the pull of Greenwich Village but never told just *why:* rather, we must rely upon our own ready-made, generic "Village-in-the-Golden-Age" associations gleaned from other sources. We know about some of Zoe's enthusiasms, all shared by Powell—city walks, window shopping, the number 5 bus that to this day travels from Riverside Drive to Greenwich Village and back—but we don't know the exact nature of their appeal. And real places that Powell frequented—such as the long-lived restaurant/speakeasy Bertolotti's, the popular Russian Inn on Thirty-seventh Street

west of Fifth Avenue, or the office towers down by Madison Square—
are mentioned only in passing, without further description, as if
every reader would know them well and be able to fill in the petty
details.

Finally, Zoe Bourne is a little too self-assured and "above the
battle" to be fully convincing. She's even rather didactic, a quality
Powell would scrupulously eschew in her later characters. And her
abiding, youthful belief that the world will reward anybody who is
hardworking and talented must have come to seem terribly naïve to
the author as she grew older.

Still, little that Powell wrote is entirely without merit, and
there are funny passages throughout *Whither*. For example, following
a dispiriting visit with an old friend who now professes to be passionately interested only in having as many children as possible, Zoe,
wearing her publicist's mantle, comes up with an absurd bit of
puffery:

BABIES!

The Love Perpetrators!

Burrowing into Your Heart! Sliding into Your Soul!

Every Baby Represents a Thousand Dollars

in the Bank of Love!

BEGIN TODAY!

"And then a poster," Zoe goes on, "saying 'A Baby a Year Keeps
the Doctor.'"

One suspects that chapter 13 may originally have been drafted
as a short story, and indeed, it can pretty much stand by itself. Julie,
one of Zoe's rooming-house friends, is summoned by her husband-
to-be to a restaurant for what he has planned as a prenuptial confes-
sional. When she arrives, Alphonse sits her down and, in a manner
that is at once maudlin and self-congratulatory, tells her about his
past affairs: "I am afraid I have had only too much experience, Julie,

to make a good husband for you." He speaks of the women he has loved: "Pepita, the belle of the Honduras," "Isabella, the most dangerously beautiful woman in all Central America," "Juanita," and others.

Julie does her best to reassure him, not by granting the humble forgiveness he is expecting but rather, to Alphonse's astonishment, by countering with the embarrassing details of her *own* affairs, such as "the time in Denver when Johnny Beekman followed me all the way into my hotel room." The litany proceeds from there, with

> Julie, her chin on her hands, scarcely paying any attention to Alphonse's words, so absorbed was she in the recollection of her own glorious adventures of the past fourteen or fifteen years. Junior proms, vacations in the Maine woods, vacations in Honolulu, two years as a co-ed, debuts in three cities, and everywhere men, men, men. Engagements on the stage because of men. All kinds of engagements because of men. Indeed, Julie began to think she had never exchanged more than a dozen words with any of her own sex until she came to [the rooming house].

The egotistical Alphonse is mortified; he hurriedly breaks off the engagement and leaves the restaurant. By the chapter's close, Julie is already flirting cheerfully with another man.

One may wonder why Powell gave Kane, who is in so many particulars a portrait of Joseph Gousha, the burden of a first wife, especially since the spouse is such a shadowy character and ultimately so easily dispatched. Even more intriguing, considering the circumstances of Powell's own early married life—with separate apartments in Manhattan and Brooklyn, and the decidedly laissez-faire attitude the Goushas took toward one another—is the section in which Zoe says, "He isn't really a married man because they don't live together."

As mentioned earlier, Powell discreetly subtracted a year from her age sometime in the mid-1920s, probably at the time *Whither* was published. A clue to her reasoning may be found in some words she gives Zoe in *Whither:* "Thirty is really the most important age for women. . . . They have to be started toward fame or a family by that time, and if they're not, they're done for. So you see it's very necessary that I should crowd the next few years." Almost thirty herself, with a marriage that was already troubled, a much-loved but frustratingly impaired son, and no fame on the horizon, Powell was likely expressing her own darkest fears.

The press notices for *Whither* were mostly brief, vaguely favorable, and fundamentally kind—much kinder than Powell herself would be toward the book in years to come. "While not glaringly original in either conception or treatment, Miss Powell's story has a refreshing naturalness and normality about it," an anonymous reviewer wrote in the *New York Times* on March 15, 1925.

> Miss Powell peoples her pages with a variety of interesting and, at times, well-hit-off types. Julie and Maisie, with whom Zoe shares rooms and a "semi-private bath," are deftly contrasted; Mrs. Horne, the landlady, really lives and moves, and the men in the book, particularly Hill and Kane, are no interpolated puppets. Their lovemaking has a healthy glow about it which separates it as far as possible from the mawkish.
>
> All in all, *Whither* should be welcomed by the large public that likes such wholesome and entertaining little yarns.

(Imagine the proud, skeptical Powell's reaction to this last line!)

The *Saturday Review of Literature* damned the novel with faint praise: "While the author writes with earnestness and evident sincerity and produces a thoroughly readable story, the book is neither searching in its insight into character nor conspicuous as a study of life. The plot is thoroughly conventional in texture and the ending departs not at all from the usual." Still, the critic conceded, Powell showed some ability: "If there be anything to distinguish the book, it is a certain freshness with which the author writes and a certain engaging air of being deeply and seriously concerned about her characters and their lives."

The warmest review came from Charles Norman, the new Village neighbor who would become Powell's lifelong friend. Writing in the *Literary Review*, he called *Whither* a "much finer conception of the jazz age than even [John Howard Lawson's] *Processional*" (!). Its author, he asserted, "has a fine satiric perception of the significances of little things in the affairs of men and women, particularly women. She is thus a dangerous creature to be let free to write of them, for she does so unmercifully, yet withal lightly, so that there is much to laugh with in *Whither*."

It is difficult to tell when Powell's distaste for the book set in; the inscriptions on the copies she presented to family and friends are jubilant, as if she felt that with its publication, she had finally *arrived*. But there can be no doubt that she soon enough decided *Whither* was a failure, scratched it from the record as best she could, and set to work on finding another home for her new book, already nearing completion.

Her search would take three years. Powell wrote the novel that was eventually published as *She Walks in Beauty* very quickly, between October 1924 and April 1925—"just six months' work," she would reflect in 1931, during one of her periodic (and usually self-punitive) retrospective accountings of time spent, this one brought on by a problematic patch in the creation of *The Tenth Moon / Come Back to Sorrento*, her fourth novel. And "no trouble in writing it apparently, with one to three short stories and two or three book reviews a month, besides. I suppose this was because it was my first year free of housekeeping. Anyway, it was my first year in the Village."

Only bits and pieces of the original manuscript are known to exist; however, through surviving diaries and letters, we do know that Powell's two working titles were "Rooms" and "The Dark Pool." When the book was finished, at ten minutes to one on the morning of April 12, 1925, Dawn and Joe sent out store-bought commercial birth announcements to friends, trumpeting a "new arrival, 'The Dark Pool.'" By 1926, it was called "Rooms"; after what Powell claimed were thirty-six rejections, it was finally published by Brentano's as *She Walks in Beauty* in the spring of 1928.

When a couple posts a birth announcement for a novel, it suggests a collaborative effort, and indeed, that was very much the case here (Powell's diary entry for April 11, 1925, reads, "Joe worked on novel at office, copying it, and I worked on editing at home"). *She Walks in Beauty* was written toward the end of Powell's initial period of contentment with Gousha, and the book is dedicated to him. Their separation and her tense visit to Cleveland with Jojo, to be followed by their new accommodation to married life, were still some months off.

She Walks in Beauty was the first of Powell's "Ohio novels," and for the rest of her life the first published work she would acknowledge. The biographical statement she provided for the dust jacket is enlightening if not entirely reliable:

I was born in Mt. Gilead, Ohio and I am twenty-eight years old. All of Ohio is simply infested with my family, the Powells and the Shermans, and at a distance I get quite sentimental about them. I graduated from Lake Erie College and no one was more amazed than myself. I had only six dollars when I came—that was nine years ago—and now that is gone so you can see the City has really got me. I did publicity and book reviewing, I married and now have a little boy and a player piano. From the time I was strong enough to hold a pencil I wrote stories in appletrees, cellars, old sleighs, under the front porch and more recently in Central Park where I completed *She Walks in Beauty.*

Here again, Powell was fudging her age. She was at least thirty and quite possibly thirty-one when she wrote this blurb (assuming authorship a few months before publication, in late 1927, or nine years after her arrival in New York). One more time, in *She Walks in Beauty*, Powell proves that the age of thirty held crucial significance for her, even more than it does for most young people: she describes a character as being "nearly thirty—too old to enjoy her opportunities." Acutely aware of the passage of time, Powell may have felt that this line applied as well to her own situation. Joe's increasing alcoholism, their son's myriad physical and psychological problems, and the crush of financial difficulties brought on by Jojo's care ensured that her accomplishments brought her only sporadic and bittersweet happiness. Moreover, despite growing recognition within her field, the fame and fortune she craved and believed she deserved still seemed impossibly distant.

Although *She Walks in Beauty* is a definite improvement over *Whither*, it is one of Powell's weakest books, and she rarely referred to it again, either. The setting is a fictional village called Birchfield, surrounded by all the real Ohio towns Powell knew so well: Crestline, Galion, Shelby, Shiloh, and Mansfield, then renowned as a roisterous, "wide-open" small city. Such interweaving of fact and fiction would become a trademark technique of Powell's; whenever she created a place, she would surround it with familiar and verifiable sites so that her readers could neither pinpoint an exact location nor mistake the general area.

She Walks in Beauty has a scanty story line; it is fundamentally a series of vignettes from a wrong-side-of-the-tracks Ohio boardinghouse, a fusion of the lodging run by Grandmother Sherman and the table Orpha May used to provide for travelers and railroad men opposite the Shelby Junction depot. In the novel, the boardinghouse is run by a woman named Aunt Jule, who, with some slight alterations, is clearly a composite of Powell's industrious relatives:

She was a splendid woman, even now in her late sixties, a woman of magnificent physique, with a fine mellow face, handsome nose, gentle golden eyes, and a sensitive thoroughbred mouth. Aunt Jule had been a belle in her day—that much at least Birchfield admitted possible. But today she was a town character, a social outcast, as any woman must be who for a period of years keeps a cheap lodging house for the tangle of driftwood washed in by the railroad trains. Yet there was a noble dignity about her in her gray percale house dress, her black hair piled in sleek coils on the top of her head, and tiny curls lying on the back of her smooth olive neck.

The central characters are two sisters, Linda and Dorrie Shirley, the one a cold beauty, the other younger, somewhat less physically attractive, but a keenly intelligent observer and budding writer. Their mother has died, their father is shiftless and irresponsible, and they have been left with the kindly and sophisticated Aunt Jule, who watches out not only for her charges but for her diverse and eccentric patrons. There are memorable cameos of visiting actors, teachers, and salesmen, and—this being a Powell novel—one guest speaks ecstatically of the pleasures to be had in far-off New York.

Linda is proper, calculating, status-conscious, and fiercely conventional in her tastes, a frosty female Babbitt. She marries the idiotic and unpleasant rich boy whom she covets, and we are left to imagine a loveless, living hell for her husband ("Courtenay kissed her hotly. Later on, Linda thought, after they were married, she could tell him she didn't like to be kissed"). Meanwhile, Dorrie watches the world, takes a wild ride with some wild company, falls in love, is disappointed by the experience, and remains, however inconclusively, in Birchfield, as Aunt Jule prepares for another season and the novel ends.

One weakness of *She Walks in Beauty* is its focus on the stereotypical and unprepossessing Linda, at the expense of Dorrie. Can

Powell really have thought that the older sister, for all her beauty, was the more compelling character? Or was this a sop to readers of what we would now label "romance fiction"?

With the hindsight provided by *My Home Is Far Away* (1944) and what Powell would sometimes confess was an essentially autobiographical representation of her family therein, it seems safe to say that Linda is patterned, at least in part, on Powell's distorted childhood image of her older sister, Mabel (the "pretty one," here endowed with a dollop of stepmother Sabra Powell's frigidity). Dorrie—smart, eager, undervalued, musical; fascinated by classic literature and remote places; lively and unpretentious but imbued with a soul of untarnished poetry—is, of course, purest Dawn.

One speech in *She Walks in Beauty* sums up Powell's philosophy so acutely that it could have been her credo:

> "For years, I have had only one desire—to get an attic somewhere and write—write at any cost. I will never be crushed by a system—domestic or economic—that much I vowed. I am going to write my novels and nothing—nothing—is to get in my way. Work will be my armor against pain. . . . I have learned to be ruthless, as you must learn to be if you're not to be hurt by life. . . . It's the only way any one can live. I've seen too many artists compromise with themselves not to know that weakness is destruction. . . . I have denied myself everything that might give me pleasure—and I could be a sybarite, I assure you, if I chose—when it took me from the work I had set for myself."

Powell gives these lines not to Dorrie but to a male character, Roger Wickley, the visiting New York writer whom she adores and with whom she engages in her first literary shop talk ("This—well, this is *me*," she says as she hands him her poetry). It has been suggested (and

sometimes decried) that Powell's vision of the world was traditionally masculine in its viewpoint. "You know, Dawn is actually a man,"
Edmund Wilson once told his daughter Rosalind, who understood
the comment to refer not to Powell's sexual orientation (or some
long-hidden biological secret!) but to the fact that she lived her life
in a manner that had long been limited to men, and was generally
happier in the company of men than in that of women.

Powell herself might have agreed: "How much sharper and better to have the central figure a man rather than a woman," she wrote
in her diary while finishing *Turn, Magic Wheel*, "a man in whom my
own prejudices and ideas can easily be placed, whereas few women's
minds . . . flit as irresponsibly as that." Increasingly, the characters
with whom Powell seemed to identify most closely (with the crucial
exception of Marcia Willard in *My Home Is Far Away*) would be men.

And until Powell was in her fifties, she did in fact prefer male
companionship. "Female friends are the greatest hazard in a working
woman's life for they cannot be casual," she wrote in 1944. She
believed that women were rarely truly committed to creative work
and that they often took a curious, selfish satisfaction in pestering
people who *were* working. In later years, Powell's attitude would
change markedly, as her close friendships with Margaret De Silver,
Frances Keene, Ann Honeycutt, Hannah Green, and Jacqueline
Miller Rice, among others, attest.

Like all of Powell's Ohio novels, *She Walks in Beauty* is stark and
rather grim. And yet the author could never completely restrain her
delight in the telling of unvarnished truths, neither complimentary
nor unduly tragic, about human beings. She begins a description of
one of her characters, the "fast" girl Esther Brown, thus: "She was an
innocent country lass—but that was solely through lack of opportunity." So far, so good—a blithe witticism out of Mae West or Noël
Coward. But then Powell proceeds to a discussion of sensual initiation that is decidedly unusual for its plainspoken honesty:

To be sure, when she was ten or eleven some boy cousins had spent a summer on the farm and out in the hayloft they had played fascinating if elemental games. Unfortunately the boys had left before Esther had mastered quite all of life's mysteries, and she was seventeen before further opportunity, in the person of Lew Mason, presented itself. Lew was forty and he was fat, but he was a man and, Esther felt, a willing enough co-worker in life's laboratory.

This is phrased straightforwardly, with clarity and humor, as one person recounting an experience to another. More important, however, is what it is written *without*—namely, any sense of sin or shame, any apology for human curiosity and desire, any effort either to shock or to titillate the reader. For Powell, as reflected in the characters of whom she seemed to be fondest, sex was simply something that *happened*, and happened relatively often, with varying degrees of involvement and satisfaction for the participants. It was a fact of life, but certainly wasn't a foundation on which to build one's life.

She Walks in Beauty is best understood as a transitional novel. It does not preach to the audience (as *Whither* sometimes does); Powell's fictional figures are here beginning to inhabit their own little lives, rather than serving as multiple mouthpieces of the author. The book shows some evidence of hasty writing, but it is sincere throughout and, at its best, gives us an inkling of what was to come.

Once again, the critical reception was mixed, though this time the articles were longer and more prominently placed than those accorded *Whither*. The *New York Times* called *She Walks in Beauty* a "triumph of atmosphere and sustained point of view."

"Dawn Powell, whose first novel this is, has caught the adolescent note and held it to the end," the unnamed *Times* reviewer wrote.

Not once does she slide over the borderline and become a sentimental adult writing reminiscently of a blurred past, and if she does write a simpering prose at rare times, it is quite in key with certain moods of her characters. A natural artist, and not a satirist, Miss Powell accepts the value of the people she is creating without any superior sneering on her part. Hence, the occasional gaucheries in *She Walks in Beauty* only add to its authentic flavor.

Margery Latimer, in the *New York Herald Tribune*, was less kind—and less comprehending. "The serious weakness of this book lies in its having no point," she stated. "With all her simplicity and hardness and understanding the author has done no more than assemble a number of snapshots of a small town and its types."

The *Saturday Review of Literature* placed the book firmly in the "Winslow-Suckow" tradition (Thyra Samter Winslow and Ruth Suckow were two novelists and short-story writers from the Midwest, popular in the 1920s and '30s and currently undervalued). The critic especially liked Aunt Jule and Linda Shirley, the "rock-bound little beauty"; Dorrie is nowhere mentioned, one more sign of the lack of emphasis the author placed on her best character.

Less successful, the reviewer felt, were Powell's "odd" people: "The mentally man-obsessed old maid, the physically man-obsessed young trollop, the gibbering and decrepit philosopher, the small-time vaudeville group, and the Main Street aristocrats have been done again, have been well done again, but only from the shiny surface slant that the talons of *Winesburg, Ohio* seem not even to have scratched."

The piece ended with a backhanded compliment: "It is unfortunate, but apparently inevitable that books with as much merit as *She Walks in Beauty* come in for harsher criticism than their inferior contemporaries because they say so briskly and explicitly what they want to say that one cannot help wishing they wanted to say something more important."

No point, no moral, "unimportant" material, "sordid" characters: this was the first time such criticism had been leveled at Powell's work, and it would dog her for the rest of her life. To some extent, the complaints linger to this day. For example, in her searching and otherwise excellent study of the Group Theatre, *Real Life Drama* (1990), Wendy Smith calls Powell a "writer who surgically dissected human weakness but felt no obligation to stitch up the wounds her literary scalpel inflicted. . . . Compassion was foreign to Powell, at least as an author; even in the cynical twenties her four published novels were notable for their matter-of-fact acceptance of life's cruelty."

Powell herself might have countered that she was merely trying to present the world as honestly and engagingly as she could, without undue sentimentality or softness. "The artist who really loves people loves them so well the way they are he sees no need to disguise their characteristics—he loves them whole, without retouching," she wrote in 1948. "Yet the word always used for this unqualifying affection is 'cynicism.'"

She knew what she was doing, even in such an immature, imperfect creation as *She Walks in Beauty*. "My plan has always been to feed a historical necessity," Powell would declare in 1938. "In the Ohio books I was not interested in making up romances, but in archaeology and showing up people and places that are or have been familiar types but were not acceptable to fiction, because of inner wars in their natures that make them confused human characters instead of standard fiction black and white types—good, bad, strong, weak."

In her next work she would excavate her own "inner war."

The Bride's House, published by Brentano's in early 1929, was Powell's first important novel. Valuable in and of itself, it is moreover another of her books with unusual significance for a biographer.

If the two earlier novels are literally autobiographical, with a clearly delineated "Dawn" figure in each, *The Bride's House* splits the author into four distinct roles across as many generations of a single troubled family. Powell's sensibility is evident in the bright child Vera, the young woman Sophie, the middle-aged (and once scandalous) Aunt Lotta, and the ancient Grandmother, who has fallen into sleepy senility and yet awakes now and then from her reveries to utter elliptical, sage commentary on the other characters.

As far as we know, the details of the narrative in *The Bride's House* have little to do with actual events in Powell's life. And yet the book seems to reveal far more of the author's inner experience than either of the first two novels, especially if (as appears likely) it was composed at the peak of her involvement with John Howard Lawson and may be seen as mirroring her own confused mixture of exultation and aching melancholy.

Like *She Walks in Beauty*, *The Bride's House* was written very quickly—begun on December 1, 1925, it was completed on July 17, 1926—but it is infinitely darker, richer, more disciplined, and more consistent than anything Powell had published before. As in her earlier books, there are a great many characters (here they are mostly women—a higher proportion than in any other Powell novel), but they all serve a purpose in the narrative. In this work, the author's quasi-improvisatory detours from her plot inevitably lead back to the main road.

Sophie in particular is both fully fleshed out and deeply ambivalent; through the cryptic utterances of Grandmother, the rumors and teasing flashes of Aunt Lotta, and the struggles of young Vera, we learn a great deal about what Sophie may have been during her girlhood and what she will likely become as an older, and then an elderly, woman. A certain timelessness—an intergenerational stream of consciousness—runs through the book: "Sophie is our blood, and we attract suffering," according to Aunt Lotta.

The Bride's House is set in Ashton Center, another invented mid-

western town; the action takes place in the closing years of the nineteenth century, around the time of Powell's own birth. Its basic story
line may be likened to the plot of any number of "bodice-rippers"
from the archives of romance fiction: Sophie Truelove marries kind,
steady Lynn Hamilton and hopes for a fulfilling and conventional
home life with him. Unfortunately, she then develops an intense passion for the dashing and elusive Jerome Gardiner and, after showing
some heroic restraint, gives herself to him.

Her husband learns about the affair, and though he is understandably less than overjoyed, he offers to go on as before; Sophie,
however, has enough self-awareness to recognize that what happened
once will happen again, and that their marriage can never be as it
was. And so she follows Gardiner to Washington, where she expects
to lead an insecure (all members of the Gardiner family are said to be
"weak with women") though fully involving and sometimes exhilarating new life.

One of the things that impresses a latter-day reader about *The
Bride's House*—in addition to its mixture of stark fatalism and informal family vignettes—is the way the book abruptly stops, neither
pointing toward a moral nor judging any of the characters, except as
fellow doomed, storm-tossed human beings engulfed in an impossible situation. The ending is neither "happy" nor "sad"; it simply *is*.
Nothing is resolved, and while we certainly care about Lynn and
Sophie (Jerome is left sketchy, as befits a mysterious icon), we are
satisfied that nothing *need* be resolved. We are not encouraged to
speculate as to whether or not Sophie will return to Lynn; nor is it
terribly important, either to author or to reader, whether she will be
content with Jerome. What matters is her discovery of her own
emotional nature, her new honesty about her desires and needs.

If this all sounds rather narcissistic—a prefiguration of the end-
less navel gazing and me-ism that would become so fashionable fifty
years hence—it should be remembered that Powell was not
attempting to endorse an ideal code of behavior. On the contrary,

she was excruciatingly conscious of the hurtful ramifications any resolution would have. Above and beyond the power of *The Bride's House*
on its own terms, the psychological undercurrents of this novel
probably express a good amount of what Powell was herself under-
going during its gestation, including the gradual perception that her
marriage to Joe was not entirely satisfying, the likely acknowledgment that she was in thrall to Jack Lawson, the gigantic question of
what to do about it all:

> It is a dreadful thing, Sophie thought, for a woman to live with
> two men, to lie in one man's arms and think of other arms, to
> smile into Lynn's clear eyes and see other eyes, dark and eager.
> Dreadful to feel that there is in the world something stronger
> than oneself, something that might leap out any minute and
> devour one's peace.

To be sure, this "dreadful thing" also seems to have been
thrilling and revitalizing, and Sophie/Powell is candid enough to face
up to that fact: she *needs* to change her life. Still, when Sophie finally
runs away from the tidy imprisonment of her "bride's house," it is
not without an awareness of what she is sacrificing:

> Lying in Jerome's arms, Sophie knew that this was her destiny.
> Peace was in a white hushed house with Lynn, but for her there
> must be ecstasy and torment. . . . Sophie, her cheek against her
> lover's throat, her body throbbing in his arms, knew that he
> would hurt her as she had hurt Lynn, and that he would hold
> her forever because of his power to make her suffer. There
> would be moments—this she knew—when she would want
> only Lynn to shield her, to console her for Jerome's wounds. A
> woman needed two lovers, one to comfort her for the torment
> the other caused her.

This is not pure lust, nor should it be casually dismissed as masochism. Rather, for Powell, it was a timeless dilemma. A popular self-help article, one that has been written over and over again by hundreds of different authors for as many publications, addresses the distinction between love and sex and offers advice to the reader on "how to tell the difference." It is a worthy question, albeit one that can hardly produce a reliable general answer. For Powell, there was love, there was sex, and there was love-and-sex; all three states were part of the human condition and had their own relative values.

Leaving aside the matter of whatever was going on between Powell and Lawson, further suggestion of a clearly autobiographical element in *The Bride's House* may be found in the book's dedication, which reads simply "For Orpha May"—the woman who was the strongest single influence on the author's early adulthood. If a strain of "wildness" may be traced from Aunt Lotta to Sophie, a similar strain might have run from Auntie May to Dawn herself, with their independent and unusual love lives. It is tempting to read the dedication not only as Powell's gift to a person who had been very kind to her but also as a token of recognition and understanding.

This is a deeply haunted book, perhaps Powell's most solemn novel. Even *Dance Night* has more witticisms, more humorous digressions. The subplots in *The Bride's House* tend to be even more somber than the main narrative. What are we to make, for example, of the suicide of ethereal Mary Cecily, Sophie's sister, who plays what is only a minor role until suddenly, late in the book, she takes center stage by walking to the river with her young son, Robert, and ecstatically drowning herself before his uncomprehending eyes? According to a diary entry from 1942, Powell's suicidal periods were "rare," but precisely in acknowledging their rarity, the author was admitting that they did exist; this fictional episode then, may point to one of them. Jojo was about the same age as the character Robert when *The Bride's House* was written; his problems were increasingly evident, and his mother was increasingly distraught. There were troubles with Joe, both of them were drinking heavily, and now she was in love with another man—who had just married *his* second wife.

The Bride's House is marred by a few corny touches: naming the family Truelove is going rather far, and portraying Jerome Gardiner as a dark horseman has a bit too much of the mark of Zorro. Still, the book is persuasive in a manner surpassing anything else Powell had yet written. *The Bride's House* has a mythic quality—the four principal female characters add up to a sort of Everywoman—and some splendid realism, too, as in this description of small-town Americana:

> Buggies and wagons lined the street of the self-satisfied little town, flags flew, bands played parading down the street, Civil War veterans marched and a group of youngsters bore a Loyal Temperance Legion banner and sang "Saloons, Saloons, Saloons must go!" But on the contrary saloons had sprung up overnight to meet the county's annual thirst. A fragrant alcoholic haze flung over the town, and tented the entire Fair Grounds. Streets were giddy with laughter and the shrill voices and megaphoned speeches of visiting politicians. There were clusters of starched white and flying ribbons here and there, groups of rosy farm girls giggling and ogling each passing man. By nighttime the groups—with good luck—would be scattered, each girl giggling with an awkward young man in some tree-shaded buggy behind the Fair Grounds, hysterically sipping from a jug of corn whiskey and abandoning herself to private yearnings. The wretched little frame hotels, supported comfortably all year by half a dozen traveling salesmen, now bulged with guests and window shades were drawn night and day, boasting of the iniquity of their bedrooms. Carnival gods rode over the city and sprinkled the orthodox with their confetti.

The reviews of *The Bride's House* were few, brief, and inadequate; this was the first time Powell could rightly claim that a novel of hers had been treated unfairly in the press. Even the favorable notices, such as the one Mary Ross published in the *New York Herald Tribune*, were surprisingly obtuse and uncomprehending (the book was "as soft and as sturdy as a pansy," Ross concluded, whatever that meant).

"There is not a wholly normal character in the book, with the possible exception of Lynn Hamilton," the *New York Times* said. "All the others seem driven by a relentless urge which strips them of peace and happiness, leaving only bitter memories in their stead." Yet the *Times* allowed that the author had written a "striking story, macabre in its intensity, painting her characters with a remarkable sureness and precision."

The most interesting—and the snottiest—critique was published by the *New York Evening Post* on April 6, 1929. The reviewer was Tess Slesinger (1905–1945), remembered today for several fine short stories and one novel, *The Unpossessed* (1934), a sprawling but perceptive and often hilariously funny send-up of New York intellectual leftism.

"Dawn Powell's new book is the exponent of a romantic theory of heredity, in which a strain of wild blood runs from mystical aunt to mystical niece," she began. She objected to the author's "stock characters: a father of the suppressed romantic type; a mother who keeps house and cannot understand the father; three brat children who utter clever and disconcerting remarks at everybody's expense. . . .

"The facts of Sophie's life are plausible as the history of a woman whose physical and emotional desires could never coincide," Slesinger wrote. "But a problem like Sophie's, in the light of the most common modern psychology, is no longer a mysterious, romantic one and must be treated, to be convincing, more or less realistically. Miss Powell's method, in 1929, is surprising. Under her sympathetic, sentimental eye Sophie becomes a sad heroine, victim not of inner conflicts but of a kind of obsolete witchcraft."

This is an unusually smug little review; one wonders which woman was really the mystic—the twenty-four-year-old Slesinger, with her belief that the "most common modern psychology . . . in 1929" could explain everything about human desire, or Powell, with her profound and somewhat horrified respect for ingrained, inborn forces beyond individual control. Today, in an era when genetics is credited with exerting an enormous influence on human development, Powell's quest for a recurring hereditary pattern in her art and her ancestry seems a lot less like "witchcraft" than it may have when *The Bride's House* was published.

Powell learned a great deal during the creation of these first three novels. Much of *The Bride's House* survives in manuscript (as do several of her later books), and perusal of the various drafts permits us a close examination of her literary process.

Even when she was not actively working on a novel, short story, or play, Powell would carry small spiral-bound notebooks in her handbag so she could jot down thoughts at restaurants, bars, or parties, in the middle of the day or night—whenever and wherever they occurred to her. She would then copy these fragments onto looseleaf sheets and eventually place them in larger notebooks where she also kept newspaper clippings, quotations from books she was reading, epigrams from the classics, conversations she had overheard, and slightly fictionalized word "portraits" of friends and acquaintances.

After some of her basic material was assembled, Powell would map out a plot in detailed (and often much-revised) outline; sometimes she went so far as to construct large fold-out cardboard charts to track her characters through the adventures she had in store for them. Then she would set to work on her book, usually beginning with the first chapter and proceeding slowly but directly to the end. Most of her early novels were originally scrawled in pencil; later, she preferred to do the initial work in pen. In the early drafts, hardly a sentence goes by without some revision, however minor; once she had literally scribbled all over her pages, she would write out a second draft of the same material, again by hand, which would itself undergo lengthy amendment.

This process would be repeated as many times as Powell deemed necessary. Once she had a complete, satisfactory handwritten manuscript, she would send it out to be typed (in later years, she often did the typing herself). Then she would add some final changes in pen or pencil and deliver the finished product to her agent—first Ann Watkins, subsequently Carol Hill Brandt—who would in turn present it to her publisher.

Powell's approach to her New York satires was frankly journalistic. She was filled with contempt for writers who claimed they simply sat down at their typewriters and made everything up. Eternally inquisitive, Powell herself was always collecting material, unsparingly scrutinizing her own behavior (and that of others) and recording her observations in thousands upon thousands of pages' worth of notebooks, diaries, manuscripts, even the backs of envelopes. Large fragments of her notebooks and diaries were incorporated, almost untouched, into her novels (*The Happy Island*, published in 1938, follows the diaries especially closely).

Sometimes she would hold on to an anecdote for many years before finding a place for it in one of her books; *The Wicked Pavilion* (1954), for example, recounts an incident involving a drunken man who puts his fist through the door of a basement men's room in a restaurant—that Joe had witnessed and reported to her almost twenty years earlier. She compared the process of writing her novels to the creation of a bird's nest—"and the bird is a magpie," she added.

In her Ohio books, Powell took a different tack. There she was likely to rely upon memories and dreams, rather than fresh observation, for her material. For her, Ohio was the past, fixed and forever, while New York was the rushing, furious, chimerical present, sweeping her along toward her destiny.

CHAPTER FOUR

Shadow on the Heart

꧁⁓

It did a very funny thing to me, that dead rocket.

DAWN POWELL, 1931

LITTLE IS KNOWN ABOUT POWELL'S day-to-day life
during the late 1920s, when her three formative novels were published. There are only rudimentary diaries for 1925, 1926, 1927, and
1930, and none at all for 1928 and 1929. This is also the stage of her
adulthood from which the least personal correspondence has been
collected; moreover, nearly everybody to whom Powell was close
during this period is now dead, and very few of them preserved any
memories or impressions. And so we must content ourselves with a
scanty recitation of facts, enhanced here and again with the record of
some crisis that spurred Powell into dashing off a letter or elongated
entry in the appointment books that then served as her diaries.

This paucity of information is especially unfortunate because it was during this time that Dawn passed her dreaded thirtieth birthday and set to work on the first of her great books, *Dance Night* (1930). These were also the years in which the full extent of Jojo's impairment came to be known and Dawn and Joe made their initial attempts to make appropriate arrangements for their damaged son. This was when Powell grew close to two people who would have an enormous impact on the rest of her life: Coburn Gilman and Margaret De Silver. And of course, there was her ongoing association with Jack Lawson.

By all accounts, Powell seems to have been a funny, tolerant, open-hearted, and altogether attractive young woman. Charles Norman, who had reviewed *Whither* so favorably, recalled his first encounter with the author in his memoir *Poets and People*:

> She was pretty, slender and shy. . . . She drank gin, and it is extraordinary that she should have produced so much and of such high quality, considering the number of tuns of gin she must have consumed in the years that I knew her. Like Joe's, her figure, in time, rounded out, while her tongue got sharper. But, unlike most literary lushes, she never attacked her friends. I see her two images in my mind—the warm, eager, pretty and ambitious young woman from Ohio, and what she became.

The young Powell was a fashionable (if necessarily frugal) dresser, and a new outfit or new hat could cheer her for days. She never allowed any trace of gray to streak her hair, consistently dyeing it an auburn brown. By her late twenties, she had begun to put on weight, which concerned her (she kept a tally in her diary); still, when she was not deliberately dieting, she was a hearty eater, and exercise regimens were regularly begun and abandoned. She smoked only on rare occasions, abstaining not so much because she feared it would harm her health as because she thought the habit wasted too much time.

Through Powell's few (and inadequate) ledgers, we know that she continued to write for magazines such as *Snappy Stories*, *Munsey's*, and *College Humor*. For the princely sum of four dollars a column, she also contributed regular book reviews to the *New York Evening Post;* unfortunately for posterity, these were usually published without a byline and are therefore now all but impossible to track down.

Her social life rushed on, amid copious alcohol consumption at such favorite Village speakeasies as 157 Prince Street, Bertolotti's, and Sammy Schwartz's, or in drawn-out parties at her apartment. In 1927, the Goushas began taking a country place every summer, most often a small, secluded, and slowly eroding shack close to the beach in the hamlet of Mount Sinai, near Port Jefferson on the north shore of Long Island. This would become a family tradition, one that persisted into the 1940s.

As a couple, the Goushas maintained one particularly close friendship, with their wedding witnesses Harry Lissfelt and Helen Kessel, now married themselves. Like Joe, his boyhood friend, Lissfelt was a successful businessman; he would soon become the regional manager for the Corning Glass Company, a position he held until his death, in 1945.

Dawn also remained in touch with three Lake Erie classmates, Eleanor Farnham, Charlotte Johnson, and Cornelia Wolfe, the latter two of whom were living in Manhattan and writing poetry. Other friends included the young poet Cornelius Burke, who would achieve a certain fame as a music critic and contributing editor of the magazine *High Fidelity*. In the late 1920s, Powell also became close to the poet, biographer, and anthologist Genevieve Taggard, but their friendship ended in a series of quarrels after a few years and is memorialized only in a few acerbic diary entries by Dawn.*

Through Dwight Fiske, she became popular within a circle of gay men, including the first drama critic for the *New Yorker*, John

---

* *For example, "Happiness has given her a sword; respectability has given her the right to be stupid."*

Mosher. Powell seems never to have harbored any sort of prejudice against homosexuals, who in fact made up a disproportionate percentage of her coterie. Her novel *The Happy Island* (1938) is one of the first books written since Roman antiquity that is filled with openly gay men and lesbians but is neither a psychological study, a plea for tolerance, a hate tract, nor an "under-the-counter" titillation. Like most of her other novels, it is simply a sharply etched and unsentimental rendering of human beings following paths that are not, after all, so terribly different from the supposed norm.

Her dearest friends were still Esther Andrews and Canby Chambers, and she was aggrieved when polio robbed Chambers of the use of his legs in the late 1920s. Andrews and Chambers subsequently relocated to Key West, where the weather was thought to be better for his health. In 1933, Powell spent several days with the couple on Martha's Vineyard during one of their rare trips north and composed an agonized meditation on their altered lives:

> Suddenly I thought, why that man, that legless man is Canby— Canby!—someone who used to dash around after the prettiest girl at the party, now figuring how few motions it takes to get a glass of water. And that gray-haired woman in the other bed, getting up now to wheelbarrow him to the toilet, waiting to wait on him, that's Esther—Esther who used to be so gay and reckless and free—and in the little dark room I thought my heart would break.

On her sporadic visits to Ohio, Dawn generally limited her itinerary to Cleveland—where her sisters were now living with their families—and Shelby. Family reunions were difficult for her. There were too many bad memories, and meetings with her sisters made her depressed about her fluctuating weight: "Both Phyllis and Mabel look young and slim and beautiful and I am the fat ugly one and I hate it."

Because of her determination to avoid further encounters with Sabra, Dawn rarely if ever visited her father. But Roy Powell came to New York in the summer of 1925, and his daughter took him out for dinner and a play. "Very drunk," she noted in her diary; the phrase had become a refrain.

The following June, Dawn was summoned to Roy's bedside; he had suffered a paralytic stroke and lay dying in his home in Oberlin. She was assigned the duty of rubbing her father with alcohol from head to toe, "greasing him and feeding him whiskey drop by drop." The death watch lasted several days, and Dawn's letters home to Joe are an affecting mixture of grim reportage and hallucinatory poetry:

> He is a skeleton. I stayed with him a good deal of the day (some one has to be with him and there is no nurse and my step-mother of course is almost a wreck). He is perfectly conscious and that's what makes his struggles to speak so pitiful. He is apt to choke any minute. . . .
>
> Today I cried thinking that once a dark, vivacious woman loved this poor wreck of a man (and she was just my age) and at midnight I saw her with long brown hair lying beside him on the bed while his second wife slept in the next room.

Roy Powell died on July 8; he was buried in Butternut Ridge Cemetery in North Olmsted, right next to Emily Helen Powell, the short-lived baby with the grisly distinction of two sequential burials. Almost exactly thirty years later, Sabra Powell herself would be interred in Butternut Ridge, alongside her ancestors. It is unlikely that Dawn ever saw or spoke to her stepmother again after Roy's funeral.

Shortly after Powell returned to Manhattan, she, Joe, and Jojo moved to 106 Perry Street, on the far western edge of Greenwich Village. A small, unprepossessing apartment building, somewhat larger than a town house, it is now one of the overlooked literary landmarks of New York, for it was here that Powell wrote all of *Dance Night*, completed most of *The Tenth Moon* (which she planned as *Come Back to Sorrento*, the title under which it would be reissued in 1997), and began *Turn, Magic Wheel*.

She loved the West Village, which was then one of the area's poorer quarters. In a letter to her young cousin John F. Sherman, who was growing up with Orpha May Steinbrueck in Shelby, she enumerated some of the attractions she found in the neighborhood, and in the city:

> Every place else but New York you have to hide all your low beginnings and pretend everybody in the family is white and can read and write and play the harp. What I mean, friend, is that you can be yourself here and it's the only place where being genuine will absolutely get you anywhere you want. If it suits you—as it does me—to live in the toughest quarter of downtown, semi-slums, because the houses are old and quaint and have little courts in back and push-carts and hurdy-gurdies go by your window with fruit and vegetables and straw hats and geraniums—well, that doesn't prevent you from being asked to Park Avenue penthouses or any place. The very *best* people think to be able to do as you damn please, not caring what anyone thinks, is the mark of aristocracy.

In 1928, Joe left his job with the H. C. Michaels Agency to go to the Paul Cornell Agency, where he was made secretary of the firm and a stockholder. By most standards, he was now very successful; however, he was increasingly discontent. An enigmatic letter Dawn sent to 106 Perry Street from the Mount Sinai cottage in the summer of 1928 suggests the abysmal state of both Joe's emotional condition and their current marital relations:

I have, loving you, been incredibly selfish and ruthless. I want so much to change and arrange our lives so that you will be the coddled, free, happy one. You were so gay and so arrogant, darling, when I first met you. That is the way you were meant to be—we both know that—not a crushed, hunted, half-defiant, half-cringing person that circumstances try to make you, circumstances that I am going to do my best to change, dear.

"Love always," she concluded, "—and what a selfish, dependent, barren sort of love it has been!"

By this time, the "crushed, hunted, half-defiant, half-cringing" Gousha had a serious drinking problem. In addition to his established pattern of long, multimartini luncheons, there were afternoons when he simply didn't report back to the office; only his acknowledged excellence in the field kept his job secure. At home, there was strife—and desperation. "Joe tight so much and mentally blurred so it's impossible to talk with him," Powell wrote in her 1930 diary. "Makes me sick at heart and so tired emotionally to see him blah-blah drunk all the time with nights of horror that make me sorry for him, yet worry so." On his fortieth birthday, Joe, reeling drunk, got into his canoe and paddled out to sea from the Mount Sinai cottage; he didn't return for several hours, leaving Dawn and the company who had come to celebrate the occasion terrified for his life.

Jojo is rarely mentioned in Powell's diaries or surviving correspondence for these years; he passed much of his time with his nurse, Louise Lee. On one country outing with her, he fell out of a tree and broke his leg. He stayed the following week in a New Jersey hospital, where he "seemed to think it was all very enjoyable even with one leg in a plaster cast," Powell told her sister Phyllis.

By the late 1920s, the boy was enrolled in the first of the many institutions for the mentally disturbed where he would spend much of the rest of his life. This one was in the coastal New Jersey town of

Seagirt, where one of his fellow patients was an older girl in her late teens, Ann De Silver, who, like Jojo had been mistakenly diagnosed as mentally retarded (she would later be reclassified as a schizophrenic). Jojo quickly became obsessed with Ann, writing letters to her, talking of her incessantly, and sometimes erupting into tantrums when he was displeased with her behavior. His obsession would continue for another four decades.

Out of this difficult situation would come one of Powell's most enduring relationships. It is unclear whether Jojo was sent to Seagirt at the suggestion of Margaret Burnham De Silver, Ann's mother, or whether the two women met through the hospital (some members of Dawn's family are convinced of the latter). However the acquaintance was made, De Silver would prove an extraordinarily sympathetic, devoted, and congenial friend to Powell; indeed, their friendship would end only when Margaret drew her last breath in a Manhattan hospital, as Dawn sat by her bedside, holding her hand.

Born in 1890, De Silver came from a wealthy and distinguished Philadelphia family; she was the daughter of George Burnham, the treasurer of the United States Foreign Policy Association. After her graduation from Vassar College in 1912, she moved to New York and threw herself into bohemian life and liberal causes. She married Albert De Silver, a successful lawyer who was one of the founders of the American Civil Liberties Union, and after his death, in 1925, ran a salon of sorts at her town house in Brooklyn Heights, where she entertained writers, artists, musicians, and stars of the political left. Her generosity seems to have been prodigious, but she was a modest and unpretentious woman who did not advertise her good deeds.

Dawn came to know De Silver just as the latter was taking up with the Italian anarchist Carlo Tresca, who published an anti-Fascist newspaper in lower Manhattan, *Il Martello*. De Silver and Tresca would live together (outsiders were told they were married) until he was assassinated in 1943, likely on the orders of one of his numerous political enemies.* According to Tresca's biographer, he contributed to the colorful life at De Silver's Joralemon Street house, filled with "parties, pots of spaghetti sauce simmering on the stove, boisterous talk and laughter. He often argued with Margaret's stockbroker brothers, but there was never any anger. Harrison [De Silver, Margaret's son] felt there was no meanness in Carlo's nature."

Powell herself spent countless hours at De Silver's, drinking and talking with the unconventional group her new friend had gathered around her. Dwight Fiske was part of the De Silver circle, as was Evelyn Scott, and it may have been here that Powell first met Edmund Wilson, who would become one of her acquaintances by the mid-1930s. His daughter Rosalind Baker Wilson (later Powell's editor at Houghton Mifflin) recalled De Silver as "beautiful and overweight, with tiny hands and feet and a sweet manner." Powell and De Silver shared a bawdy sense of humor; the only time Dawn ever used four-letter words was in her correspondence with De Silver (even in her private diaries, she refused to completely spell out the word *f--k*, and she complained about the use of obscenities in the books she reviewed). Powell designated De Silver a fellow *"forte* woman." *Forte* can be defined as either "strong" or "loud"; Powell likely meant it in both senses.

Over the years, De Silver provided support for Powell on several occasions. She took her along to Bermuda on a family vacation in 1930, sent her on a trip to Haiti in 1949 and to Paris in 1950, and bailed her and Gousha out during a disastrous period of complete financial collapse in the late 1950s.

Powell also made another lifelong friend about this time: the Colorado-born magazine editor and translator Coburn Gilman, always a hapless and delightful presence in her diaries. He has been

---

Tresca had the singular honor of aggravating Stalin almost as much as he did Mussolini, but recent research suggests that the hit may have been ordered by New York businessman Generoso Pope.

described as Powell's lover, and he probably was, at least upon occasion, at the start of their friendship. But Powell's purported domestic arrangement with Gilman—sometimes described as a ménage à trois—has been much overstated; the two of them certainly never lived together, and he was never a serious rival for Joe over Powell's deepest affections.

Indeed, there is no evidence that Powell ever really "fell in love" again after her great heartbreak over Lawson in the late 1920s; she would not permit herself to relinquish self-control. She nonetheless became markedly casual about her sex life as she grew older: "I never know whose shoes will be under my bed in the morning," she once told her horrified sister Phyllis. The writer and editor Frances Keene, who would become a close friend in the 1940s, said that Powell was never forthcoming in discussing her affairs—"She always had the attitude that you live your life and I'll live mine"—though she gave the "clear impression" that she had been a sexual enthusiast in her youth. Joe, too, seems to have joined in the revelry; when he made an aggressive, drunken pass at the artist Peggy Bacon at a party in 1935, Edmund Wilson shrugged it off with the comment that "this was the thing to do in Dawn's set." "I don't make beds, I break 'em," Powell would tell Sara Murphy in 1949.

However easygoing Powell may have been in her choice of lovers, she was highly selective about her social cohorts. To her, an exciting lovemaking partner was one thing; a true, steady, sympathetic friend was something else indeed. Whatever physical intimacy she may have enjoyed with Gilman, those who knew Powell well in later life are united in the opinion that he was always first and foremost her favorite drinking buddy—a witty, uninhibited, and original companion for a night on the town.

Gilman, always known as Coby, had been born in Denver in 1894 to well-to-do parents, Ephraim and Mary Ward Gilman. He moved to Manhattan and graduated from Columbia with the class of 1915. For most of his life, he lived in an apartment at 428 Lafayette

Street, in the neoclassical Colonnades building, directly across from what is now the Public Theater. He began his career as an editor at *Harper's*, moved on to the early *Cosmopolitan*, and became editor in chief of *Travel* magazine from the mid-1930s through the early 1950s. He edited at least one guidebook, *The Weekend Book of Travel*, translated novels by Cecil Saint-Laurent and Colette, and, according to Powell, was essential in placing the memoirs of convicted rapist turned anti–capital punishment activist Caryl Chessman with Prentice-Hall.

He took his greatest happiness, however, in his strenuous social life. "Over a long period of years, Coby Gilman was everybody's favorite barfly in the Village taverns," Matthew Josephson wrote, "ever speaking with aplomb in well-rounded sentences, carrying himself with dignity to the end of the night."

Charles Norman described Coby as looking like a cross between a country squire and a man-about-town, adding that he "possessed one of the most boisterously cheerful personalities I have ever known." He continued, "Merely to be near him was to banish gloom. . . . Even his accidents had their cheerful, hilarious side."

But not always. According to Josephson, a sketch that John Cheever wrote for the *New Yorker*, entitled "The Peril in the Streets" and printed in the issue dated March 21, 1942, was based on Gilman. This grim vignette, set in a bar at three in the morning, shortly after the onset of World War II, is essentially a monologue/harangue directed at a newly enlisted soldier by a highly educated, deeply cynical, and very drunk middle-aged man; it concludes with the besotted pseudo-philosopher's collapsing to the floor and losing consciousness.

Powell was infinitely fascinated by Coby and wrote more about him in her diaries than she did about any of her other acquaintances: "I sometimes think a writer could become immortal merely as a chronicler of Gilman," she would observe in 1940. But while he appears throughout her personal papers as the star of some of the funniest set pieces, there is not a single entry that even hints at a passionate involvement. "I never thought there was much of a romance there," Frances Keene recalled in 1994. "No. Coby had a specific duty. He was a very kind and funny man, and it was his job to keep Dawn out of trouble, to lift her out of her depression when she was unhappy about her son, to keep her laughing when she needed to laugh."

Rosalind Baker Wilson believed that Gilman appealed to strong maternal instincts within Powell: "She was a very nice person, you know—that's something everybody forgets, just how *nice* she was—and she felt it her duty to care for Coby, who wasn't any good at caring for himself." Even within this hard-drinking crowd, Gilman's alcoholic intake was legendary, and the travails that make for such amusing reading must have been rather less amusing to live through.

In the fall of 1929, Powell herself needed care. One night at the Mount Sinai cottage, she began to experience terrific pains in her chest. As there was no phone, Joe had to row across the inlet to call for help. When the doctor arrived, he immediately ordered Powell rushed into New York by taxicab ("$30 and me ready to pass out any minute," she told Phyllis), where she was admitted to a private hospital. She would spend the next three months there.

This was the beginning of a long and mysterious nightmare. At the time, Powell's affliction was diagnosed as a heart attack, but in hindsight it seems more likely that it was the first blatant symptom of a teratoma—a rare and grisly type of tumor that often includes vestiges of hair and a toothlike mineral deposit—that had been building up on her heart and lungs, probably since infancy.

All anybody knew was that she was very sick. The whole experience was terrifying:

> They thought at first my heart was permanently crippled but
> so far they see no damage. The right lung filled and jammed the
> heart out of place but they gave me stuff—icebags and morphine—and I was only in real pain about four days and four

nights, and the X-rays showed it was pleurisy causing the peri-
carditis and that as soon as it got well the heart would be all
right.

The pain subsided but never really went away; thereafter, she
would regularly complain that her "heart hurt." This was not hypo-
chondria; in the mid-1930s, her doctor would inform her that she
had a cyst in her chest and that she would have to wait until it grew
large enough to be cut out. "I walked down Madison Avenue not
looking in shops for the first time because I thought it extravagant to
buy or even want things for so short a while," she wrote after that
appointment. "It doesn't matter what the corpse wears." A satisfactory explanation of her malady would not be forthcoming for
another two decades.

Meanwhile, in 1929, at the age of thirty-three, Dawn believed
that she had suffered a heart attack and could likely expect another
one in the near future. If she had always been conscious of her own
mortality, her sense of urgency now became acute.

Despite the worry of it all, her convalescence in the hospital
may have had its welcome aspects—it meant three months away
from Joe, away from Jojo, away from alcohol, the chance to be a pampered patient day and night. Apart from the actual ailments that
necessitated them, Powell usually enjoyed her hospital visits—"telephone at bedside, broiled squab, live lobsters, broiled sweetbreads,
crab meat, delicious French soups, orange juice," she reported to her
sister. "These things do help you to get well."

Shortly after Powell was released, her professional future
started to brighten. A new publishing company founded by John
Farrar and two brothers named Stanley and Frederick Rinehart
had set up offices in Manhattan's Murray Hill (as their early books
proudly announced on their title pages), and the house offered her a
contract for three novels, with an advance against royalties of $3,500
for the lot.

Farrar and Rinehart was already a much more prestigious company than either Small, Maynard or Brentano's had been; moreover, not only was the advance larger than any Powell had received before, it was possibly the first one she had ever been offered.

We do not have specific figures on the amount of money (if any) Powell was paid for her first three books, but we do know from a 1934 diary entry that she made $545 from *all* of her work in 1925 (the year *Whither* was published), $2,335 in 1928 (the year *She Walks in Beauty* finally saw print) and $2,133 in 1929 (when *The Bride's House* came out). Since we are certain that she had many other sales during those years—making up to two hundred dollars for a single story in *College Humor*, for example—it is at least possible that she simply *gave* her early books to their respective publishers, in the hope that royalties and reputation would eventually result in some income.

However, Powell does refer to a character's "$500 advance from Brentano's" in *The Happy Island*, and because she so frequently incorporated facts from her own life into her fiction, this may be an indication of what she herself had received from that publisher. Whatever the case, an advance of more than a thousand dollars per book from an impressive new house such as Farrar and Rinehart must have been enormously reassuring. It was, after all, the first year of the Great Depression, and Joe's salary had been temporarily cut by a third.

So Powell set to work with redoubled intensity on *Dance Night*, since the company's terms called for no payments to be made until the first novel was done. The contract was signed on April 9, 1930; Powell, writing furiously, finished the book on June 15, and in what will seem to contemporary authors an uncannily short turnaround, it was in the stores less than four months later.

Powell often reflected upon the books she had written, rereading and reevaluating them in comparison to her present work. In her diary, she selected three novels for her highest praise: *Come Back to Sorrento / The Tenth Moon* (which she called a "beautiful book—the best writing I ever did and technically flawless" in her entry for March 18, 1943), *Turn, Magic Wheel* (which she described as "very likely my best, simplest, most original book" on February 18, 1954), and—repeatedly—*Dance Night*.

"I still think it was a good book and probably better than anything I could write right now," she said of her fourth novel on March 23, 1931, still spinning from what she perceived as its critical and commercial failure. And on April 4, 1933: "I can never write so good a novel as *Dance Night*. Nobody thought it was of the slightest value." A decade later, "a re-reading of *Dance Night* persuaded me it is my best book—material, mood, prose and structure by all odds the best," she wrote on December 1, 1943. Finally, in 1957, with all of her novels completed except *The Golden Spur*, when Maurice Dolbier of the *New York Herald Tribune* asked her to name her favorite out of her books, she answered, without hesitation, "*Dance Night*."

Powell apparently began *Dance Night* in the summer of 1928 and worked on it throughout 1929. She plotted it carefully, making a long fold-out graph as a skeleton guide for the novel, a plan of action she would also use for several, but not all, of the works that were to follow.

This seems to have been a very difficult book for her, particularly as she approached its conclusion, working under the deadline imposed by her new publisher. "Hate novel as if it were a personal foe—it's so damned hard and moves so slow. . . . Can't conceive of having energy ever to attack a novel again," she wrote in her diary on March 10, 1930. But when it was finished, she was exultant. Farrar and Rinehart had promised her a large printing and a generous amount of publicity; now, perhaps, she would finally receive the broad recognition she had sought since childhood. Certainly, with the creation of *Dance Night*, she had earned it.

Dance Night is a bleak book, from its grim opening panorama of a factory town on the edge of a summer evening through the blunt, matter-of-fact treatment of the only scene of direct mortal violence in any of Powell's novels.

Once again, the outline of the plot can be summarized handily. The action is set in a dingy village called Lamptown, in the years just prior to World War I. On a balmy night, Morry Abbott, eighteen years old, meets a young orphan named Jen St. Clair. They establish a friendship based largely on the imagined futures, far from Lamptown, they have created for themselves.

Morry's mother, Elsinore, runs a millinery shop in town. She is tormented by her husband, a vicious and abusive traveling salesman named Charlie Abbott, whose occasional visits home she dreads; she has, in the meantime, developed a passion for an itinerant dance master, Mr. Fischer. When Charlie brutalizes Elsinore once too often, she shoots him dead. The townspeople assume that the dissolute Charlie has killed himself, and they take Elsinore to their heart; Morry knows and accepts the truth, feeling only compassion for his mother. Shortly thereafter, recognizing that Lamptown cannot comprehend ambition and will never allow him to realize his dream of becoming a serious architect, he prepares to leave for a distant city.

Typically, Powell gives us many minor but engaging characters, from simple, kindly, baby-faced Mrs. Pepper (Mr. Fischer's secret lover) to the barroom philosopher Hogan (with his eternal hymning of Robert Ingersoll, the evangelical nineteenth-century agnostic), on through Jen's beautiful younger sister, Lil St. Clair, locked away in an orphanage for most of the book. (When Morry suggests that potential adoptive parents usually prefer "those little yellow-haired blue-eyed dolls," Jen angrily interrupts him: "The hell they do. . . . They always pick somebody that looks like a good worker. Once in a while some woman that's had her pet cat run over picks out one of those pretty ones. There aren't that many of them.")

A spiritual claustrophobia haunts *Dance Night*: throughout the novel, we are aware of a painful sense of constriction, whether in the corsets fitted in Mrs. Abbott's shop or in the martial counting of the dance master (ONE-two or ONE-two-three or ONE-two-three-four). Sex is omnipresent but inevitably furtive and disturbed—with the wrong partners, at the wrong times. Only their visions of escape sustain Jen and Morry through the greasy, bug-ridden summers and numbing, desolate winters:

> Trains whirred through the air, their whistles shrieking a red line through the sky behind them[;] they landed on Jen's bed without weight, vanished, and other trains, pop-eyed, roared toward her. Trains slid noiselessly across her eyelids, long transcontinental trains with diners, club cars, observation cars. The people on these trains leaned out of their windows and held out their hands to Jen. "California, Hawaii, Denver, Quebec, Miami," they chanted, "oh you dear child, New Orleans, Chicago, Boston, Rocky Mountains, New York City."

At the conclusion of *Dance Night*, Elsinore Abbott is suspended in a strange and ambiguous state. After shooting her husband, she feels, we are told,

> neither glad nor sorry. The revolver shot had blown out some fuse in her brain. She couldn't remember why it had seemed so important to silence Charles, the thoughts that had made her quiver with fanatic delight a few days back were lost, Fischer ceased when Charles ceased, all feeling died with that explosion. Now, night and day, she was only the proprietor of a thriving millinery store, in her numb memory ran color combinations, arrangements of hand-made lilacs on milan, her heart had become a ribbon rosette worn with chic a little to one side.

Later we are informed that Elsinore and Mrs. Pepper, her long-time assistant, have become very close friends, successful businesswomen and highly popular with men throughout the area. Judith Faye Pett, who in 1981 wrote the first dissertation examining Powell's work, suggests that Elsinore "blossoms into a gay, lively, independent, full-figured counterpart of Mrs. Pepper," and others have agreed with this view.

My own reading is more pessimistic. It seems to me that Elsinore may indeed have won her freedom, but at a terrible price— namely, the loss of her human feelings. She is still able to function, but she has become cold and impatient, lacking in ideals of any sort—calculating and absolutely hard-boiled. Her final line is particularly cryptic. Having learned that a mutual acquaintance, Dode, is now working in a Toledo whorehouse, Mrs. Pepper tells Elsinore the news "in their room that night while they took turns manicuring each other. Wasn't it a shame, she said, the way Dode turned out?

" 'There's worse things,' Elsinore said."

At least one reader has taken this to mean that Elsinore herself has become—or will become—a prostitute. I think Powell deliberately left the matter unclear, though I find this second interpretation more convincing than that positing a pseudo-liberated "happy ending" for Elsinore. For Powell herself, the only plausible happy ending for any character in such circumstances was flight. The lines she had written in "What Are You Doing in My Dreams?" bear repeating: "What you have to do is walk right on down the street, keeping your eyes straight ahead, pretending you're on your way someplace a lot better. And that's the way it turns out, too; wherever you land is sure to be better than the place you left."

She meant every word of it.

However far away she landed, Powell herself never forgot the places she had left behind. *Dance Night* includes some extraordinarily evocative descriptions of America's lost "Lamptowns":

The humming of this town was jagged from time to time by the shriek of an engine whistle or the bellow of a factory siren or the clang-clang of a red street car on its way from one village to the next. The car jangled through the town flapping doors open and shut admitting and discharging old ladies on their way to a D.A.R. picnic in Norwalk, section workers or linemen in overalls, giggling girls on their way to the Street Carnival in Chicago Junction. As if hunting for something very important, the car rattled past the long row of Lamptown's factory boarding houses, past the Lots, then on into long stretches of low, level hay fields where farm girls pitched hay, stopping to wave their huge straw hats at the gay world passing by in a street car.

There was gray train smoke over the town most days, it smelled of travel, of transcontinental trains about to flash by, of important things about to happen. The train smell sounded the "A" for Lamptown and then a treble chord of frying hamburger and onions and boiling coffee was struck by Hermann Bauer's kitchen, with a sostenuto of stale beer from Delaney's back door. These were all busy smells and seemed a six to six smell, a working town's smell, to be exchanged at the last factory whistle for the festival night odors of popcorn, Spearmint chewing gum, barbershop pomades and the faint smell of far-off damp cloverfields.

Powell told her sister Phyllis, to whom *Dance Night* is dedicated, that Lamptown was "sort of a combination of all the factory sections of all the factory towns I ever knew." The one she knew best, of course, was Shelby, and even today, with most of its industry long gone, we can recognize some landmarks. Shantyville, the poorest section of Lamptown, was based on an area then known as Irish Town, where most of the workers at the Ohio Steel Tube Company and the Shelby Electric Company lived; Powell was well acquainted with the neighborhood, for it was not far from 121 North Broadway, Orpha May Steinbrueck's house. At the other end of the spectrum, Clover Heights, the fine residential section that Morry Abbott longs to develop, was modeled on the real Grand Boulevard, for generations Shelby's most prestigious address.

Perhaps the most outstanding memory that Powell took with her from Shelby was the cry of the locomotive: Shelby Junction was then an important transfer point for several lines, and she must have heard hundreds of whistles every week while growing up across the street from the depot. Train sounds permeate all of her novels, but they are rarely so potent or poignant as in *Dance Night*.

The value Powell placed on this book cannot be overstated. A dozen years after it was published, its author began a slightly fictionalized version of her own life story called *My Home Is Far Away*. During one period of self-doubt, she regretted her decision to mingle truth with invention: "Although I set out to do a complete job on my family, I colored it and, even worse, diluted it through a fear of embarrassing my fonder relatives, also a distaste for throwing away my own privacy.

"A writer, for purposes of future collecting of material, needs personal privacy and disguises," she continued.

> Since telling the truth is merely a version of events anyway and nobody else's "truth," the essential thing is to convey similar effects, similar emotions and in my own case arrive at artistic truth by artistic means, instead of handicapping myself by withholding some facts and enlarging or distorting others. . . . *Dance Night* was completely fiction as I was working on it. Yet it is more autobiographical (with facts translated into their own value emotionally and structurally) than any autobiography I can imagine.

However positive Powell's own evaluation, the critical reviews of *Dance Night* were mixed. The smartest and most appreciative notice came from an anonymous reviewer at the *New York Times:*

> *Dance Night* is fiction unobscured by moralizing or any psychological or sociological analysis of the people and the town, and hence takes on an atmosphere of realism seldom achieved in a novel of its setting. Miss Powell has painted in sure, even strokes the dreary boarding houses, the roisterous saloons and poolrooms, the cheap factory girls and the gaudy dance hall which make Lamptown. . . . Out of *Dance Night* emerge unforgettably real people, drawn with an unerring instinct for characterization. Nor has Miss Powell made the mistake of merely gathering together a group of unusual people to describe. Each one belongs definitely to Lamptown. The reader feels that should he visit Lamptown's prototype he would inevitably meet each of them.

Mary Ross, the same critic who had so memorably pronounced *The Bride's House* "as soft and sturdy as a pansy," weighed in with a favorable if sentimental and largely uncomprehending review of *Dance Night* in the *Herald Tribune:* "To call the story 'realistic' is to risk a connotation of drabness which somehow has come to be associated with that word," she wrote. "Such an implication would be wholly unjust to the atmosphere which this author brings to her favorite Ohio setting. . . . It is unusually direct and unassuming work, clear and sturdy in its grasp of homely, even hateful things. But in this sturdiness there is a kind of joy in living, in feeling experience whole, that gives illuminating delicacy to its handling of emotion." Ross partially redeemed herself with her final line: "It has that fundamental respect for human nature which is the essence of sympathy."

The unsigned review in the *New Republic* was savage. It read, in full:

> There seem to be in America as many professional observers of small-town life as there are small towns, or else this particular one, entitled Lamptown, Ohio, would never have been singled out for attention. It is a dirty and dreary little place, filled with unprepossessing people about whom the author has little to say; moreover, she has said it in a dull and undistinguished manner.

Although *Dance Night* was nothing like the success Powell had hoped it would be, it was almost certainly her best-selling book to date. An accounting she entered into her diary on November 21, 1935, suggests that the novel had sold 4,972 copies in what she called a "regular edition" and that another 7,500 had been ordered up in an elusive "reprint," probably a cheaply bound popular edition. (How many of these copies actually made it onto the market is unknown; it has been my experience that *Dance Night* is one of the scarcest of Powell's books.)

It is, however, important to put things into perspective. There are no sales figures extant for *Whither, She Walks in Beauty*, or *The Bride's House*, but *The Tenth Moon/Come Back to Sorrento* (1932) sold only about 3,000 copies, and *The Story of a Country Boy* (1934) a mere 1,842 in its first year on the market. Thus, at least by Powell's sorry standards (which would improve only moderately during her lifetime), *Dance Night* could be regarded as the most substantial success among her early novels—a modest advancement for her career, but an advancement all the same.

Still, Powell herself considered the book a commercial failure and was deeply depressed by it. "It seems to me that ever since I finished *Dance Night* I have been marking time, waiting for something that doesn't happen," she entered in her diary in the summer of 1931, almost a year after its publication. "I can't buckle down seriously to a big job but just do little odd pieces—marking time, really, in my mind, waiting for *Dance Night* to come out with great *éclat*. As if it had never come out—a rocket that only sizzled because it was rained on. Still wait for the blaze in the sky. It did a very funny thing to me, that dead rocket."

Powell didn't yet know it, but even at that moment she was already working on another "big job"—one of her grandest creations, in fact. This was her massive, magnificent diary, which she began in earnest in early 1931. It differed dramatically from the painfully intimate "Woggs" journal she had kept in 1915, and not only because the author was now a full-grown woman. If Powell had seen herself as writing for a far-off biographer in that earlier record, she seemed now to be writing for far-off *readers*. There is the sense throughout that she has one eye on posterity, and in fact, in her will, she specifically named the diaries among the "unpublished documents . . . manuscripts, papers, notations, letters, sketches and memoirs" that might be sold or published posthumously. An edited version of her diaries was accordingly issued in 1995; it brought Powell more attention than anything she published in her lifetime.

In her diaries, Powell valued the opportunity to observe human behavior—her own and that of other people—and put it down on paper while it was still fresh. Some of these scenes found their way into her novels; others were perfect vignettes on their own, flashes of long-ago reality, as vivid and vital as the best photographs by Weegee. Some entries were frankly trivial; still, precisely because yesterday's trivialities are so fleeting and quickly forgotten, it can be an eerie delight to listen, with Powell, to a conversation that took place in a nightclub bathroom half a century ago, to travel to the top of the Empire State Building when it was brand-new, to eavesdrop on a cosmopolitan Manhattan party in the middle of the Great Depression.

Many of the entries are decidedly impersonal—playful, fascinated reporting rather than searching self-revelation. Nor was Powell especially interested in recording her own reactions to the events of her time: Pearl Harbor, Hiroshima, and the assassination of President Kennedy would all go unremarked.

But from the very first entry—dated January 1, 1931, and presented here unedited—it was unmistakably an author's diary:

> The tragedy of people who once were great or glamorous—now trying in their mediocre stations to modestly refer to their past to kind, stupid friends who pity their *lies*—until your grand-relic must shout and brag until at the end everyone says he is a little crazy—no one should brag that way. You see me in this little town—ah, but Bernhardt told me I was a great actress—I tell you she did—she said. Yeah—well Bea, why didn't you —. I don't know, she says—and she doesn't. They brag only because no one believes anyone is more than he seems at this moment.

This would become the theme of Powell's next novel, *Come Back to Sorrento* (originally published as *The Tenth Moon*).

Over the next thirty-five years, the author would fill her diaries with many such ideas for novels and short stories, as well as songs, dreams, observations, one-liners ("Never give a guest Dexedrine after sundown"), gossip, philosophy ("No such thing as present sight. Hindsight and foresight"), and her own agonies. As far back as 1915, Powell had acknowledged that she was usually unhappy when she addressed her diary (in this case personified as "Woggs"):

> It's too bad that I'm always confiding in you on those days I feel the bluest. This book is enough to make a stone weep and if anyone should read it they would think the writer was indeed in pathetic straits. But no one will ever read it so I think I'm really wiser to do it this way—tell my blue, weepy thoughts to you, who will never reveal them to another soul, instead of inflicting them on the people around me—and when I'm in a flip, gay mood, I take it off on other people.

This was to remain her pattern: as late as 1959, she would regret that her diaries lacked "rich joy, which I have but for some reason never write about."

The physical diaries comprise thirty-five separate prefabricated volumes, their pages dated and their years embossed on their covers. Powell was not scrupulous about keeping up with her diary, so whereas the volume for 1931 is at least twenty-five thousand words long, others (the one for 1964, for example) contain only a fraction of that number. She regularly skipped days, sometimes even months, at a time. She was careless about chronology; for instance, her entry on the murder of Maxwell Bodenheim was scribbled on the page allocated to February 3, 1954, even though the Village poet and novelist was not killed until February 7. Many more such misdatings may be found throughout the entries, as Powell wrote when and where she felt like it. As a result, the diaries do not present anything like a balanced portrait of her; the glimpses they *do* provide, however, are priceless.

When she began keeping the 1931 diary, Powell was laboring over two different projects, one of which she called the "Lila" novel, a sharp picture of sophisticated New York that would eventually evolve into *Turn, Magic Wheel* (1936). The other book she usually referred to as "Madame Benjamin"; finished in 1932, the retitled *Come Back to Sorrento* is the gentlest of Powell's novels, a soft, melancholy narrative of lost dreams and thwarted ambitions set in yet another of her Ohio towns.

Gentle though the book may be, the author's moods were nothing if not mercurial while she was working on "Madame Benjamin." It began promisingly enough: "As soon as this new book came to life, my other one ["Lila"] seemed too stiff," she recounted on March 31, 1931. "This one—'Madame Benjamin'—laid in the little town, is known to me. I smell the town, with its bonfires of autumn leaves, the meadows far off with wild flowers in them. Every person is familiar to me."

Three months later, though, her faith had begun to wane. "This new novel seems to ring true but it is not anything important or unusual," she observed.

> It runs along easily and solely by intuition, unlike the careful, solid planning of *Dance Night*. It is very slight—as thin and usual as the works of Ellen Glasgow or Isa Glenn—so easy I scarcely miss what goes out of my brain. I neither like nor dislike it. I only feel that if I were stronger and not so crippled by the disappointment of *Dance Night*, my domestic panic and responsibilities, I could do bigger stuff than this light lady-writing.

By the next year, she had decided that her new novel simply wasn't any good. Her displeasure was compounded when Farrar and Rinehart rejected her chosen title—*Come Back to Sorrento*—and issued the book in the fall of 1932 as *The Tenth Moon*, taking the name from a line by Shelley that served as its epigram. "How I hate the empty, silly, pointless title!" Powell complained. A year later, distraught over the lack of serious critical attention paid to her work, she determined to give up her higher literary ambitions and write in such a way as "to find a public somewhere for something, if it's only in *Snappy Stories* or *The New Yorker*. Write *Tenth Moon* crap if that's as much reality as people can stand."

A present-day reader can only wonder what Powell could have been thinking. *The Tenth Moon* is a wise, sorrowful miniature, intricately shaded, filled with subtle and memorable characters. Anybody who has ever doubted the extent of Powell's compassion for human suffering has only to behold what she makes of her two central figures here, Connie Benjamin and Blaine Decker.

In her youth, Connie wanted to be a professional singer; the "great Morini" once complimented her artistry. However, her career ended before it even began: pregnant and abandoned, she married a cobbler and settled down to raise two daughters in the hamlet of Dell River.

Blaine is Dell River's newly appointed music instructor; having studied in Europe, he has come to town with a ready-made legend. The author and the contemporary reader (though not Connie or the villagers) understand that Blaine is homosexual; without malice, Powell repeatedly uses such coded expressions as "queer," "gay," and "strange" in connection with him, while other characters speak of his dandy "mannerisms." Blaine, too, is caught in the past, in the fond recollection of an idyllic year in Paris, where he lived with a successful novelist, Starr Donnell.

The two small-town sophisticates become friends and create their own exclusive clique, one built largely on fantasy lives, past and future, far beyond the borders of Dell River. They discuss music and literature, pass judgment on visiting artists, and generally behave with an intellectual pride that crosses over into snobbery. It all ends in tears, of course: Connie dies of tuberculosis (in a simple and memorable death scene told from the dying woman's perspective, a difficult trick that Powell pulls off beautifully), and though Blaine does indeed embark for Europe, it is only as a sort of paid amuser and tour guide for the area's wealthiest matron:

> He wandered around the deck, his muffler flying in the breeze, his new topcoat flapping about his knees, his tie—as always—flying gaily from side to side. In six more days he would be in Paris—oh terrifying thought! It was no longer a city of dreams set in the silvery mist of romantic memories but a strange unfriendly place that had once found him not good enough; it was only in Dell River that Paris belonged to him completely, a tender place that loved him, that perpetually held out arms to him.

From the opening of the book, the author's tone is compassionate. She has already presented us, in earlier works, with the gritty, industrial side of Ohio; now she gives us the state's more bucolic qualities. Living amid the honeysuckle, morning glories, and bonfires of fallen leaves is a typically diverse group of Powell characters, including Connie's husband, Gus ("She was fond of him because he seemed somehow the very kind husband of a dear friend, not her own husband at all"); Mrs. Busch, who takes in washing ("Her casual references to her work made it seem that her long days of laundering were only a gentlewoman's hobby"); and Mrs. Busch's mysteriously disturbed daughter Honey, who resembles Jojo in some particulars ("The loveliest child she had ever seen, dancing around a group of the other children, thumbing her nose at them, and finally whirling herself dizzily round and round down the street, screaming with laughter").

Come Back to Sorrento has no sharp edges. There are no real villains, and Connie and Blaine themselves are decidedly fragile heroes; neither has what Powell calls the "god-like ruthlessness so necessary to the genuine artist." The book is poignant, not tragic, with a tender fatalism pervading the action. "I've gone over the whole thing dozens of times and I always come to the same goal," Connie tells Blaine at their first meeting, when he asks about her aborted career. "There never is any real choice about your life . . . just the one door open to you always. . . . You can't say you're sorry."

Both Connie and Blaine hide their deepest fears and hauntings from each other, a reticence that has its roots in Powell's own sensibility. One of the odder quirks of her diary is the way it dismisses the deaths, over the years, of her father, her sister, and the aunt who raised her from late childhood in clipped, simple, declarative sentences, without any emotional elaboration. A passage in Come Back to Sorrento might have served as her excuse: "You cannot talk about real things, there are no words for genuine despair, there are not even tears, there is only a heavenly numbness for which to pray and upon that gray curtain words may dance as words were intended to do, fans and pretty masks put up to shield the heart."

The novel is marred by one misstep: toward the end of the book, when Connie is already very ill, she meets by chance the man who had seduced her so many years before. Not only has he forgotten her name, but he has grown so fat and repulsive that Connie's older daughter is horrified that her mother even deigns to speak with him. The scene is handled carefully and with subtle pathos, but it still seems a pat and predictable form of closure, never entirely believable.

The Tenth Moon sold fewer than three thousand copies and garnered only a smattering of reviews, most of them short and poorly placed, albeit generally positive in tone. The most insightful notice was by the distinguished critic and editor Harold E. Stearns, writing in the *New York Herald Tribune*. "It is neither the characters, nor their fates, pathetic or gay, which linger in one's memory after closing the book," Stearns said, "but rather the peculiar penumbrae of feeling in which they are enwrapped, like melodies not quite remembered nor yet wholly lost. Compared with the clatter of events, the almost aggressively picaresque flow of episode, in most current fiction, *The Tenth Moon* comes as a particularly compelling, a particularly gracious interlude."

The *New York Times* was also warmly receptive: "Every small town has its Connie Benjamins and Blaine Deckers, people whose lives do not fit into the conventional pattern, who are speculated about, misunderstood, ridiculed and resented by the rest of the town. It is a high tribute to Miss Powell's ability that she can create out of their pitiful frustrations and impossible hopes as sustained and moving a story as *The Tenth Moon*."

The *Saturday Review of Literature* published a mixed report: "Miss Powell chooses to employ her talents this time on a theme more interesting to the technician than to the general reader; you may admire the way she does it without being persuaded that it was worth doing at all." This anonymous critic seems to have missed the homosexual subtext altogether: "What was drawing these two together was soon obvious enough, even to them, but each of them resolutely thrust it into the background and kept it there," the reviewer wrote. "To concede that they were attracted as man and woman and that their emotion could have been discharged in an ordinary human satisfaction would have destroyed the dream world each had built for the other, the only thing that made life worth living. These are not important people and the theme, once stated and recognized, is no longer particularly interesting."

For years, Powell would consider this one of her poorest books. Then, in 1943, finding herself stymied in the middle of composing *My Home Is Far Away*, she would go back and reread *The Tenth Moon*, hoping that it might provide some direction, and would be shocked by her response:

> I was actually absorbed in it and read it all the way through weeping and moved to my depths. The fact is that it is a beautiful book—the best writing I ever did and technically flawless, with the most delicate flowering of a relationship that grips interest far more than my dramatic plots such as *Country Boy*. I then examined my notes in my journal and found all the way through references to the pleasure of writing something that left my emotions absolutely uninvolved, a mere craftsmanship job, a literary joke—okay, critics, I won't give you a pound of flesh, I will cheat you.

The "result," she concluded, was a "quivering book filled with pain and beauty."

CHAPTER FIVE

Movies, the Theater, and Literary Philosophies

꧁꧂

The theater has a harsh truth.

DAWN POWELL, 1933

"DAWN WROTE TWO PLAYS," the actor, director, and teacher Robert Lewis recalled in 1995. "One was *Big Night*, which was ruined by the Group Theatre. The second was *Jig Saw*, which was ruined by the Theatre Guild."

Powell actually wrote several other plays as well, but *Big Night* (1928, revised 1932) and *Jig Saw* (1933) were indeed the only two of her mature stage works presented during her lifetime. Another, unproduced play, *Walking down Broadway* (1931), based on her first days in New York, was turned into a film entitled *Hello, Sister!;* a novel, *The Story of a Country Boy*, was filmed as *Man of Iron* in 1935; and Powell herself spent at least two extended—and unhappy— periods in Hollywood under contract turning out film scripts. But all

of these efforts to write for the stage and screen unquestionably mis-
fired—though again, as Lewis suggested, that was, in large measure,
not her fault.

Ever since her days at Lake Erie College, Powell had been a
serious student of the drama. After moving to New York, she
attended the theater as often as she could; her early appointment
books are filled with blithe, one-line critiques of whatever she might
have seen the night before. She revered the classics—her favorite
play was *The Cherry Orchard*, which she would see many times
throughout her life—but she also took a strong interest in contemporary American theater, an interest encouraged by John Dos Passos,
Jack Lawson, and their colleagues at the New Playwrights Theatre.

In 1927, Powell decided to try her hand at playwriting herself.
She turned an early novella called *Women at Four O'Clock* into a self-
consciously experimental play and made some not very systematic
attempts to sell it. This brought her back in touch with Barrett
Clark, who, as a visiting lecturer on modern drama, had made an
enormous impression on her at college.

Little remembered today, Clark was nonetheless an influential
figure in the theatrical world of his time. He edited dozens of books
(including the annual editions of *The World's Best Plays* from 1915 to
1926 and a twenty-volume series called *America's Lost Plays*) and published early and significant studies of Eugene O'Neill, James Branch
Cabell (the once notorious author of *Jurgen*), and others. He seems
to have been a kindly and responsive friend to Powell, meeting with
her on numerous occasions in the late 1920s and early 1930s.

Clark didn't think much of *Women at Four O'Clock*—"This particular kind of impressionistic, nervous, high-power thing is a bit shop-
worn today," he told the author. Still, he allowed that the play had
some "corking good dialogue," encouraged her ambitions, and
promised to look at any work she wanted to show him.

In 1928, during a period when Joe was between jobs, Powell

wrote a scathing play called *The Party*, about an advertising executive named Ed Bonney. Over the course of one long, boozy evening, Bonney introduces a valuable client, "Schwartzie," to his wife, Myra, and pressures her to go to bed with him in order to help his business. Powell must have wanted to leave the outcome of this intrigue deliberately hazy; though later versions of the play have Myra briefly denying that anything has actually happened, this may have been a rather timid stab at keeping what was already a shocking piece from vaulting past the furthest bounds of popular sympathy. (A film dealing with a similar situation, *Indecent Proposal*, would cause much controversy and public discussion in America more than sixty years later.)

Clark liked *The Party* and helped Powell sell an option to an established and respectable troupe, the Theatre Guild, in 1930. "Can't imagine they will do it," she noted at the time. She was right; two years later, when there were still no plans to produce it, Clark called Powell once more and told her that a new company called the Group Theatre needed a play for January 1933, then only seven months off. Powell felt some genuine ambivalence about how to proceed—the Theatre Guild "bawled [me] out as a louse and [said] no good could come of such a dirty way of doing business—all of which I was aware of but I've been a sucker so long and been loyal up to the minute I get the kick in the pants"—but finally, after two days of negotiations, it was agreed that the Group Theatre would produce *The Party*.

The troupe had been founded in 1931 by Harold Clurman, Lee Strasberg, and Cheryl Crawford, all recent alumni of the Theatre Guild themselves. Modeling itself on the Moscow Art Theatre and, in particular, adopting the acting theories and methods of Konstantin Stanislavsky, the Group was a strange mixture of artistic innovation and proto-cult. "There were to be no stars in our theatre, not for the negative purpose of avoiding distinction, but because all distinction—

and we would strive to attain the highest—was to be embodied in the production as a whole," Clurman explained in his memoir *The Fervent Years*.

> The writer himself was to be no star either, for his play, the focus of our attention, was simply the instrument for capturing an idea that was always greater than that instrument itself. The playwright too could be worked with, the power of his play could be enhanced by the joint creativity of the theatrical group as a whole, which saw in the play a vehicle to convey a motif fundamental to the theatre's main interest. The director was the leader of the theatrical group, unifying its various efforts, enunciating its basic aims, tied to it not as a master to his slave, but as a head to a body. In a sense, the group produced its own director, just as the director in turn helped form and guide the group.

It was all terribly utopian—the company lived together during summer retreats outside New York, and a star actor in one play might find himself transformed into a stagehand for the next—and like most utopias, it didn't work for very long. Still, in the ten fractious years of its existence, the Group Theatre created some legendary productions, presented more than twenty new plays, helped launch a number of distinguished careers (not only Clurman's, Crawford's, and Strasberg's, but also those of directors Robert Lewis and Elia Kazan, actors Franchot Tone and Stella Adler, and playwright Clifford Odets), and established "method acting" as an eminent force on the American stage.

The Group renamed the play *Big Night* and, according to Lewis, doomed it from the start through their attempts to give it a proper staging. "Nobody understood Dawn's characters, her sophisticated dialogue, her wit," he said.

I don't want to say that the Group was full of Communists, but they were certainly leftists of one sort or another. If you wanted to talk about workers or bosses or something, they could talk to you, but if you wanted to talk about all those aspects of life that didn't necessarily have anything to do with Karl Marx, they were at a loss. They were much more in sympathy with John Howard Lawson or Clifford Odets and all these solemn social plays.

Lewis described the young Powell as being "very pretty, plumpish all over but in a very nice, squeezable way—not fat. . . . She was jolly company, but that wasn't all she was—you'd get tired of somebody like that," he continued.

Dawn was a *pal*—you could talk to her about anything. She could make fun of everybody because she really wasn't mean, you see. If you're mean, you make fun of people you don't like or whom you disapprove of. But if you're not mean, you can make fun of people you like, too, and they'll understand. She was a very rare person, very much ahead of her time.

The friendship between Powell and Lewis developed during the rehearsals for *Big Night* and lasted until her death. "This was a rather small play, and the Group Theatre had twenty-eight members," he recalled. "If you weren't in the show, well, you had to do something—that was the way we worked—and so I became the assistant stage manager for *Big Night* and I was there for every rehearsal."

Cheryl Crawford was designated as director (though Clurman would take over for the last few weeks), and Stella Adler chosen to play Myra; the cast also included Lewis Leverett and J. Edward Bromberg. "I remember sitting in a dress rehearsal, just before *Big Night* opened, and Dawn was right beside me," Lewis said in 1995.

And she had written a line for this model type, something along the lines of "I like to think of myself as a cultured person who loves music and art and books—and then I'm walking along Fifty-seventh Street and I see a fur coat in the window and I say, no, *that's* what I like." Now this line was supposed to be spoken by somebody pretty ordinary, certainly not by a great actress like Stella Adler with all of her emotional capacity. So we came to that line and Stella gasped it out, with tears and weeping and apology and this terrific intensity—Stella cried through all of her parts anyway, she was a famous crier. And Dawn was sitting there, looking on, sort of amazed. And she turned to me and said, "Isn't that strange? When I wrote that line, I thought it was *funny.*"

Throughout its preparation, Powell complained that the show wasn't being played "nervously enough." Four days before the premiere, she feared the worst:

> The Group has put on a careful production with no knowledge whatever of the characters—as they might put on a picture of Siberian home life—made up bit by bit of exact details but [with] the actual realism of the whole missing. People have one drink and therefore they are drunk. People are unconsciously selfish or cruel, therefore they are consciously selfish or cruel. People strive blindly and vaguely for something, therefore they are intelligently striving for a definite thing. This heavy-footed literalism weighted the play down.

Big Night opened on January 17, 1933, and the reviews were vicious. "Miss Powell's drama is even more tiresome than the odious little microbes with whom it is concerned," John Mason Brown wrote in the *New York Evening Post.*

"Miss Dawn Powell, author of 'Big Night,' broods bitterly about the twin arts of commerce and publicity and proclaims them and their practitioners to be immoral and debauched," Percy Hammond reported in the *Herald Tribune*. "In as sordid a play as I have seen since the Muscovites were here she parades them in all their merry squalor, drunk, disorderly, lustful and mean."

Brooks Atkinson, theater critic for the *New York Times*, spent most of his review limply describing the social aspects of the opening night, throwing in a few lukewarm complaints about the play and a few mild compliments about the players.

Robert Benchley, in the *New Yorker*, was the sole major critic to come to Powell's defense, albeit somewhat shamefacedly: "My reaction to 'Big Night' was apparently one which marked me as not only obtuse but calloused. I liked it." He called Powell a "keen and humorous observer" and, in his final line, showed an acute understanding of her art: "I thought I detected not only humor and bitterness but a fine and delicate sadness."

Powell was perplexed by the reaction to *Big Night*. "Those of my friends who laughed most at the script of 'Big Night' are jovial souls who take human frailty for granted," she wrote in an article published in the *Post* just before the opening. "The reformers insisted that what the characters do or say can't possibly be funny because the way they live is wrong.

"Naturally," she continued, "by the time any play reaches production, most of New York has read it and the rest come to rehearsals. Such readers and rehearsal guests have astounded me by referring to some of my characters as 'persons of that class.' I'm far too polite to answer, 'Why, honey, that class is *your* class.'"

Big Night closed after only nine performances. It was a disaster for everyone involved, and its failure plunged the Group Theatre into another of its chronic financial crises. Clurman himself would later admit that the troupe's whole approach to *Big Night* was wrong from the beginning. "The play was one we should have done in four swift weeks—or not at all," he wrote in 1957. "We had worried it and harried our actors with it for months."

Powell would never forgive the directors of the Group for the way they mangled her play. She nonetheless remained resolute in her determination to succeed at playwriting:

> The accumulation of stupidity challenged and even flattered me—to be attacked as a menace to the theater was the first real sign that I had a contribution to make there.
>
> The theater has a harsh truth about it that appeals to my own desire for truth. It doesn't soften its blows or its cruelties for me and I need not pull my punches for it. It is a worthy foe—no false excuses or restraints—no *politesse* but back and forth honest blows. It is an open battlefield, not a discreet exchange of notes, and the old Sherman fighting blood smells raw meat—always a damn sight more exciting than the faint fragrance of the pressed rose.

Four months after the *Big Night* debacle, she completed her next play, *Jig Saw*, a likable but much less daring and abrasive work that would open at the Ethel Barrymore Theater near Times Square on April 30, 1934, under the auspices of the Theatre Guild. While the production could hardly be described as a huge success—it closed after forty-nine performances—the notices were kinder, the audiences were friendlier, and Farrar and Rinehart thought sufficiently highly of the play to release it in book form. (A brief notice in *Variety* suggests that the early closure may have had nothing to do with the quality of the play itself: "Show made money from operation, but last week's business was not profitable for the house," the magazine reported. "Shuberts sought a change in the sharing terms but the Theatre Guild refused to accede. House share was not enough, it was contended, because fifteen stagehands were needed.")

Jig Saw is a slight, amusing work to skim through (until late 1997, that was the only way to experience it—there had been no subsequent staging of the play, professional or private, since its original run). Julie, the innocent daughter of a wealthy divorcee, appears unexpectedly at her mother's Manhattan penthouse, only to find herself an unwelcome intruder in what has become a boozy series of cocktails and lovers. After three acts of comic mishaps, Julie surprises everyone by eloping with the philandering Nate Gifford, who just happens to be the man her mother has selected as her next conquest.

Powell seems to have been fairly content with the production, directed by Philip Moeller and imbued with an easier wit than the Group Theatre had brought to *Big Night*. She particularly admired the work of actors Cora Witherspoon and Ernest Truex, but found Spring Byington (who played the mother, Claire Burnell) solipsistic, observing, "[She] studies her own role with the greatest care and intelligence, reads it with every pause studied, each merry laugh, but has nothing to do with the other characters, does not listen to them and doesn't know what they've just said."

The critical reception for *Jig Saw* was much more enthusiastic than that for *Big Night*. In yet another dull, earnest notice, Brooks Atkinson commended Powell's "flair for breezy patter and topsy-turvy sophistication"; Percy Hammond, who had all but branded Powell a Communist in his review of *Big Night*, found "many flashes of wit, wisdom and wickedness." The new play, Hammond continued, "is fun . . . and when I suggest that its cold glitter sheds amusing beams on light, New York places, I voice the opinion of all my neighbors present last evening at the premiere." Gilbert W. Gabriel, writing in the *New York American*, was of two minds; he thought *Jig Saw* contained "enough wit for seven plays—and not quite plot enough for one."

Joseph Wood Krutch, then the drama critic for the *Nation* (later a Columbia University professor and the author of a fine biography of Samuel Johnson), turned in the most thoughtful critique:

What gives Miss Powell's play the strong flavor of originality which it undoubtedly has is a certain elusive individuality in the tone of the remarks which her characters make upon the set themes of "sophisticated" farce. In the first place, she has achieved a casualness which removes any distressing suggestion that she considers herself unusually naughty and is deliberately trying to shock. In the second place, she eschews the more or less established techniques of both the Wildean epigram and the Broadway wisecrack in favor of a slightly drunken irrelevance of phrase which, in so far as it resembles anything, resembles the manner of Frank Sullivan or James Thurber rather than that of more formally literary wits.

Krutch, too, had his reservations: "The dialogue is by far the best part of 'Jig Saw,' which limps noticeably in its action and, incidentally, includes some of the most awkward exits and some of the most painfully obvious clearings of the stage seen here in a long time."

On this point Powell probably agreed with Krutch: she does not seem to have considered *Jig Saw* a substantial work in any sense. "My plays have the difficulty of my short stories—an excellent real treatment of character and dialogue on a structure of contrived, exaggerated and strained story," she wrote in her diary on May 9, 1934, while *Jig Saw* was still running.

And then, in a bitter afterthought, she added, "Except that 'Big Night' wasn't."

Powell's experiences with Hollywood were equally bleak. However, here there was one crucial and redeeming factor, the same factor that has kept hungry writers venturing to California ever since: a chance to make some real money.

Indeed, Powell's movie career began with an astonishing bit of luck: *Walking down Broadway*, a play she wrote quickly and easily in early 1931, was sold, unproduced, by her agent, Ann Watkins, to the Fox Company for the sum of $7,500. This was more than twice what she had been paid for three novels by Farrar and Rinehart, and many times the average per capita income in the United States at that era—and all for a work that was already finished.

In late December that year, Powell traveled to Los Angeles with Watkins. Precisely why she went is unclear: she does not seem to have done any work on the script of *Walking down Broadway* (or any other film, yet), and her only known meeting was with Carl Laemmle, Jr., then head of Universal Studios, one of Fox's principal rivals. But she visited with the newly wealthy Lawsons ("[Jack] is, as near as I can figure, the belle of Hollywood," she wrote), became friendly with novelist and screenwriter Eric Hatch (best remembered today for *My Man Godfrey*), and—briefly—surrendered to the charms of southern California.

She lived in a Hollywood hotel called the Château Elysée and wrote home delightedly of its luxury. But what astonished her most was the environment—"the sheer geographical excitement of being on the edge of the world high up with trees shooting past your windows in the sixth floor and the heavenly June air."

Within a week, however, she hated it all. "Now impossible to sleep," she wrote in her diary. "The gaiety of early morning brilliant sunshine, immense green trees and singing birds leaves me depressed and weepy by noon. This climate picks you up and throws you down in the most amazing way." Several days later, she headed home by train, stopping in Ohio to see her sisters and Auntie May. The gray skies over Cleveland must have come as an enormous relief to her; Powell was perennially exhilarated by leaden winter clouds and stormy weather.

In the meantime, *Walking down Broadway* was making its way into motion-picture history, for reasons that had nothing to do with Dawn Powell. Eventually released as *Hello, Sister!* in 1933, it was the last work directed by Erich von Stroheim, that painstaking master of the ornate whose few surviving films have ensured his place among the most original of screen visionaries.

It would be hard to think of two geniuses who needed one another less than Powell and von Stroheim—and indeed, the director seems to have set to work immediately on destroying the author's modest little play. According to Fox staff writer Leonard Spigelgass, who worked on the film, Stroheim was "chiefly interested in the neuroses of the characters," whom he altered from "simple American characters into far more complicated ones, Viennese oriented"(!).

Stroheim completed his film in the summer of 1932 and delivered it to Fox. In February 1933, the *New York Sun* announced that *Walking down Broadway* was being remade, "now that Erich von Stroheim is no longer directing." In April, *Variety* announced the change of titles and the fact that $62,000 had been spent on retakes. When *Hello, Sister!* was finally released, later that year, it carried no directorial credit whatsoever.

For years it was thought that most, if not all, of Stroheim's contributions to the film had been cut. However, after a 1970 revival of *Hello, Sister!* in New York, film historian Richard Koszarski suggested that "what actually occurred was a brief reshooting, amounting to most of the final reel and perhaps a few intermittent episodes elsewhere in the film, a total of perhaps twenty-five percent of the running time." Still, he added, "it must be kept in mind that [Stroheim's] original version was considerably longer than the six reels of 'Hello, Sister' and much violence has necessarily been done to his original conception."

Powell is nowhere mentioned in Koszarski's article; though she received screen credit as the author of the play, the film had very little to do with her conception. Her funny, bittersweet drama is about innocent young women in New York trying to impress equally innocent young men with their worldliness in sexual matters, and the unfortunate estrangements that result from their deception. Stroheim turned this into a much more elaborate narrative, complete with a suicide attempt that leads to a fire and ultimately an explosion (when some dynamite that a drunken tenant has hidden blows up an apartment building). There is much to admire in *Hello, Sister!*—rich detail, intricate characterization, a vivid fight scene in which characters tumble downstairs raging and clawing at one another—but it has nothing to do with *Walking down Broadway.*

The notices were mostly poor, filed by critics who may not even have known that the film had been directed by the uncredited Stroheim and who were unlikely to have recognized the name Dawn Powell. One anonymous reviewer in the *New York Times* called it a "stupid little trifle, aimless and dull." *Variety* was equally underwhelmed: "As screen entertainment, the picture has little to recommend it. Direction and dialogue are particularly feeble. Or else whatever punch the yarn had was lost in the adaptation."

Powell's second experience with Hollywood came when First National Productions Corporation and Warner Brothers bought her novel *The Story of a Country Boy* in 1934. Here again, the financial windfall was extraordinary—$12,500 for the rights to a novel that had sold barely two thousand copies. The director, William McGann, though hardly of Stroheim's caliber, did at least observe the etiquette of remaining somewhat faithful to Powell's original plot, and there was a fair cast, including Barton MacLane as the self-made tycoon Chris Bennett, Dorothy Peterson as his wife, Bessie, and Mary Astor as a pretty stenographer. The film itself, however, entitled *Man of Iron* and released in late 1935, was a terrific flop, receiving reviews almost as scathing as those for *Big Night.*

"Since it is generally acknowledged that the cinema is technically proficient, it is almost inconceivable that a film bearing the Warner–First National seal could so completely violate the standards of motion picture production as does 'Man of Iron,'" the *New York Times* railed. "Here is an example of a hackneyed story presented with a minimum of action and excessive dialogue."

Variety predicted that *Man of Iron* would "just get by on double bills," though "a few minor laughs can be found," the critic conceded. Powell herself never referred to the film, either in her diaries or in surviving letters.

It is a pity that *Man of Iron* turned out so poorly, for *The Story of a Country Boy*, which was published in 1934 by Farrar and Rinehart, might have made a good movie. It is probably the most traditional, the most carefully plotted, and (to put it bluntly) the most formulaic of Powell's novels. *Country Boy* is not all "bad," by any means, and in some ways it is quite skillful, but many of the worries Powell had about *The Tenth Moon / Come Back to Sorrento*—that it was tailored too consciously for public taste, that it was overly tidy and almost academic in its construction, that it was lacking any strong personal impetus—apply more directly to this book.

Powell was attempting something new with *Country Boy;* she seems to have envisioned it as a sort of Ohio epic, a novel of the soil in the realistic manner of Frank Norris. It was planned on a grand scale and is in fact the lengthiest of her works, though in book form it didn't appear massive enough to satisfy its author. ("Disappointed in the page proofs," she wrote as the book was about to come out. "Only 303 because of fine print, when it is ¼ longer than anything else I've done").

The idea for *The Story of a Country Boy* had come to her during that first visit to Hollywood in 1932. As she basked in the decadent luxuries of the Château Elysée, a world away from her Mount Gilead roots, she was reminded of a cousin who had become a successful businessman. "I should write a novel about a boy like Charlie Miller," she mused on January 1, "who works himself up from class to class to factory head, then [is] unable to understand the strikers, explaining he's one of them—there *are* no classes."

And so, carefully, methodically, she sketched out a sort of rags-to-riches-to-rags story about Christopher Bennett, a young man with a rural Socialist background who starts off as a laborer at the Balding Company, rises steadily through the ranks, and becomes wealthy. Ultimately he finds himself in the middle of a nasty labor dispute, takes to drink, nearly destroys his marriage, loses his fortune, and finally goes back to the farm, where he may or may not find happiness—Powell was too honest to completely compromise her basic skepticism about such matters.

"The *new* Ohio must be the keynote," Powell wrote as she set to work, "the dizziness of speed through broad auto highways, hot dog stations, not the tranquil hayfields of my recollection." Some of Lawson's social beliefs crept in, too: "Jack is talking and thinking so much more clearly and directly than ever before," she wrote in August 1932, "owing, he says, to Trotsky and a study of Marxian theories applied to creative work. The business of thinking straight—what do you want to prove and what type of protagonist will best prove your idea and is the idea sound to begin with?"

In another five years, Lawson would be a dutiful Stalinist who rooted out "Trotskyism" wherever he could find it and cheered on the Moscow show trials. But the winds had not yet shifted, and Powell was still very much in his thrall. "Began plotting Christopher Bennett's story," she wrote on August 29.

Jack's system of Marxian criticism and his insistence on right ideology before work is attempted very helpful on this. For that reason I should like to dedicate it to him. He actually has influenced me enormously in all my work since *She Walks in Beauty*. I have talked over all my plans with him and each time he knows exactly, from the most casual outline, what I must watch out for and what main direction I must stick to. That is why, as I grow older and more egotistical, more centered in my work, I would sacrifice almost anyone for a little hour with him going over these quite selfish matters.

By temperament, however, she was not a dogmatic thinker—it is almost comical to envision the not-very-political Powell concerning herself with "right ideology"—and she soon began to stray from her outline. By mid-1933, she could state contentedly that the novel was "flying along as it should but on a different line than I expected." Her characters, it seems, had asserted their rights: "The people have taken charge of it," she observed. "I only hope they continue to run it themselves; after all, it's their business."

In time, she came to regret her meticulous planning. "Odd about the benefits of that complete outline and chart I made for this book," she noted. "Like any other support, it weakens intelligence. I faithfully and fairly easily do all the scenes and climaxes as arranged but the results of each one are blank. Scene goes to scene with no connecting link or character change or effect."

She finished *The Story of a Country Boy* on December 12, 1933, having written the vast majority of it within the preceding six months. At some point before publication, she suddenly canceled the original dedication to Lawson and gave Jacques LeClercq the honor instead. After reading the proofs, she commented, "It isn't as good a book as *Dance Night* but is much more compelling since its people are real and living and contemporary." She reassured herself, "It will probably sell around twenty thousand no matter what the reviews, since it has the basis for popularity."

Wishful thinking; in fact the book sold wretchedly—just 1,842 copies over the course of the first year—and was deleted from Farrar and Rinehart's catalog shortly thereafter. The reviews were mostly lukewarm. *"The Story of a Country Boy* is one of those American novels which is without special distinction but which adds an honest bit to the mosaic of contemporary American life that our fiction is creating," the critic for the *New York Times* wrote. The *New York Herald Tribune* printed a small but basically flattering notice by Phil Stong, author of the novel *State Fair*, who added a mischievous aside: "There is so much truth so delightfully managed in *The Story of a Country Boy* that it seems almost malicious to remark that when Miss Powell is compelled to touch on matters of farm technique, she is not really the Old Pioneer Mother she pretends to be."

In the end, many latter-day readers will no doubt agree that the *Saturday Review of Literature* found an appropriate and judicious tone with its observation that "Miss Powell has done better work than this in her *Tenth Moon* and will do so again."

By the time these articles appeared, Powell was already working on her first satirical novel, *Turn, Magic Wheel*—the resuscitation, after four years, of the "Lila" book set in New York that she had started concurrently with *Come Back to Sorrento / The Tenth Moon.* "I want this new novel to be delicate and cutting—nothing will cut New York but a diamond," she wrote in February 1934. "It should be crystal in quality, sharp as the skyline and relentlessly true. No external details beyond the swift, eager glance over the shoulder."

It was, perhaps, an odd time to be turning to comedy, for 1934 was to be an excruciating year personally for Powell. As noted earlier, she had suffered some enormous emotional hurt, presumably involving Lawson, in the early-morning hours of January 1. Then, too, Jojo was out of control much of the time, though every new doctor, every new treatment, filled his parents with desperate and exhilarated hope. Finally, there was the chronic and mysterious pain in Powell's chest, always accompanied by the frightening prospect of another "heart attack":

> Dr. Witt examined me with X-rays and fluoroscopes and said the tumor *in* my lung and *on* my heart is slowly, almost imperceptibly growing—faintly ominous—slowly crowding the heart, filling the lung until one day I will strangle—unless it's cut out before. No maybe. It terrifies me, even though in sensi-

ble hours I see that this may move as slowly as any glacier and not fulfill its destiny for centuries.

Notwithstanding the failures of *Hello, Sister!* and *Man of Iron*, Hollywood remained interested in Powell; in June 1934, Paramount offered her $1,500 a week, well above the journeyman average, to come to California, and in August, United Artists tried vainly to convince her to undertake a screen adaptation of L. Frank Baum's *The Wonderful Wizard of Oz* (the company eventually abandoned the idea; the classic film would be made five years later by Metro-Goldwyn-Mayer). She refused all such offers, preferring to put her every effort into *Turn, Magic Wheel*, despite the fact that she and Joe were once again having financial difficulties.

By all external signs, they should have been doing very well indeed. In 1934 alone, Powell made $13,845—her best year yet, by far—while Gousha earned some $14,000 at his firm. But Joe spent a good portion of his salary on meals out, often at some of the fanciest restaurants in Manhattan, such as "21," the Rainbow Room, and the Stork Club. Powell, too, preferred to eat and drink out, at the Hotel Lafayette or the Brevoort, two ancient establishments located almost back to back on East Ninth Street, between Fifth Avenue and University Place. Jojo's doctors needed to be paid, as did his full-time nurse. There was also a maid, Marie Jeffers, who, like Louise Lee, would remain a faithful employee for decades. On top of all these costs, Dawn and Joe had taken a new, much larger, and more elegant apartment, located at 9 East Tenth Street. With the exception of brief sublets and some occasional hotel stays, Powell would live within three blocks of that address for the next thirty years.

At just about the same time that Powell broke off her association with John Howard Lawson, her friendship with John Dos Passos deepened. Dos Passos was then a Marxist, and some of Powell's letters to him touch on their political differences. In 1935, for example, she attended the initial meeting of the Communist-dominated American Writers Congress and sent back a lively report:

> I feel all my old Elk and Modern Woodman blood sweeping through me. This came partly from the crack in the Writers Congress creed—"defend the Soviet of Russia with our bare bodies." Suddenly five or ten generations of bigoted Republicans popped out of me as well as an old American Legion button and I was raring to defend my old Steubenville steppes instead of Max Gorelik's. I hesitate to broadcast these sentiments because no one will give me proper credit for them— anything that pig-headed gets a Mencken or Nathan credit line and it's no fair. I went to two or three meetings which sounded very bright but I swear I couldn't figure out what it was all for or who until it ended with a parade plan and the singing of the "Internationale" with little hot hands up to little hard heads.

Dos Passos was the first correspondent with whom she could also swap literary opinions and gossip on a high level (Edmund Wilson would soon become another). Of some poems published by a mutual friend, the short-lived Berenice Dewey, Powell told "Dos":

> They are really excellent, I think. I always feel so relieved and grateful when lady poets don't write about what vagabond lovers they are—especially when you have generally only to see them to realize they're only old Aunt Minnie who had all she could do to bed Uncle Eph, and any vagabonding they ever did was about as light and charming as Lizzie Borden's coquettishly peeping over the handle of her axe.

As this excerpt suggests, Powell could be unusually hard on women writers. There were a handful whom she admired greatly, especially the Norwegian Sigrid Undset, best remembered for her medieval Catholic trilogy, *Kristin Lavransdatter*, which won the Nobel Prize for literature in 1928 and has never since gone out of print. Powell was most attracted to Undset's dark early novels about modern Scandinavian women, especially *Jenny*. She revered the writing of George Eliot and Edith Wharton (*The Reef* was a favorite) and respected Virginia Woolf's artistry without much liking her work. Frances Trollope's *Domestic Manners of the Americans* was always one of her favorite books; she read it over and over again, inevitably finding fresh delight in the author's acid, hilarious impressions of the United States in the 1830s. "Mrs. Trollope didn't attack America," Powell insisted in one of the many defenses she wrote of this controversial memoir. "She loved it and wrote truly about it."

Among her contemporaries, she admired Djuna Barnes (she described *Nightwood* as a "sad, brilliant book"), the Anglo-Irish Norah Hoult, and—more surprisingly, perhaps—the enormously successful novelist, essayist, and short story writer Katherine Brush, whose humor she esteemed and whose facility she envied. In later life, Powell would read the works of Iris Murdoch, Muriel Spark, and Brigid Brophy with pleasure (one wonders if she ever came across the early novels of Honor Tracy, which share some of her own unflinching humor). But she had little but contempt for most of the fashionable women authors of her time, including Marcia Davenport, Lillian Hellman, Margaret Mitchell, and, later, Françoise Sagan. And she would find the inspiration for one of her best satires, *A Time to Be Born*, in the career of Clare Boothe Luce.

Powell's relationship to Dorothy Parker was necessarily an awkward one. She believed Parker's celebrity was largely a matter of publicity, and she resented it when they were compared to one another.* Powell's ingrained work ethic may have had something to do with her attitude toward her "rival": from 1928 to 1944, she

---

* *Such comparisons were inevitable — not only were both women cosmopolitan New York wits, they even had the same initials.*

herself produced at least one novel every other year, while Parker's far grander reputation was built on her slight collections of poems and short stories and some reported one-liners. And yet the two were friendly whenever they saw one another, and there was a period when that happened often, particularly in the early 1940s. In 1963, Dawn would reminisce in a postcard to her sister Phyllis: "Yes, I used to have some good times with Dorothy Parker who gets too much credit for witty bitchery and not enough for completely reckless philanthropy—saving many people really, without a thought."

She was not much easier on men than she was on women. In 1935, shortly after the publication of Thomas Wolfe's 912-page autobiographical novel *Of Time and the River*, she wrote a wicked eight-line parody called "Wolfe's Pocket Apostrophe," with the subtitle "Of Time and the River on My Hands":

> *Oh Boston girls how about it*
> *Oh Jewish girls, what say*
> *Oh America I love you*
> *Oh geography, hooray*
> *Ah youth, ah me, ah beauty*
> *Ah sensitive, arty boy*
> *Ah busts and thighs and bellies*
> *Ah nookey there—ahoy!*

Although she enjoyed the occasional company of Ernest Hemingway and was understandably flattered when he breezily informed her, in passing, that she was his "favorite living novelist," she detested Hemingway's writing and thought *The Sun Also Rises* "thin and feeble, lacking in human depth, mean-spirited." She seems to have taken small interest in the work of F. Scott Fitzgerald or William Faulkner and to have actively disliked the novels of John O'Hara and John P.

Marquand. It is even difficult to tell what she thought of the writing of her friends John Dos Passos and Edmund Wilson; her personal affection for them is clear enough throughout her diaries and letters, but she had few words for their books, and those words were often dubious.

In 1953, Powell made a list of the novels she liked best. Probably in no special order she named Theodore Dreiser's *Sister Carrie*, Sinclair Lewis's *Dodsworth*, Gustave Flaubert's *Sentimental Education*, the *Satyricon* of Petronius Arbiter, George Eliot's *Daniel Deronda* ("partly," she qualified, for she thought it devolved as it went on), Nicolai Gogol's *Dead Souls*, two novels by Honoré de Balzac, *Lost Illusions* and *The Distinguished Provincial*, two novels by Charles Dickens, *Our Mutual Friend* and *David Copperfield*, and Undset's *Jenny*. Later in life, Arthur Koestler's *Darkness at Noon* and Malcolm Lowry's *Under the Volcano* would also move her greatly, while her admiration for the classic Greek and Roman writers, and for Chaucer, Shakespeare, Henry James, and Ivan Turgenev, would increase with every passing year.

Is there a pattern here? I think so. Powell esteemed a hearty, stoical pessimism, leavened whenever possible by wit, worldly pleasures, and sophisticated camaraderie. For Powell, the bad news was already in: life was an absurd, bloody, and brutal business—always had been, always would be—but there would be compensations along the way, and a wise person would grab as many of them as possible, without complaint. She was never a crusader, and she mistrusted idealism of any kind (one notes the absence of authors such as Tolstoy and Dostoyevsky in her canon, despite her love for Turgenev and the Russian drama). Her favorite books are characterized by a steady, unblinking realism of one form or another; each of them presents us with an intelligent person's take on life as it is, not as it should be or might have been.

Powell would have seconded Turgenev's autobiographical statement: "I am, above all, a realist and chiefly interested in the living truth of the human face; to everything supernatural I am indifferent, and I do not believe in absolutes and systems; I love freedom more than anything else, and so far as I can judge I am sensitive to poetry. Everything human is dear to me."

A case could be made for seeing Powell as a kind of early, idiosyncratic existentialist, albeit one gifted with an unusually keen sense of humor. She seems to have concurred with many of existentialism's defining premises, especially the crucial tenet of personal responsibility for one's actions, twinned with a knowing recognition of their probable insufficiency. In some ways, however, Powell went most of the official existentialists one better, in that her recognition of an "absurd" universe did not push her work into either gloom or didacticism.

Moreover, her frank pessimism and her innate mistrust of human motives did not rule out compassion; with Samuel Johnson, she believed that the cure for worldly ills was not radical but palliative. Once, when a friend accused her of oversentimentalizing the young, she replied:

> My seeming sentimentality is based largely on the empty exhaustion I feel in a party of older people—being nice to someone because they are through, have failed, are poor—all requiring a kind of painful dry pity, because there is nothing you can do about it. You can't bring back their dead or give them fame or love or whatever the hell they want.
>
> With young people, you can't make their loves be true or pass out wedding rings if that's their passion. . . . But with some young people, you *can* give them an address to get a job or some money or a walk-on part or a hearing—and this is exhilarating and alive.

"True gaiety is based on a foundation of realism," she would write in 1939:

All right, we know we're dying, we know we're poor, that is off
our minds—we eat, sleep, make merry, but we are not kidding
ourselves that we are rich and beautiful or that Santa Claus and
two blondes will soon come down the chimney. There is only
sorrow in people making believe—sorrow and sordidness in
stories of [an] invincible, Peter Pan fairy-godmother world.
Gaiety should be brave, it should have stout legs of truth, not a
gelatine base of dreams and wishes.

In short, for Powell, even if humankind was a "futile passion" (as
Sartre would put it), living was still worth the effort.

CHAPTER SIX

The Escape into Satire

⚜

Satire is people as they are;
romanticism, people as they would
like to be; realism, people as they seem
with their insides left out.

DAWN POWELL, 1936

POWELL HAD MADE A TENTATIVE START on what
would become *Turn, Magic Wheel* in 1930, but she had shelved it to
write *Come Back to Sorrento/The Tenth Moon* and then immersed herself in stage and screen work. Exasperated by the slow pace of her
progress, she gave up even trying to work on the project in May
1931. "If I could get away—people are driving me crazy—I could
work on this novel," she scrawled, noting that she was "perpetually
teased by trifles of New York life."

When she took up the book again in mid-1934, after the Lawson debacle, her worldview had changed, and she now decided to
incorporate those "trifles" of New York life into her fiction. "New
novel must be burningly contemporary, even libelous if necessary—

no words to be spared, no feelings saved, no recognition softened," she said in December. And then, the following month:

> Since I can write so fluidly and with such pleasure about real people and my surmises, it seems increasingly an effort to step from this reality into a storybook world. On the other hand, I hate to use real people and hurt them but I have reached the point where I must sacrifice my tender feelings for reality. It's a decision against personal life for the crueler pleasures of artistic exactness.

She seems to have worked on *Turn, Magic Wheel* in a state of creative jubilation. Her diary for this period abounds with commentary such as "I never felt better, more alive, keyed up to impressions in my whole life"; "Believe, in spite of unusual facility in this new novel, that have something here rather unique"; and "I think this is much my best book, expresses more of my own self than anything else I ever did and furthermore I enjoy writing it."

Her initial three-book contract with Farrar and Rinehart had been satisfied by this time. After some hesitation—she disliked the way the company had presented and promoted her work—she agreed to produce two more novels at $2,500 apiece for the same publishers, provided that her advance was sent to her in monthly installments of $250.

However, when she submitted the first forty-four pages of her new book to Farrar and Rinehart in late February 1935, the editors were dissatisfied with both the scant quantity and the changed quality of her writing—the easy, breezy contemporaneity of *Turn, Magic Wheel* must have come as an enormous shock to them on the heels of *Dance Night*, *The Tenth Moon / Come Back to Sorrento*, and *The Story of a Country Boy*. A dispute of some sort ensued over the contract, and Powell was given permission (or perhaps simply told) to take the project elsewhere. Her new agent, Carol Brandt, made overtures to

Boston-based Little, Brown, but that house was no more interested in the book than Farrar and Rinehart had been.

At this point, Powell became dispirited: "Fear is such an utterly disrupting force—fear of no publisher, fear of cringing once more before debtors, fear of being trapped in the Middle West again and dependent on relatives—so that this panic creeps in my pen or typewriter, and nothing is possible." By the end of April, several other rejection letters had trickled in, and Powell's anxiety had redoubled. Not until May did author and publisher make their peace: Farrar and Rinehart agreed to continue her stipend and to look once more at *Turn, Magic Wheel* when it was closer to completion.

She finished the novel on November 2, delivered it, and was then forced to wait almost three weeks for any word from the company. When the response finally came, she was furious; John Farrar himself seems to have told her flat out that the manuscript was hopeless. "John wrote 'Better put aside—not necessarily destroy,'" Powell would recall eighteen years later—and this about "very likely my best, simplest, most original book."

Farrar and Rinehart ultimately did accept the manuscript, and by December, Farrar himself was even willing to allow that it was a "fine" novel—though he added hastily that "it probably wouldn't sell." Despite this lack of enthusiasm on the part of her publisher, *Turn, Magic Wheel*, released at the beginning of February 1936, would become far and away the fastest-selling volume Powell wrote for the company.

The book derives more directly from Powell's plays *Big Night* and *Jig Saw* than from any of her earlier novels; it is a fleet, unsparing send-up of Manhattan high life and low life, at once funny and sad, raucous and realistic, with an opening epigram by the third-century B.C. bucolic poet Theocritus and a dedication to Dwight Fiske—an appropriately scrambled pedigree for a dazzling creation.

Many readers will agree with Powell that *Turn, Magic Wheel* is indeed her "best, simplest, most original book." Here at last, more than a decade after the embarrassment of *Whither*, is her full-hearted exaltation of NewYork City in all its multiplicity—and Powell needs scarcely a single exclamation point to prove her love.

From its opening paragraph, the novel is written in a breathless, exhilarated style that pulls the reader immediately into the action:

> Some fine day I'll have to pay, Dennis thought, you can't sacrifice everything in life to curiosity. For that was the demon behind his every deed, the reason for his kindness to beggars, organ-grinders, old ladies, and little children, his urgent need to know what they were knowing, see, hear, feel what they were sensing, for a brief moment to *be* them. It was the motivating vice of his career, the whole horrid reason for his writing, and some day he warned himself he must pay for this barter in souls.

The novelist Dennis Orphen will reappear in several other Powell books. He is both a supreme egotist and something of a rotter, yet he is obviously the character with whom Powell feels the greatest affinity. One of the themes that *Turn, Magic Wheel* addresses, however airily, is the dilemma facing any writer who would use friends and acquaintances for inspiration—namely, when does artistic license cross the line into personal betrayal?

In this case, the answer may be found on page four of Orphen's new novel, *The Hunter's Wife*. Orphen has appropriated the love life of the older woman he squires about town—Mrs. Andrew Callingham, née Effie Thorne, whose famous husband deserted her some years ago—and constructed a thinly disguised roman à clef:

> Past youth, the sweet creature lies about her age, not through ordinary female coquetry but in the way men lie, men who

having failed to do the great deed by the given hour, ease their desperate fear of failure by cheating with the calendar. Fifteen years and he has not come back to me, she says, perhaps never, then, and this cannot be borne so she swears she is only thirty-nine, this year the miracle must happen, he will come back, the hunter will return and see the wise gentle wife she has become in his long absence.

The character of Andrew Callingham is based loosely on Ernest Hemingway (whom Powell knew only slightly at the time). A hunting-and-shooting type who lives in Paris, Callingham is arrogant, self-obsessed, badly behaved, publicity-hungry, and disdainful of the women who adore him. He appears only momentarily (and then in a deliberate anticlimax), but his meticulously crafted legend pervades the narrative.

Hemingwayesque though he may be, Callingham is presented mostly as a celebrity, rather than an active creative artist. The "author" character in *Turn, Magic Wheel* is Dennis Orphen, and by the end of the book we know quite a lot about him—about his vanities, his fantasies, his fears ("the growing conviction that his genius was no more wondrous than an old file"), and his rare but sincere flashes of self-reproach ("How clever I was, how damnably clever, Dennis thought, furious with his own demon now that made him see so savagely into people's bones and guts that he could not give up his nice analysis even if it broke a heart, he could not see less or say less"). We have also been introduced to a staggering array of New York grotesques—Belle Glaenzer, a "monument to Hollandaise in [a] black velvet chair," rivals anyone in Evelyn Waugh—and two sympathetic heroines, both of whom have been "Mrs. Andrew Callingham" and who now come to a mutual understanding that helps one of them die in peace and the other rejuvenate herself.

Still, the most vivid force in the book is the city itself:

Magically the five o'clock people came to life, bounced out of
their subways, jumped out of their elevators, bells rang, elevator bells, streetcar bells, ambulance bells; the five o'clock
people swept through the city hungrily, they covered the sun,
drowned the city noises with their million tiny bells, their five
o'clock faces looked eagerly toward Brooklyn, Astoria, the
Bronx, Big Date Tonight.

There are scenes set in Fifth Avenue mansions and in crumbling
garrets, at Carnegie Hall and at Luchow's restaurant; as Powell had
once promised her cousin Jack Sherman, we are right at home wherever she takes us in New York. The story is told not only in straight
narrative but also in interior monologues, flashes of conversation,
snatches from letters, clippings from gossip columns, posted adver-
tisements, the cries of newspaper boys, advice from fortune tellers,
and publishers' blurbs, among other things. Old and young, bar-
tenders and nurses, socialites and Communists, dandies and lascivi-
ous young women all come along to join the dance.

The set piece in which Dennis and his young mistress, Corinne,
speed to the top of the recently opened Empire State Building has
been rightly celebrated:

> Clouds as white as if the sky was baby-blue instead of black
> swam softly about them, stars were below and above, glittering
> through the plumes of the moon, listening for compliments
> from the Tower visitors. . . . New York twinkled far off into Van
> Cortlandt Park, spangled skyscrapers piled up softly against the
> darkness, tinseled parks were neatly boxed and ribboned with
> gold like Christmas presents waiting to be opened. Sounds of
> traffic dissolved in distance, all clangor sifted through space
> into a whispering silence, it held a secret, and when letters
> flamed triumphantly in the sky you felt, ah, that was the secret,
> this at last was it, this special telegram to God—Sunshine

Biscuits. On and off it went, Eat Sunshine Biscuits, the message of the city.

Powell herself believed she had created the "perfect New York story" in *Turn, Magic Wheel*. It was, she said,

> one woman's tragedy viewed through the chinks of a writer's book about her, newspaper clippings, café conversations, restaurant brawls, New York night life so that the story is tangled in the fritter of New York—it could not happen anyplace else. The front she keeps up is the front peculiar to the New York broken heart: people's deeds and reactions are peculiarly New York. "What? Our friend committed suicide—that's terrible . . . that's the kind of suit I'm going to get, there in Altman's. . . . She jumped out the window? No!—are you getting out here, why don't you get a gold belt . . . ?"
>
> Publisher and critic (but not public which—once it can be reached—is always more sane and sound than critical interpreters) would say these women, discussing the deaths of their friends, must be hard, bitter. The truth is that in New York, a city of perpetual distraction—where superficial senses are perpetually forced to react to superficial impressions—the inner tragedies, no matter how intense, are viewed through the tawdry lace of New York life.

In fact, many critics were impressed with *Turn, Magic Wheel*, and the reviews were placed far more prominently than those for any of her earlier works. The *New Republic*, which had so viciously attacked *Dance Night*, published a short but perceptive and appreciative appraisal by Jerre Mangione:

> Of the half-dozen novels that Dawn Powell has written, *Turn, Magic Wheel* is the first to reveal her vast talent for writing good

burlesque in fiction form. What makes Miss Powell as a lady wit seem more promising than either Tess Slesinger or Dorothy Parker is that, as an experienced novelist, she has developed a sense of structure, shown in her ability to go beyond the *bon mot* and invent characters and situations that are comic in themselves. Thus, although her main target is the dizzy literary world of Manhattan, her comedy emerges from original people and predicaments, rather than from mere caricatures of well known writers in better known quandaries.

Herald Tribune critic Mary Ross seemed more attuned to Powell's New York books than she had been to the Ohio cycle. "Dawn Powell's novels show the unusual combination of a clear head and quick sympathies," she wrote. "She sees the foibles of her people, their funniness and inconsistency and pettiness, and she also not only sees but feels their desires. Her stories have both warmth and wit."

The book seems to have made Edith H. Walton, who wrote about it for the *New York Times*, rather uncomfortable. Although she conceded that *Turn, Magic Wheel* was a "barbed and immensely entertaining satire on a certain phase of New York's literary life," she was bothered by the "peculiarly sharp and ruthless edge" of its author's wit. "[Powell] has some deadly things to say about the cormorant aspects of the intelligentsia," Walton concluded, "and though her actual story—despite its moving moments—is a little synthetic, her book as a whole rings savagely true."

For his part, Charles Hanson Towne, writing in the *Los Angeles Examiner*, sounded homesick: "It is a story with the pulse and feeling of the New York I love in every roaring page of it; a sparkling satire on the publishing business with a group of characters clearly and humanly drawn."

Turn, Magic Wheel was the first Powell novel to be published in England; Michael Sadleir, John Galsworthy's great champion and a novelist himself, bought the rights for John Constable, Ltd., which released its edition in the summer of 1936. Powell was delighted by the enthusiasm of the British reviews, with the marked exception of the *Times Literary Supplement*'s, which said it had "all been as well or better done by other writers."

From this time onward, Powell would always have a small but avid following in the United Kingdom. She herself believed that the "blunt, down to earth realism of the Middle West" had much in common with British humor. There were reportedly informal "Dawn Powell clubs" at several English universities; even sixty years after the publication of *Turn, Magic Wheel*, the London-based novelist and editor Francis Wyndham would beam as he recalled the pleasure the novel had given him as an undergraduate.

Powell was especially happy to be forwarded a note from the Irish poet, novelist, and historian Helen Waddell, whose translations of *Medieval Latin Lyrics* she had always admired. "I have just finished Dawn Powell's *Turn, Magic Wheel*," Waddell wrote to Sadleir. "It is the same kind of experience as watching Elisabeth Bergner act for the first time. Odd, to discover again the Comic Muse in Radio City, sorrowful, impish and wise."

As usual, Powell was perplexed by those critics who (as she herself had predicted they would) found her fictional people mean-spirited and distasteful, and she wrote a little essay in her diary defining and defending her approach:

> In my satire (except for stage satire which admits of little or no nuances) I merely add a dimension to a character, a dimension which gives the person substance and life but which readers often mistake for malice. For instance, take the funeral of a much-loved family woman, a mother. Treating this romantically, one writes only of the sadness in the people's hearts, their woe, their sense of deprivation, their remembrance of her. This is true, but it is not as true as I would do it, with their private bickers over the will in the garage, as they all gorge themselves

at the funeral meals, as the visiting sisters exchange recipes, confidences (for they haven't seen each other in many years), as pet vanities emerge.

Yet in giving this picture, with no malice in mind, no desire to show the grievers up as villains, no wish more than to give people their full statures, one would be accused of "satire," of "cynicism" instead of looking without blinders, blocks, ear mufflers, gags, at life. Satire is people as they are; romanticism, people as they would like to be; realism, people as they seem with their insides left out.

With the triumph of *Turn, Magic Wheel*, Powell immediately contemplated doing a follow-up in the same general style. But she put the idea aside in September 1936, having decided, after almost five years of entreaty from the studios, to try to make her name in Hollywood once more.

She lasted only about a month, again staying at the Château Elysée, working on scripts for the Samuel Goldwyn Company. She received no screen credit for any of the films on which she labored, but Goldwyn did offer her a three-year contract, which would require her to spend six to eight months a year in California, at a salary of $1,250 a week the first year, and $1,500 a week the second, rising in the third year to $1,750 or $2,000 (she gave conflicting figures in different documents). This was a staggering amount of money in the midst of the Great Depression; moreover, the studio pampered her utterly. "I do what I like, come and go as I please, stay in bed all day if I like—in fact, the oddest job imaginable," she wrote. "If I could only get my brain together, I might get it done."

But her distaste for the movie industry persisted, and eventually prevailed. She turned Goldwyn down—"DEFINITELY REFUSED ON GROUNDS OF INSANITY," she cabled to Joe on October 15—and returned to Manhattan on the train.

Thereupon, she began once again to write short stories, which she sold to *Mademoiselle*, the *New Yorker*, and *Harper's Bazaar* for a fraction of what she might have made in just one week in Hollywood. She finished a play she had started several years earlier, *Red Dress* (based loosely on *She Walks in Beauty*), and made an effort to peddle it to the Theatre Guild. Theresa Helburn, the Guild's executive director, remained an admirer for many years and would regularly ask Powell to submit works for consideration, but none of the four plays that the author registered with the U.S. Copyright Office after *Jig Saw* would be performed during her lifetime. Her last involvement with a show that would actually make it to the stage was to be a disastrous collaborative effort.

Powell's diary entries for the middle and late 1930s are unusually rich. Here, more than at any other time in her life, she preserved lengthy examinations not only of herself and her troubles but also of the daily life that surrounded her. Those who have read the diaries may recall Powell's piercing description of the sudden death of a young woman at a cocktail party; her repeated encounters with a sorrowful, sardonic antiques dealer in the East Village; and her despairing reverie upon overhearing a lovers' quarrel one steamy summer night. All of these were lived, observed, and recorded during this time.

In January 1937, Powell was hospitalized for three weeks with a case of jaundice; as usual, she was grateful for the attention she received from the doctors and nurses and—especially—for the enforced escape from the turmoil at home. "Hanging over the hospital can with not a care in the world but whether I could stop upchucking was the gay carnival of my year," she would report in September.

The pubescent Jojo was in wretched shape. "He requires the most intense control for from morning till night he bursts in, plants himself before me and shouts meaningless sentences over and over," she wrote. "It's too horrible a life, waking up to the jabbering of a noisy maniac, a dreadful future for all of us to face—ten thousand days of hopeless work to pay for hopeless treatments."

Still, thanks to the help of Louise Lee, Powell retained a fair amount of free time, which she spent writing and socializing. By the mid-1930s, the critic and historian Edmund Wilson had become a good friend, and a long correspondence ensued, with much intellectual teasing and role-playing over the years. Sometimes he would sign his letters "Wigmore"—"a seedy literary man," by Wilson's description—and Powell was "Mrs. Humphry Ward" (the author of that name, rediscovered in the late twentieth century, was then generally considered an embarrassing relic of the Victorian era). Later on, they would assume the characters of a flirtatious French couple, Raoul and Aurore; these notes are flowery and effusive, filled with intimate terms of endearment sometimes written in a sort of Dada French ("Je souffle pour vous, Raoul, ah!" Powell concluded one such letter).

Surprisingly, perhaps, given Wilson's reputation for womanizing and Powell's generous attitude about sex, their relationship seems to have been a platonic one. There is, however, one intriguing diary entry for October 4, 1937: "Bunny Wilson called up from hotel. 'Come over here right away,' he urged. 'I just had a dream about you and I want to go over it with you.'"

"Dawn had two personae with men," Rosalind Baker Wilson said in 1997. "One was the Mae West persona. She had the figure—which was then very much in style—and she knew how to flirt. This was mostly an act, a sort of comic routine—but not entirely. With my father, I think, she was always in her other persona, which was simply that of a sort of buddy."

Powell's association with Coburn Gilman, meanwhile, continued, and if there was ever a point when friendship crossed over into genuine romance between them, it was probably around this time. But Gilman remained a pathological drinker (he seems to have imbibed even more than Joe Gousha, though he was much more convivial when in his cups). Powell wrote regularly of him, but always with an exasperated mixture of amusement and pity that is not the customary tone of a lover; take, for example, her account of the time Coby, drunk, stayed over on the couch in the Gousha apartment:

> In the morning Joe came in and said "Who is that in the living room?" I said, in surprise, that I didn't know, having forgotten. Later Coby said he woke up with no idea where he was, then out of one bleary eye saw Joe and wondered what he was doing in his house, then what he was doing in his house in a bathrobe.

To judge from this 1939 diary entry, rumors of some sort of ongoing, easygoing ménage à trois among Dawn, Joe, and Coby would seem to have had little basis in fact.

It is certainly true, however, that Powell remained sexually active, and that activity may well have included Coby; to be sure, he was her closest companion in these years. But her approach toward affairs was fundamentally sportive, and if she was not exactly promiscuous, she was nonetheless uncommonly cavalier for a woman of that era. Once, according to Matthew Josephson, she shared a taxi cab with the English biologist and author J. B. S. Haldane:

> "Mr. Haldane was tight, he became playful," she related with her puckered smile—like Fanny Brice playing Baby Snooks — "and suddenly there I felt his hand going up under my skirt. Well, it was very confusing for me. On the one hand I didn't want our visitor to think that American girls were easy to make; but on the other hand I didn't want him to think I didn't like it!"

Powell's journals from this period are filled with anecdotes of sexual variance, which clearly fascinated her. Many of the friends Powell would make in later life—including Rosalind Wilson, Hannah Green, and Jacqueline Miller Rice—have expressed strong doubts that she had bisexual leanings, but the editor and translator Frances Keene, who spent a good deal of time with her in the 1940s and '50s, believed that Powell's love life included "multiple partners of both sexes." "It was always my impression that she found women more attractive than she did men," Keene said in 1994. "But she surrounded herself with men because she thought they were more interesting to talk to. Forty years ago, there were fewer women of high caliber."

Whatever her own experience may have been, Powell was well acquainted with a number of lesbians, among them Cheryl Crawford, Djuna Barnes, and especially Virginia Pfeiffer, Ernest Hemingway's sister-in-law and the companion of Laura Archera before Archera's marriage to Aldous Huxley. Powell's feelings about Pfeiffer were decidedly mixed—"A worthless woman who should marry and support some worthy gigolo," she called her in one particularly acerbic diary entry—but the two women traveled together regularly in the late 1930s, taking a three-week motor trip down U.S. 1 to Florida in 1939.

"Fairy" was Powell's customary term for a gay man, and she used it with affection: "Fairies as an oasis in midst of country villages; alone you find them—sure of some intelligent conversation and wit. Little cosmopolitan posts on the prairie, a little lamp. Here is conversation, here is imagination for the weary traveler, worn down by Babbittry."

About 1936, she began to sketch out a novel based on the "fairy" circle around John Mosher and Dwight Fiske (with whom she had continued to write monologues). "The bachelors of New York in the Satyricon style," she noted. "Do in swift fierce style of a race descending on the enemy—'The Joyous Isle.'" Although Powell often modeled her characters on real people, she rarely provided such a direct key as may be found in her diary entry for March 2, 1936:

John Mosher, unattractive to women, silent in the home, finds balm in getting the pale silent young man in borrowed evening clothes away from Dwight. He has him in his home where he encourages him to go on with his cooking, gets him Escoffier, Brillat-Savant [sic], Sabatini, Moneta, brings him home little gadgets, egg slicers, canapés, entertains, proud of his pompano in fig leaves, his duck *à la presse*. John talks, educating him culturally; Dopey listens, says salad too wet. . . .

John encourages Dopey to write cook book à la Brillat-Savarin but week after week Dopey gets gloomier. Presently sees manuscript. "Cooking is the art of making something to eat. Everybody likes to eat. People mostly put too much water on in cooking vegetables." John's heart sank. "You ought to get out more."

She worked on "The Joyous Isle"—the title was an English translation of a piano piece by Debussy, *L'isle Joyeuse*—through 1937 and the early part of 1938, finishing up on May 31; it was published that September by Farrar and Rinehart as *The Happy Island*.

It is a busy, daring, provocative, and, in the end, unsatisfying novel. One wishes *The Happy Island* were stronger, for Powell would never again set out so deliberately to create a twentieth-century answer to the Roman satire. Almost all of the characters are either gay or bisexual, and they change partners every few pages or so in what amounts to a latter-day bacchanal, complete with winking references to cocaine and marijuana amid the feasting and heavy drinking.

Such a description makes *The Happy Island* sound brighter and racier than it really is; unfortunately, despite some marvelous moments, it reads like a draft for a great book that was ultimately never written. The whole endeavor is suffused with a curious satiety, as if Powell's amusement at human foibles had turned into annoyance. We recognize some of the flashing wit of *Turn, Magic Wheel*, but here it has taken on an exhausted, earthbound quality, and the author seems to be trying awfully hard to keep the party going.

The novel has one notable quirk: more so than any of her other books, it relies extensively on Powell's diaries for inspiration, with whole sections often being lifted and transferred into the narrative. Almost without exception, these vignettes are more potent and convincing in their quickly jotted original form than in their polished fictional transformations.

Although Powell provides many subplots and minor roles, the story is a simple one. Jefferson Abbott, a passionate and rigorously upright young playwright from Silver City, Ohio, comes to New York (on the *bus*, for once, instead of riding those beloved rails). He looks up his hometown friend Prudence Bly, who, unbeknownst to him, has become a celebrated nightclub singer in the years since she fled Silver City. She was his childhood sweetheart, but disgusted by her new world, he dramatically insults her, then moves downtown to concentrate on his writing.

As it happens, his play is a flop, but he doesn't much care because he believes in the integrity and ultimate value of his art. Such confidence dazzles Prudence, and after a number of affairs (the longest with her addlepated best girlfriend) and a few career setbacks, she decides Abbott is the one she really loves; after he returns home, she moves to Silver City to be with him. Powell, of course, could never countenance such a tidy ending; the idyll lasts all of a few minutes before Prudence comes back alone to the city, to throw herself once more into the festivities on the "happy island" of Manhattan.

Larded throughout are many and disparate secondary characters, among them a washed-up alcoholic pianist and his estranged wife; a radio crooner with a ridiculous, sub–Charlie McCarthy prop dummy; libidinous young marrieds; old roués; Broadway agents; Armenian chefs; autocratic dowagers; thin-skinned gossip columnists who take public revenge after every imagined slight; and a pet dog named Sofa. All of these individuals are, as William Soskin put it in his *New York Herald Tribune* review, "involved in such a series of promiscuities, adulteries, double-crossings, neo-perversions and Krafft-Ebing exercises as would make the towns of Sodom and Gomorrah seem like mere suburbs of li'l old New York."

Soskin enjoyed *The Happy Island;* most of the other critics did not. "I am afraid that *The Happy Island* is greatly inferior to *Turn, Magic Wheel,*" Edith Walton wrote in the *New York Times.*

> It is neither so trenchant nor so funny. While it would be impertinent to suggest that Miss Powell is less familiar with the café crowd than she is with the literati, that is certainly the impression she creates. Her caricatures in this case are overdone, over-farcical, monotonous. . . . There is hardly a character in her book who seems really human. Stinging contempt and a wicked sense of humor have gone into the making of *The Happy Island.* Somehow or other, Miss Powell's material has betrayed her. One is left with a covert suspicion that it was hardly worth her time.

The *New Yorker* published a brief, anonymous review that read, in its entirety: "Night-club life of New York. Plenty of heavy drinking, perfumed love affairs and in general the doings of a pretty worthless and ornery lot of people. Miss Powell serves it up with a dash of wit and for good measure throws in a couple of boys named Bert and Willy, who nearly steal the show from the main characters."

In recent years, *The Happy Island* has won some distinguished admirers, most notably Gore Vidal, who compared its closing lines favorably to Thackeray's work in his essay "Dawn Powell: The American Writer." Certainly the characters no longer seem so "worthless and ornery"; instead, they come across as fragile and unconventional, and so quite naturally rather defensive. Still, for many readers, *The Happy Island* remains heavy going. According to Samuel Johnson, the first duty of a book is to make us want to read it through, and it is more difficult to do that with *The Happy Island* than with most of Powell's other novels; it simply doesn't have "legs." Nor do we return to it with the same joy that the prospect of a fresh encounter with *Turn, Magic Wheel, A Time to Be Born*, or *The Locusts Have No King* may inspire.

The Happy Island sold poorly on its first publication, and it was the last of Powell's mature New York novels to be reissued when interest in her work was revived. Powell herself never regarded it as one of her better books, though she was nothing like so embarrassed by it as she was by *Whither* or the later *A Cage for Lovers*.

Michael Sadleir's enthusiasm for Powell's work ensured *The Happy Island* an English publication. During contract negotiations, however, the editor became anxious that Great Britain's strict libel laws might leave his firm open to a suit brought by one of the book's real-life models. Powell hastened to alleviate his fears:

> There are no portraits in *The Happy Island*. Aside from fear of libel suits, I find no profit or pleasure in straight portraiture. There are frequently snatches of this or that person cautiously pinned to other persons' bodies and love-life, and it is true I have changed one real man into a woman but as he has done this himself so often I cannot see that he should object and have furthermore combined him with two other people. . . .
>
> One young man called on me, very upset, and said he recognized himself in my book and wondered if everyone did, as there were some rather sacred thoughts exposed. As he has been far from my thoughts I was embarrassed, then realized that here was the pallid pansy whose whole career had accidentally fit into the Bert/Willy pattern. I was horrified. But it turned out the figure he recognized as himself was, of course, the splendid hairy-chested young playwright from the West.

But I had a bad twenty minutes of apologizing frantically in the dark.

The Happy Island marked the end of Powell's association with Farrar and Rinehart. The author was discouraged by her sales, which had begun to climb with *Turn, Magic Wheel* and then dropped off again sharply with the new novel, and she decided to publish elsewhere (her editors at Farrar and Rinehart, mystified by her evolving style, were probably not sorry to see her go). As it happened, she landed exactly where most serious American writers of the time wanted to be: at the august firm of Charles Scribner's Sons, with editor Maxwell Everts Perkins.

Max Perkins had spent most of his professional life at Scribner's: fresh from Harvard, he had joined the advertising department in 1910 and become an editor four years later. In 1919, he signed up an unknown young author named F. Scott Fitzgerald; the following year, Fitzgerald's first published novel, *This Side of Paradise*, became an international best-seller and the first literary emblem of the "Jazz Age." Over the next decade, as Perkins published Fitzgerald's subsequent books (including *The Great Gatsby*) and signed and worked with Ernest Hemingway, Thomas Wolfe, and Erskine Caldwell, among many others, Scribner's became the "hot" publishing house, and the editor himself became a legend.

A gentle, fastidious, somewhat old-fashioned man, Perkins divided his time between a town house on East Forty-eighth Street and a country home in Connecticut. His working manner with his writers was tender, intuitive, and supportive. As A. Scott Berg, Perkins's biographer, put it:

> His literary judgment was original and exceedingly astute, and
> he was famous for his ability to inspire an author to produce the
> best that was in him or her. More a friend to his authors than a
> taskmaster, he aided them in every way. He helped them struc-

ture their books, if help was needed; thought up titles, invented plots; he served as psychoanalyst, lovelorn adviser, marriage counselor, career manager, money-lender. Few editors before him had done so much work on manuscripts, yet he was always faithful to his credo, "The book belongs to the author."

Powell, for her part, worshipped him and met with him regularly for long teas and working luncheons. When she adopted a stray cat out at her country place on Long Island, she immediately christened it Perkins ("I named him before I found out her arrogant nature," she assured her new editor). She even went so far as to dedicate *Angels on Toast*, the first of her books for Scribner's, to Max Perkins, a tribute she paid to no other colleague.

Scribner's was a conservative house, and Powell was given an advance that was drastically less than what she had been used to at Farrar and Rinehart—only a thousand dollars apiece for her next three novels, as opposed to the twenty-five hundred she had received for both *Turn, Magic Wheel* and *The Happy Island*. Still, she must have decided that being in understanding and creative hands was worth it. She worked enthusiastically on what would become *Angels on Toast* throughout much of 1939, spending part of that period holed up at the Half-Moon Hotel on Coney Island, a throwback to her days at the Hotel Traymore in Atlantic City.

But Powell never possessed the sort of temperament that would have allowed her to devote herself exclusively to a single project, and so she wrote a few short stories and a new play, *Every Other Day*, on the side; she began another play as well, based on *Dance Night*, but quickly abandoned it. For a few months in late 1939, she took a job scripting and reading "song analyses" for a radio program on New York's WOR, "Music and Manners," starring Ann Honeycutt, an author and broadcaster who was also James Thurber's longtime love. Powell had never liked Thurber much, and her initial, necessarily subservient encounter with Honeycutt irritated her enormously

("There is no fighting mediocrity when it is in authority," she wrote in exasperation when Honeycutt mangled one of her scripts), but the two women would eventually become close friends. No recordings of "Music and Manners" are known to exist—a pity, for it would be interesting to hear what Powell made of "Three Little Fishies," one of the songs she "analyzed."

"Three Little Fishies" had been planned for the broadcast of August 25, 1939, but it was postponed because of a news report about the impending war in Europe. By then, Nazi Germany and the Soviet Union had in fact been practicing regimented terror on a hitherto unimaginable scale for the better part of a decade. From the vantage point of the 1990s, the Spanish civil war seems a somewhat murkier and more complicated affair than was believed to be the case at the time; in the late 1930s, however, it was nothing less than a struggle between good and evil, democracy and fascism, the past and the future—or so it appeared to many bright and idealistic young people, some of whom gave their lives for the cause. Lawson and Hemingway became partisans for the Spanish Loyalists; they were among the many onetime friends who turned on John Dos Passos when he broke ranks and published his doubts about Stalin's influence and intentions in Spain.

Powell stuck by Dos Passos; his apostasy meant nothing to her. Friends were friends, and were not to be judged by their politics. In any event, she herself had become disenchanted with communism early on—her familiarity with John Howard Lawson and his capitulation to the party line had seen to that. However, there is some evidence that she may have been momentarily intrigued by fascism in the months before the war.

One of her old friends, the Spanish-American author Felipe Alfau (whose all-but-forgotten fantastical novel *Locos* [1936] would be republished to critical acclaim in 1988), was a passionate Francoite—for which stance, Powell noted, he had been as thoroughly ostracized as any conscientious objector in World War I. Powell thought Alfau a likable, unconventional, and highly intelligent man; to the horror of some of her acquaintances, she had kept up her friendship with him throughout the polarized 1930s. After one lunch, on February 18, 1939, she wrote that Alfau "talked so brilliantly of Totalitarianism that is based on human weaknesses, human error, human conduct, that it almost convinced me":

> Certainly its admission of individual woe and personal problems is wonderfully relaxing after the Communists' rigid belief in paper theories and a love of masses that excuses them from making personal loans or any emotional duty to a wife or friend; their uncompromising belief in theory excuses their startlingly variant lives, their greed, egotism, callousness and personal betrayal.

At some point thereafter, somebody—almost certainly Powell herself—ripped out the four diary pages that immediately followed this entry. It is the only such drastic emendment in any of the volumes. What could she have written that might later come to bother her so? We can only speculate; it might have been anything, perhaps something to do with Lawson, perhaps something completely apolitical.

My own guess is that Powell, who sounds as if she were just warming up in the passage quoted, may have taken her line of thinking a bit further, perhaps even so far as to shock and shame her on a rereading after the full horrors of fascism had been made known. Although she was undoubtedly capable of being swayed, however briefly, by extreme political thinking (recall her attempt to plot *The Story of a Country Boy* along Trotskyite lines), she was generally a consistent if skeptical centrist throughout her life.

Ultimately, the content of the destroyed diary entry, while tantalizing, is of little importance. Whatever Powell may or may not have written privately on February 18, 1939, she was solidly in the

Allied camp by the time World War II began in earnest, and she had much less to apologize for in her political history during the 1930s than did many of her contemporaries.

Now almost twenty years into their marriage, Dawn and Joe continued to live basically separate lives within the same apartment, while Jojo stayed at the Gladwyne Colony, a remedial school for disturbed people outside Valley Forge, Pennsylvania. In the summers, however, the family would regroup and gather at the cottage on Long Island, where Dawn would read a chapter of *David Copperfield* to Jojo every day. He eventually memorized the entire book but never stopped asking his mother to start over again; outside of favorite passages from the Bible, he rarely wanted to hear anything else.

Dawn's sisters came east most summers, and Dorothy Chapman, Mabel's daughter, has vivid memories of Jojo's behavior at such reunions. "He was very strange, very distant," she recalled in 1997.

> I remember he would suddenly disappear into the water by the cottage and sink to a level where you couldn't see him at all. He'd stay under until you started to get scared and then suddenly he'd explode from the water, his eyes all bugged out, and shout something incomprehensible like "God *damn* these Chinese!" He had an incredible fascination with maps—maybe he knew that the Chinese were on the other side of Earth from us and wanted to impress me by pretending he'd just been there.

In early 1940, after an unusually severe tantrum, Jojo was hospitalized again. "Obsessed this time with Ann [De Silver] and very close to serious breakdown," Powell wrote in her diary. She visited him in Brooklyn Hospital in February and took him on a walk through Fort Greene Park, where she was once again struck by his innate intelligence:

Say what you will—there is something superior in a child who
stops breathless, glowing-eyed, before street intersections, fig-
uring out where they come from correctly, wondering where
they must lead, wide-eyed with the thrill of it. . . . He was better than I ever knew him—in the thrill to his mind his walk
changed from institutional shuffle to perfectly normal.

Slowly, surely, amid strife and distraction, *Angels on Toast* took
shape. It was finished by June 1940 and slated to come out in September.

Just before the publication of one of her merriest satires, Dawn
Powell wrote a despondent and affecting self-portrait of the artist in
middle age, a passage that should be required reading for any brash
young critic out to skewer the older generation:

Fear is a primary factor in life—either one begins courageously
with no fear and slowly learns to cringe, or one begins fear-
fully, so afraid that bravado is necessary for everyday routine, a
shell [that] eventually serves as well as genuine courage for
meeting the monsters of life. But, unless the shell is constantly
rebuilt, it melts like some Dupont imitation glass and then one
is too old for new bravados. One can only quiver and hide and
scamper finally to a grave where They cannot find you.

I never realize how lost my defenses are until the crisis
comes and now I only want to run and hide. A new book coming out no longer rouses any hope. As the day approaches, I
look at the book section and think with a sudden horror that
this is the last Sunday I will be able to look at a book review
without sick misgiving—no review, bad review, or the patron-
izing review of another illiterate lady reviewer. There is a
dreadful week now of the usual worst fears ahead, and after
that the nervous, weary effort to pick up and begin again after
another disappointment.

Scribner's released *Angels on Toast* on October 7, 1940. It sold very poorly—only 2,267 copies through 1951—but was much admired within some influential circles. As Gore Vidal would put it, "*Angels on Toast* was the first of Powell's novels to become, if not world famous, *the* book for those who wanted to inhabit the higher, wittier realms of Manhattan where Truman Capote was, later and less wittily, to camp out."

The novel shares many qualities with *The Happy Island*. It has very little plot, the characters are unusually hard, and the tone is rather clipped and cold. We know that the author wrote both of these books quickly, working through much of the night with the aid of prescription diet pills such as Maxitrol and Benzedrine; it does not seem unreasonable to suggest, then, that such speedy, emotionally insulating medication may have affected the writing.

But *Angels on Toast* is a much better book than *The Happy Island*—tighter, faster, funnier, more linear, and altogether more engaging. One more time, Powell captures some of the rushing breathlessness that makes *Turn, Magic Wheel* so appealing.

Like many of her other books, *Angels on Toast* begins in full swing, as Lou Donovan and Jay Oliver, traveling businessmen, charge eastward toward New York on a high-powered locomotive. "I wanted to convey the sense of speed, changing geography with no change in the conversation, the sense of pressure behind the ever-evanescent big deal, and behind these adventurers," Powell wrote to Perkins shortly before the novel's publication. "These are normal people saying one thing and doing another, warning a neighbor of danger while stepping into it themselves."

Neither Lou nor Jay is a particularly distinctive character—indeed, the two are so interchangeable that the dust jacket for the first edition accidentally refers to them as "Jay Donovan" and "Lou Oliver"—but we nonetheless willingly follow both of them for 273 pages as they wheel and deal, juggle wives and girlfriends, drink too much, double-cross one another, and end up pretty much where they began. Their tone is slangy, self-assured, materialistic, and impatient throughout; it is impossible to imagine either one of them except in motion.

For once, in a Powell novel, the women characters are more winning and attractive than the men. Ebie, a smart, charming commercial artist, is among the brightest and most self-aware of Powell's heroines. Her mother, a bizarre and bibulous eccentric who dabbles in real estate and poetry, is no less vividly drawn. Best of all, though, is Mary Donovan, patrician and high-minded but deeply and achingly in love with a vulgar man. Mary has some of the resigned, abiding sorrow of the Countess Almaviva in *The Marriage of Figaro*, and her desperate self-transformation into a raucous party animal toward the end of the novel makes for bittersweet laughter as she sinks, however comically, into the same mire as the other characters. Sooner or later, Powell seems to be suggesting, this happens to us all.

The association with Scribner's and Perkins helped ensure a prominent reception for *Angels on Toast*, which was reviewed extensively—twice in the *New York Times*, at length in the *Herald Tribune*, and in many other publications. Not everybody liked the book; still, it could not be ignored. Charles Poore of the *Times* called it

> a blistering and hilarious story of latter-day Babbitts on wheels, a warm-hearted and yet singularly penetrating piece about raucous, expansive men of affairs who shuttle constantly between New York, Chicago and points south or west, who are constantly in hot water with their wives, mistresses and competitors, who, in short, inhabit a wit-and-glitter world where, as *Time* magazine said of a recent musical comedy, morals are so loose as to be practically detached.

Also writing in the *Times*, Robert Van Gelder, while acknowledging Powell's "exceptionally keen ear for dialogue," found the novel "formless and inconclusive," if "amusing."

OVERLEAF: *My home is far away*: Hattie Sherman Powell with her daughters, Mabel, Phyllis, and Dawn, in Cardington, Ohio, about 1901. *(Collection Tim Page)*

Roy King Powell as a young man.

(Collection Tim Page)

The only known photographic portrait of Hattie Sherman Powell, Dawn Powell's mother.

(Collection Tim Page)

Dawn Powell as a baby. *(Collection Tim Page)*

Mabel, Phyllis, and Dawn Powell around the time of their mother's death in 1903. *(Collection Tim Page)*

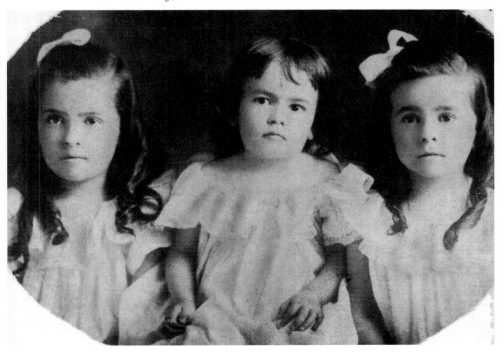

Roy Powell in later life. *(Collection Tim Page)*

Dawn's stepmother, Sabra Stearns Powell.
(Collection Tim Page)

Orpha May Sherman Steinbrueck, who raised Dawn from adolescence, here shown in front of the Shelby Junction railroad station with her young nephew John F. (Jack) Sherman, who also grew up in the Steinbrueck home. *(Collection Tim Page)*

Dawn Powell (*seated at right*) and the editorial staff of the Shelby High School *Tatler*—"before and after" photographs.

(Collection Tim Page)

Powell as Puck in an outdoor production of *A Midsummer's Night Dream* at Lake Erie College, 1917.

(Collection Lake Erie College)

Joseph Roebuck Gousha as a young man. *(Collection Tim Page)*

Joseph Roebuck Gousha, Jr. ("Jojo"), shortly after his birth in 1921. *(Collection Tim Page)*

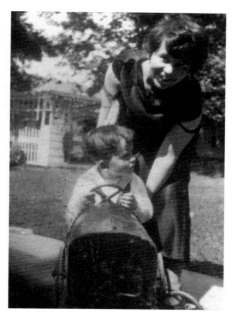

Dawn and Jojo during their visit to Ohio in 1925. *(Collection Tim Page)*

Jojo as a young boy, at the Long Island beach cottage. *(Collection Tim Page)*

Louise Lee ("Deesie"), Jojo's nurse, outside the beach cottage. *(Collection Tim Page)*

Powell's first promotional portrait, probably issued with *Whither* in 1925.

(Collection Tim Page)

John Howard Lawson in the mid-1940s. *(Collection Jeffrey Lawson)*

Mary Ross, in the *Herald Tribune*, thought *Angels on Toast* an "intriguing book, compounded of wit and hardness and satire." She expounded:

> With the exception of Mary Donovan, all the characters are on the make, and if they are not sweet and beautiful, they are devastatingly real and human. Miss Powell pulls no punches, plays no favorites. When the little comedy she develops with acid acumen is finished, as far as the book is concerned, there are neither victors nor spoils. They're all ready to start over again with the same problems, the same shabbiness of spirit, the same greed.

Like many artists, Powell was never as reassured by positive critiques as she was vexed by negative ones. "There are, I have now learned, rigorous rules for wit," she wrote in her diary on October 8:

> If there is to be satire it must not bite at the bread-winner—but at those who interfere with his getting ahead. The rules for satire as laid down by reviewers are purely materialistic. Let no mockery interfere with the budget! Flay with "good-natured fun" the antics of the poor or the rich, but never say the pleasures of the middle class are a little ridiculous, too. The middle class comes in large families, and if you must record them, say they are earnest; say they eat simple apple pies and honest roast turkeys; say they till the soil, quibble over wills, snub new neighbors, juggle their accounts, cheat their partners (through family necessity), disown sons for unsavory marriages—but show that these vices are necessary, and are accompanied by worry, harassment and groans, never by laughter. Say that these sins (if sins they be, since they are at least *solemn* sins) are done with dignity, unlike the sins of the rich or the very poor.

In breaking these rules, *Angels on Toast* apparently had some unpleasant repercussions for Joe Gousha's brother Harry—his wife accused him of being Powell's model for Jay and Lou! In fact, the type is a common and distinctly American one. Intense, boorish business executives, with nothing more on their minds than the next city, the next love affair, and, above all, the next dollar, the descendants of Donovan and Oliver may still be found in any busy U.S. airport, dressed in spiffy suits and racing for their planes, all the while barking frantically into cellular phones.

CHAPTER SEVEN

Wars—at Home and Abroad

᷄᷄

This was no time to cry over one broken heart.

DAWN POWELL, 1942

THE FRENCH AUTHOR ROMAIN ROLLAND once described his working philosophy as "pessimism of the intelligence, optimism of the will." Whether or not Powell codified it so elegantly, she adopted a similar approach herself. No matter how she might despair over her family tribulations, her professional setbacks, the precarious state of her health and finances, something in her psychology always impelled her to go on working.

The disappointing sales of *Angels on Toast* naturally made her gloomy. "Depressing year but not as depressing as the thought of a new one, and the weariness of perpetually beginning at the bottom," she summed up on the last day of 1940:

From the appalling lack of momentum in my progress I gather I must have originally started several ladders below bottom and have not yet struck bottom rung. There is an effort, certainly, for those who must keep their ball rolling uphill, but that is nothing compared to the ever-increasing work for us whose efforts keep nothing going up, merely keep the ball from crushing us in its downward roll. Every book, every play, every story, seems to have less chance than ever, and the factor of luck seems to have nothing to do with me—merely work to no avail.

And yet hardly a month had elapsed after the publication of *Angels on Toast* before she began making notes for what would develop into another of her finest, funniest satires, *A Time to Be Born*. Then, less than three months later, she had a vivid dream about her childhood that led directly to the first sketches for one of her finest literary accomplishments, *My Home Is Far Away*, the final book in her Ohio cycle and the closest thing she wrote to pure autobiography. By the age of forty-five, she had published nine novels, none of which had been particularly successful; undaunted, she would go on to create six more. However sorely she may have been tempted to abandon her writing, she kept going; diary entries to the contrary, Powell never quite allowed herself to hit bottom.

It was the same way in her domestic life. If her relationship with Joe was not what she had imagined it would be at twenty-three (and the two were never more distant from one another than in the early 1940s), the pragmatist within her pressed Powell to seek her necessary personal satisfaction elsewhere, in parties, friendships, and occasional affairs, even as she remained unshakably committed to the continuation of her marriage.

After the Goushas moved once again, this time into an elegant and spacious duplex at 35 East Ninth Street (complete with a mezzanine overlooking the living room, where the couple would occasionally send up *Romeo and Juliet* for amused guests), Powell was only a few steps from the Hotel Lafayette—so close, she told Malcolm Cowley, that she could look out the window and watch her own checks bouncing there.

The Lafayette had long been among Powell's favorite restaurants, and it would now become her court. Located at Ninth Street and University Place, it was just around the corner from the Hotel Brevoort, which was owned by the same family. There the two establishments had stood for almost a hundred years, so ancient as to be believed permanent. (In the early 1950s, both would be summarily demolished to make way for a gigantic new apartment building; this charmless usurper would in turn be christened the Brevoort, an appropriation that would revolt old Villagers.)

Matthew Josephson has left us a vivid picture of the Hotel Lafayette, a "low, rambling, Federal-period structure only three stories high":

> It was a place where after a sumptuous meal in the adjoining restaurant a man could come to the café and game room, read his newspaper, and consume his cigar at leisure over French coffee and cognac. The café was a wide, high-ceilinged room with tall windows giving on the street: it had mirrored walls, green shaded lamps, and marble-topped tables, some of them reserved for players at dominos and chess; in a corner there used to be a rack filled with French magazines and newspapers. In short it looked exactly like a café in a provincial city of France.
>
> The Lafayette was rather ill served by aged and surly waiters who were not French but usually Swiss or Belgian. While one could order a variety of French aperitifs, the drinks were not only dear but mediocre. Yet a distinguished clientele persisted in coming here, many of them because of Dawn Powell.

The Lafayette was indeed more expensive than most of the neighborhood's other bars and restaurants; it had a sort of antique elegance far removed from the studied informality of *echt* Village Bohemia. Powell preferred a corner seat where she could keep an eye on the comings and goings within the café. Her cronies included not only Coby and her literary friends but a number of visual artists as well, among them Reginald Marsh, Peter Blume, Niles Spencer, and Peggy Bacon, the last of whom sketched several portraits of Powell.

There were three entrances to the Café Lafayette, and when Powell spotted somebody she liked walking through one of the doors, she would call that person over to her table, "just as if she were the hostess," as Josephson relayed it. By all reports, she was an animated, hilarious, and uninhibited raconteur—even funnier in person than in her books. "Her words were calculated to amuse or shock, at all events to make an impact on her hearers," Josephson said. He believed she tried out her best anecdotes and witticisms on her friends before incorporating them into her work: "She improvised her stories, listened to the tales and the gossip of the others, and out of the talk and gossip, the intrigues of every day, the couplings and uncouplings, she shaped her novels."

Despite her innate conviviality, Powell was not fond of going to other people's homes for dinner—"You have to eat or drink what they have and if the company is dull you are trapped for the evening," she said—though she made a few exceptions. One of these was for the American actress and torch singer Libby Holman, who occasionally invited her to join the group of weekend visitors she entertained at her home in Stamford, Connecticut. And then there were Gerald and Sara Murphy.

This fabled couple—wealthy, attractive, and gracious, the dedicatees of F. Scott Fitzgerald's *Tender Is the Night*—presided over a social circle that ranged from southern France to the Hudson Valley and the Hamptons and included Ernest Hemingway, John Dos Passos, Dorothy Parker, Archibald MacLeish, and many other gifted people. Gerald Murphy was himself an artist of distinction.

Powell had met the Murphys during the 1930s, but it wasn't until 1940 that she became a regular visitor in their homes in East Hampton and Snedens Landing, New York. Although she sometimes made withering comments about them in her diary—the impoverished girl from across-the-tracks Ohio maintained an intrinsic mistrust of people born rich and privileged—the Murphys would prove to be generous and supportive friends to her for the rest of her life. She completed one book (*My Home Is Far Away*) and was inspired to write another (*The Wicked Pavilion*) while a weekend guest at one of the Murphys' homes.

In June 1941, Powell embarked on her last serious attempt to win favor on the Broadway stage. She was approached by a producer named George Hale and asked to help rewrite a musical comedy entitled *The Lady Comes Across*, slated for a December opening at the Forty-fourth Street Theatre.

"[Playwright] Fred Thompson wrote the original idea a few hundred times by himself first, then I joined in and we wrote it a few more dozen times," she later told the *Boston Post*. From the beginning, she found the form difficult and disliked having to squeeze in a few lines of compressed dialogue as filler between the all-important musical numbers:

> Nowhere in the field of writing is the printed word regarded with such alarm as in the musical comedy field. A few type-written pages are bound to creep into the theatre from time to time but the unhappy authors who bear these printed words, either immortalized in typescript or spelled out on bits of confetti, are heading to certain unpopularity.

The plot was a dubious one, a spy story of sorts culminating in an FBI raid on a Manhattan boutique where a foreign agent is caught hiding purloined papers in a black and silver girdle. Despite this unpromising concept, an extraordinary number of talented people were signed on to *The Lady Comes Across*. Vernon Duke wrote the music, John Latouche provided the lyrics, and the choreography was by George Balanchine. Romney Brent was the director, and frequent Marx Brothers collaborator Morrie Ryskind the production supervisor; the original cast included Jessie Matthews, Mischa Auer, and Joe E. Lewis, with the young Gower Champion in a supporting role.

It was an absolute and unqualified disaster, one of the most spectacular flops in the history of the American theater. After the first preview, Ryskind all but rewrote the second act, to the immense irritation of both Thompson and Powell. Matthews left the cast after tryouts in New Haven and Boston; Ray Bolger had agreed to take on a leading role when the show came to Broadway, but he was so dissatisfied with the play that he changed his mind and pulled out. The New York premiere, scheduled for December 30 (with a gala performance on New Year's Eve), was delayed for more recasting and rewriting. *The Lady Comes Across* finally opened at the Forty-fourth Street Theatre on January 9, 1942. The reviews were brutal; the play closed the following night, at a cost to the producers of two hundred thousand dollars.

Thompson and Powell took the brunt of the criticism. *Variety* called their work "deplorably childish and confusing"; John Mason Brown, in the *New York World-Telegram*, said it was but "one step ahead of the average Hasty Pudding, Mask and Wig and Princeton Triangle libretto." Brooks Atkinson, writing in the *Times*, thought the book "highly superfluous," while the *New York Post* partially excused leading lady Evelyn Wyckoff's uninspired performance with a caveat: "Considering what she has to work with, we doubt very much if a combination of Katharine Cornell, Ethel Merman, Vera Zorina and an incendiary bomb could have made much effect on it."

The whole experience was exceedingly unpleasant, and Powell left the show with a detestation for both Hale and Ryskind; as far as she was concerned, the only good thing that came out of it was a new friendship with John Latouche. The multitalented Latouche was only twenty-three when he started work on *The Lady Comes Across*, but he had been a professional lyricist since his undergraduate years at Columbia. Over the course of his short career—he would drop dead of a heart attack at the age of thirty-eight—he would collaborate with Duke Ellington (*Beggar's Holiday*), Jerome Moross (*The Golden Apple*), Leonard Bernstein (*Candide*), and Douglas Moore (*The Ballad of Baby Doe*), in addition to a more celebrated endeavor with Vernon Duke, *Cabin in the Sky*. He would also write the lyrics for the populist anthem "Ballad for Americans," set to music by Earl Robinson and memorably sung by Paul Robeson.

Latouche quickly became one of Powell's closest companions. They shared many qualities: wit, facility, an openhearted warmth, a fondness for the high life, a penchant for working hard and partying harder. However, Latouche was an immediate and prodigious success, which only redoubled his professional demand and activity as he took on more projects than were good for him. Powell thought he worked himself to death. "Talented but shrewd users pursued him always," she would reflect after he died, in 1956. "Contracts, advances, deals, love offers were all around—trying to get him in a corner room, lock him up and get out the gold when he wanted only to talk all day and all night." Latouche was, she said, a "natural gusher that grim syndicates tried to harness for the stock exchange. Ending up now an incorrigibly sweet, indestructible little ghost."

However diluted and unrewarding it may have been, *The Lady Comes Across* was the last work in which Powell was involved that made it to the stage. Still, she kept trying. Later on in 1942, she temporarily took on the revision of a show for nightclub singer and producer Peggy Fears. The following year, she attempted another musical, this one a collaboration with producer Irvin Graham based on Shakespeare's *Taming of the Shrew*. Although their version was never presented, Powell and Graham were unquestionably on to something: a few years later, *Kiss Me, Kate*, Cole Porter's adaptation of the same play, would become one of the decade's greatest hits.

Then, in 1944, legendary producer and director George Abbott asked Powell to rewrite her 1939 play, *Every Other Day*, as a vehicle for actress Leonora Corbett. Greatly impressed by Abbott's courtesy and professionalism, the author worked on this project for some time, but it ultimately went nowhere; the next year, Abbott endeavored to interest ZaSu Pitts in the same play, with the same unsatisfying results.

Thereafter, Powell's engagement in the theater waned, with the exception of her work on an incomplete play that occupied her for more than thirty years. She had started it by 1934, when she referred to it by the working title *The Brooklyn Widow* in her notes:

> The Brooklyn Widow (Mrs. Flack)—very happily married before with average moron intelligence—to Mr. F., an Elk, O.F., K.P., K.K.K., ad salesman, proud of his home, its electric devices, etc. His death leaves her not grieved but the envy of the neighborhood because of insurance, etc. She, bored after a while with mere envy, wants to do something gay with money, feels herself in class with Astors. Meets foreign orchestra violinist in N.Y.—invites him over—he comes, drunk, to scoff at respectability (she, too, is ashamed of it) [and] ends by being earnest upholder of her dead husband's standards while she has no further chance at glamour. All the super solid things he had once asked, Juan now asks and she does.

Something about this vignette appealed to Powell, and she would go back to it again and again, though it never seems to have progressed much beyond a formative state. By 1948, the play was called *The American Widow*, but it retained the same basic plot: "Widow ends slowly chilled; he [i.e., her lover] has turned into [her husband] Harry." In a note to herself, "This is very good," she wrote determinedly. "Should be mapped out and should be done." By 1953, she was contemplating a drastic simplification, for a modern audience, of what was once again called *The Brooklyn Widow*; in 1964, the last full year of her life, she began to transform it into a short story. None of these variations on her original theme was ever completed; only a single fleshed-out scene, an undated fragment from what was then entitled *West Side Widow*, has yet been found among her papers.

By the early 1940s, Powell was overextended and frustrated. Over the previous few years, she had been featured regularly on a weekly radio program and had worked for several months on a doomed musical comedy. In 1941, she agreed to become the book critic for *Mademoiselle*, a position she kept for almost a year, though she hated her "kindergarten" job from the start (she had barely a paragraph in which to sum up her impressions of each book).

The worst of it was that she felt alienated from what she termed her "lawful wedded mate"—the novel. A touching diary entry from January 1942 shows both how badly she needed reassurance and how grateful she was for the simplest praise. Within the space of a few days, she had received two passing compliments from acquaintances and a fan letter from a stranger in Mexico. Apparently that was all she required: "If these things [had] happened at a time I needed them for encouragement, a lot of my time would have been saved. I would not have felt my novels were private luxuries and failures so I had to desperately search for other mediums and flounder around."

Yet she also regretted her proud refusal of the "big money" in the movie industry, noting in her diary, "Curious conviction that my fate was offered me in 1936—three years in Hollywood—$1250, $1500, $1750—and on rejecting it I must pay forever for not being commercially opportunistic."

This was, in fact, one of Powell's rare suicidal periods. Her mysterious internal ailment had begun to torment her again—"Heart hurt for the first time in years," she wrote on February 25. Jojo, who had been living at home for a while without incident, fled coatless one day into a Manhattan blizzard, leaving her frantic with worry; it took hours to find him, and the next day he was readmitted into a sanatorium. Joe, for his part, was drinking more heavily than ever and grew soggier and less coherent as the evenings wore on; "Fire in beautiful new sofa due to Joe's falling asleep with cigarette," Powell recorded mournfully. Moreover, America had entered World War II on December 7, 1941, and the situation, particularly in Europe, looked bleak.

How extraordinary, then, that the author should have been able to finish a novel so airborne and exhilarating as *A Time to Be Born*, one of her great books, amid such despair. Although this is, along with *The Story of a Country Boy*, the longest of Powell's works, it flies by almost as breezily as *Turn, Magic Wheel*. It is enormously playful, yet it is also built against a more somber background than her preceding satires, and shot through with a fundamental seriousness. Where *Angels on Toast* contains some prefigurations of World War II—and the later *The Locusts Have No King* would be plotted very specifically as a postwar novel—here the author gives us the war itself, viewed nervously from across the ocean (the book was completed less than six months after Pearl Harbor). The brilliant opening paragraphs set the scene:

> This was no time to cry over one broken heart. It was no time to worry about Vicky Haven or indeed any other young lady crossed in love, for now the universe, nothing less, was your problem. You woke in the morning with the weight of doom on your head. You lay with eyes shut wondering why you dreaded the day; was it a debt, was it a lost love?—and then you remembered the nightmare. It was a dream, you said, nothing but a dream, and the covers were thrown aside, the dream was over, now for the day. Then, fully awake, you remembered that it was no dream. Paris was gone, London was under fire, the

Atlantic was now a drop of water between the flame on one side and the waiting dynamite on the other. . . .

This was a time when the artists, the intellectuals, sat in cafés and in country homes and accused each other over their brandies or their California vintages of traitorous tendencies. This was a time for them to band together in mutual antagonism, a time to bury the professional hatchet, if possible in each other, a time to stare at their Flower Arrangements, Children Bathing, and privately to weep, "What good is it? Who cares now?" The poet, disgusted with the flight of skylarks in perfect sonnet form, declaimed the power of song against brutality and raised hollow voice in feeble proof. This was no time for beauty, for love, or private future; this was the time for ideals and quick profits on them before the world returned to reality and the drabber opportunities. What good for new sopranos to sing "Vici [*sic*] d'arte, vici d'amore," what good for eager young students to make their bows? There was no future; every one waited, marked time, waited. For what? On Fifth Avenue and Fifty-fifth Street hundreds waited for a man on a hotel window ledge to jump; hundreds waited with craning necks and thirsty faces as if this single person's final gesture would solve the riddle of the world. Civilization stood on a ledge, and in the tension of waiting it was a relief to have one little man jump.

It is the most immediately arresting opening in any of her novels. And though the tone grows more intimate, the pace scarcely abates over the next three hundred pages.

Despite the author's own repeated disclaimers, there need no longer be any doubt that Powell modeled the character of Amanda Keeler Evans in *A Time to Be Born* on the early life of Clare Boothe Brokaw, the beautiful, ambitious American playwright and journalist who married Henry R. Luce, a cofounder of *Time* magazine.

It is easy enough to understand why Powell did not want to

leave herself open to a lawsuit by publicly identifying the wealthy and powerful Clare Luce as the inspiration for the fraudulent, pretentious, publicity-hungry, and ghost-written Amanda. However, even privately, Powell seems to have vacillated about the origins of one of her most memorable characters. "I have been denying for years any basis in *A Time to Be Born* that [Amanda] is Clare Luce," she wrote in a 1956 entry in her diary, where, one presumes, she could and would be honest with herself:

> I swear it is based on five or six girls, some known personally and some by talk, and often I changed the facts to avoid libel with resulting character a real person evidently and libelously Luce-ian. I insist it was a composite (or compost) but then I find a memo from 1939—"Why not do novel on Clare Luce?" Who can I believe—me or myself?

Nevertheless, as early as 1943, after the newly inducted Congresswoman Luce attacked Vice President Henry Wallace for what she called his "globaloney" internationalist views, Powell made another diary entry that suggests she had known exactly what she was doing all along: "After Clare Luce made such evil use of her new Congressional power I was glad I had slashed her in my last book and realized that my immediate weapons are most necessary and can help. The lashing of such evil can only be done by satire and I am the only person who is doing contemporary social satire."

Moreover, there is teasing internal evidence throughout the book that Powell was well aware of the parallels between the fictional Amanda and Julian Evans and the real-life Clare and Henry Luce. One example: "But time—time—time!" Julian explodes at his wife when she tells him she has to meet someone at the train station (*Time* magazine was, of course, the source of Luce's fortune).

Ernest Hemingway reappears in this novel in his guise as Andrew Callingham, covering the war for Julian's newspaper and eventually becoming Amanda's coveted new conquest. Powell knew Hemingway well by now (through her association with the Murphys and with Virginia Pfeiffer, and from visits to Canby Chambers and Esther Andrews in Key West), and the two were quite friendly. Callingham is vividly rendered, and the resultant portrait is much more obviously patterned on the real Hemingway than was the same character's short but much-heralded walk-on role in *Turn, Magic Wheel*.

Yesterday's literary gossip cannot by itself sustain a novel. What continues to hold our attention in *A Time to Be Born* is the drive and hilarity of the narrative (reminiscent of the best 1930s "screwball" comedies), blended with engaging and recognizable characters—including the return of novelist Dennis Orphen—all set against the anxious, almost palpable representation of New York City at the beginning of the war.

Amanda Keeler has migrated from Lakeville, Ohio, to Manhattan, where she has since seduced a leading newspaper baron away from what was, by all indications, a happy marriage. "At thirty, Amanda had all the wit, fame and beauty that money and publicity could buy," Powell wrote in a synopsis that she provided to Scribner's in 1941. "Even the coming of the New War could not detain her, for she adjusted her ambition to the times and rode the world's debacle as if it were her own private yacht."

Vicky Haven, a lovelorn classmate of Amanda's from Ohio, shows up uninvited on the doorstep of the Evans mansion. Amanda arranges a job for her on one of her husband's magazines and then adopts her as a sort of protégée, but Vicky promptly falls in love with the taken-for-granted boyfriend her "mentor" keeps on the side. As Powell summarized it:

> Amanda, in the midst of flying inspections of London war-raids, sponsoring titled refugees, adopting orphans, making clarion calls to arms, and wangling literary favors, is so wounded by this personal blow as to endanger recklessly all that she has

hitherto built. As soon as she permits herself human weaknesses, her public structure is weakened, and the latter part of
the book deals with her frantic efforts to indulge private emotions without surrendering her public position.

Powell finished the book on May 18, and publication was scheduled for late summer. But the author was already beginning to sour
on Scribner's—and on her editor. On July 6, she dashed off an
unusually cross letter to Perkins that merits quotation in its entirety:

Dear Max,

I hope the jacket for my book is a plain lettered one without
figures, and I should like to check the copy on it, since the last
jacket had characters mixed up in the blurb.

I do not like at all the approach called to my attention
recently in *Publishers Weekly* which refers to the book as "slightly
wacky" and uses other deprecatory phrases that would come
better from an angry reviewer than from the publisher. There is
nothing wacky in the book, nor is there anything to be gained
by suggesting it is a jolly little book for the hammock. It is
serious satire in the way Dickens or Thackeray built satire—the
surface may be entertaining but the content is important
comment on contemporary affairs. There are very few American writers today who are writing satire on the present age—
or on any age for that matter—and if I did not think such
work was important I would not engage in it. I am sure there
must be readers for a novel whose mood follows the tempo of
the news they are reading, even though, like the news, it does
not always take the point of view they would prefer. That is why
I think the book's contemporary scene value should be
stressed, and if it is "slightly mad," it is merely reflecting the
times.

Powell signed the letter with a cool "Best wishes." Despite the commercial failure of *Angels on Toast*, her Scribner's debut, she knew her own worth and was willing to speak bluntly when she felt slighted.

Scribner's gave Powell her plain, lettered cover and released the new novel on August 3. It sold very well from the beginning— almost nine thousand copies over four printings—and the press reception was far more appreciative than that for any of her previous works. "The difficulty with reviewing Dawn Powell's new novel, *A Time to Be Born*, is that, first of all, you want to quote from it continually," Rose Feld wrote in the *New York Herald Tribune:*

> To say it's brilliant, it's witty, it's penetrating, it's mature isn't enough. You want to prove it by giving examples but then, having chosen your quotes, you find they do not add up to all the book holds and means. Because there is something more in this volume than the exercise of a mind that is as daring as it is keen; there is emotional flavor and pungency which make it greater than an intellectual tour de force.

Beatrice Sherman, writing in the *New York Times*, was hardly less positive: "Dawn Powell's new book maintains and probably tops her record for writing very enjoyable books about very disagreeable people. Her wit is sharp, shrewd and biting, and it finds a pretty mark in the stuffed shirts, male and female, of *A Time to Be Born*."

Diana Trilling, who was briefly and brightly the book critic for the *Nation* in the early 1940s, was ultimately disappointed with the novel's outcome—she found it too *romantic*, a quality rarely associated with Powell's sensibility. But Trilling made it clear that she admired the author's gifts enormously, calling her "one of the wittiest women around . . . the answer to the old question 'Who really makes the jokes that Dorothy Parker gets the credit for?'"

Astonishingly, even Henry Luce's *Time* magazine weighed in with a favorable review (is it possible that the editors didn't get the joke?).

This was probably the moment of Powell's greatest celebrity, and she relished it—even "this usual but new business of people *I* know but am sure don't recognize me waving to someone behind me and bowing and finally coming over and saying, 'Well, well, *Dawn*'!" Nonetheless, she was still "amazed at the brazenness of people—completely New York people—who only remember you when you've gone into your fourth printing," she observed pointedly.

Nineteen forty-three started with a shocking tragedy: the anarchist journalist and editor Carlo Tresca, Margaret De Silver's lover for more than a decade, was assassinated as he left his office on lower Fifth Avenue on the night of January 11. There remains some question as to who was behind the murder—Tresca had "all the right enemies," as Dorothy Gallagher would put it in the title of her biography—but the actual hit seems to have been carried out by the young mafioso Carmine Galante, who would himself be similarly dispatched thirty-six years later. Powell and De Silver had long been close friends, but their affection for one another now deepened.

Throughout that year, Powell's medical problems intensified. In February 1944, an X ray revealed that the growth in her chest, now described as a "dermoid tumor," was half the size of one of her lungs. It was placing an enormous amount of pressure on her rib cage; shortly thereafter, her ribs would start cracking, one by one. Ever since her "heart attack" in 1929, Powell had lived with this ticking bomb in her body. She was now almost fifty years old. It was a time for reflection, a time to feel mortal. And so the writer turned her gaze homeward—toward Ohio and toward her past.

In the early morning of January 27, 1941, Powell had awakened from an unusually vivid dream and made the following entry in her diary: "Unfortunately my fever brought back so many childhood memories with such brilliant clarity that it seems almost imperative to write a novel about that—the three sisters, the stepmother, Papa. . . . Wrote a start from 3 to 5 A.M. with temperature."

In an undated section of the same volume, there are perhaps a thousand hastily scrawled words that likely represent this feverish, aurorean "start"—an outpouring of reminiscences of small-town Ohio at the turn of the twentieth century, of surreys and steam engines, of general stores with chocolate mints and jelly beans behind their counters, of a loving aunt who stood up to familial tyranny, of a loathed stepmother with her silver-handled whip. Over the next three years, Powell would take this material and mold it into a unique mixture of novel and testament that would be published as *My Home Is Far Away*.

Most of Powell's work is in some way autobiographical, but in *My Home Is Far Away*, fact and fiction blur. Lena, Marcia, and Florrie Willard are clearly Mabel, Dawn, and Phyllis Powell; in preliminary drafts, Powell even used Phyllis's lifelong nickname, "Fuffy," for the character based on her younger sister. Harry Willard, the footloose traveling salesman, is Roy Powell, and the girls' mother, Daisy, is modeled after Hattie Sherman Powell. Idah Hawkins embodies a devastating but fundamentally accurate portrait of Sabra Stearns Powell, while the character of Aunt Lois is obviously a loving tribute to Orpha May Steinbrueck.

But *My Home Is Far Away* is a novel, not a straight history, and so there are a number of authorial inventions. Young, sweet, lovestruck Bonnie Purdy, who so earnestly pursues Harry Willard, does not seem to have had a specific counterpart in reality, though her character was likely inspired by Powell's memories of her aunt Dawn Sherman Gates, and the tragic and unnecessary early death she shared with her sister Hattie. Sabra worked as a schoolteacher and cashier rather than as a nurse, like the fictional Idah Hawkins, and she probably didn't meet Roy Powell until well after Hattie Sherman died. The grandfather, locked out of the house by Idah and subsequently electrocuted at the train station, is pure (and not very convincing) fabrication. Thorburne Putney is probably a composite of the many Chautauqua-circuit lecturers who passed through midwestern towns during Powell's youth. Finally, Vance Hawkins, Idah's wastrel brother, who sets the final tragedy into play, is an entirely invented character: there were no boys in Sabra's family.

These exceptions aside, *My Home Is Far Away* is painfully close to unvarnished autobiography, told in the third person and recast as a novel in thirty-four chapters. It is a book written for adults, with an adult command of the language, that nonetheless manages to maintain the vantage point of a hungry, serious child throughout. The agonizing tale of the dissolution of a family, it might be compared to a memoir penned not with the usual tranquillity of distance but rather with the sense that everything happening to the characters is happening *right now*, without any promise of deliverance, without any assurance that childhood, too, shall pass.

Because the story so closely mirrors the actual events of the author's life, its essence has already been told in the first chapter of this biography. Three sisters—Lena (like Mabel, the "pretty one"), Marcia (like Dawn, the "smart one"), and Florrie (like Phyllis, the "baby")—lose their mother at an early age (in the book, Daisy/ Hattie dies of consumption). Their father abandons the girls to a succession of relatives all over Ohio, then suddenly calls them back together after his remarriage and installs them in the "grandest house in town."

The children's new stepmother proves a horror, mistreating them with psychopathic severity. Marcia, brilliant and sensitive, eventually discovers in herself a passion for words, written and spoken, which is encouraged by the love and support of a kindly aunt. Upon learning that her stepmother has burned all her compositions and drawings (and after uncovering a sordid and fatal romance between the fictional Vance and Bonnie), Marcia, just barely a teenager, boards a train for Cleveland, determined to put her past behind her. The book concludes with a passage written directly from the heart, a wrenching mixture of the sorrow, apprehension, and insistent self-affirmation the young Dawn Powell must have felt after her own escape:

> She was still scared, but she felt light-headed and gay, the way Papa did when he was going away from home. She thought she must be like Papa, the kind of person who was always glad going away instead of coming home. She looked out the window, feeling the other self inside her, the self that had no feelings and could never be hurt, coming out stronger and stronger, looking at the fringe of London Junction and the beginnings of Milltown with calm, almost without remembrance. In a backyard past Milltown Village, a woman was chopping off the head of a chicken, and Marcia thought if Florrie was along this would make her cry. She thought she ought to cry just a little, out of loyalty to Florrie. She'd come back and get Florrie someday, just like she promised. But maybe Florrie would never leave Papa. It was as if Florrie would always have to protect Papa instead of the other way around. . . .
>
> The rain came louder, beating across the window. Marcia rubbed a spot on the pane and saw they were already at Union Falls, miles and miles from London Junction. The rain covered the spot, and Marcia took her forefinger and wrote "MARCIA WILLARD" across the foggy pane.

In much the same way that John Farrar had reacted to the first of her satires, *Turn, Magic Wheel*, Powell's agent Carol Brandt—and, to a lesser degree, Max Perkins himself—seemed befuddled by the direction her new book was taking. Brandt's efforts at tact were not particularly delicate: "Carol called to say she 'liked the new book very much,'" Powell wrote in December 1946, adding, "Maybe after the second part was finished she could tell more—'and then the first part could be cut.'" Powell's working titles included *There Were Three Children*, *There Was Another America*, *London Junction* (the name of the book's fictional town), and *Once Upon a Time*. Her final selection, *My Home Is Far Away*, was taken from an old song she remembered from her youth, about a lonesome Irish immigrant unable to get work in the new land.*

By this time, Powell was drafting some of her novels by hand and others on a typewriter; she constantly debated the merits of the two approaches and firmly believed that the choice made a difference in the end result. *My Home Is Far Away* was written mostly by hand, and as with *Turn, Magic Wheel*, she enjoyed the creative process more than usual. "I write and rewrite each chapter half a dozen times with pleasure—perhaps because the material is so limitless," she observed on March 8, 1944. "There is always something more to say, to touch up. This is again proof of the advantage of doing by hand instead of typewriter. The latter always seems so final I hate to change the pretty neat page, and a certain magazine style creeps in." By May 18, she had changed her mind: "Working on typewriter now for clarification purposes and to tense up plot, which sprawls forever over pen and ink."

She completed *My Home Is Far Away* on July 24, while spending a weekend with the Murphys, and submitted it to Scribner's the next day. In retrospect, some of the hesitations Brandt and Perkins had about the manuscript seem understandable. With her last few books (and especially after the success of *A Time to Be Born*), Powell had attained a reputation for high sophistication, and nothing could be less "sophisticated"—at least in the glittering, all-knowing, furiously present-tense, big-city manner Powell had perfected—than *My Home Is Far Away*. This is meant not to disparage the book, but merely to point out that it is not a typical Powell novel by any means, and that

---

* In 1997, Powell's nieces could still sing this melody, which had been passed on through the generations.

readers who pick it up looking for barbed cosmopolitan wit may be
disappointed.

There are many consolations, however, including the lush, lyri-
cal writing about a remembered countryside; the reacquaintance
Powell offers us with our own youthful secrets and yearnings; and
the rare sense of a creative artist's treading in dangerous proximity
to her raw material, to the very crises that helped determine the
course of her life and artistry.

My Home Is Far Away is not flawless: the fictional material often
seems arbitrary and grafted on, and the Idah/Sabra character seems
almost unbelievable in her monstrosity (though if anything, Powell
seems actually to have *understated* Sabra's cruelty). But if this book is
not so perfectly polished as some of Powell's others, it nonetheless
remains a wrenching and potent narrative, unsparing in its emotional honesty. Indeed, as Terry Teachout wrote in the *New York Times
Book Review* when *My Home Is Far Away* was reissued in 1995, it must
be counted "one of the permanent masterpieces of childhood, com-
parable with *David Copperfield*, *What Maisie Knew* and the early reminiscences of Colette."

The book was published in late October 1944. Once again,
Scribner's seems to have had no idea how to promote Powell's new
work—though at least it made an effort this time, taking out adver-
tisements in the *New York Times*, the *New York Herald Tribune*, and other
publications. But the campaign stressed the wholesome, "homespun"
quality of the novel, a misrepresentation that seems downright farci-
cal today:

> The scene is Ohio in the early 1900s; the main characters are
> the members of the happy-go-lucky Willard family—always
> on the move, always seeking the home that is always far away.
> You'll laugh with the Willards and sympathize with them in
> their moments of tragedy. They're a family you'll like—espe-

cially Marcia, the "middle one." Meet them today. You'll be glad you did.

"Happy-go-lucky?" A dying mother, a delinquent father, a stepmother with her silver whip, a charming young girl dead as the result of an abortion—can this publicist have read the book? Fortunately, most reviewers saw through the insipid presentation. "The characteristic of novels which warm the cockles of the heart is their sentimentality," Ruth Page noted in the *New York Times* when the book was first published. "There is nothing sentimental about *My Home Is Far Away*, except that it is set in an era which we tend to regard with sentiment. Miss Powell does not. Her view of the world and of human character is sharp and uncompromising."

Kenneth Fearing, writing in the *Herald Tribune*, predicted that the book would "furnish sociologists with a controversial field day." He summed up: "Home is always somewhere else, regardless of age, place or period, is the essential theme of this novel that is poignant as an accidentally rediscovered souvenir."

Edmund Wilson weighed in with a review in the *New Yorker* that was meant to be helpful but instead came perilously close to severing a long friendship. The article was in many ways astute and not entirely dismissive by any means: in it Wilson compared Powell to Sinclair Lewis, for example, and found that she took "human life more calmly, more genially and less melodramatically." However, he had some reservations—and those reservations stung:

> Miss Powell has so much talent and of a kind that is so uncommon that one is always left rather disgruntled at her not making more of her work than she does. Three of her recent novels—*Angels on Toast* and *A Time to Be Born,* as well as this latest one—have all been in some ways excellent, but they sound like advanced drafts of books rather than finished productions. It is not only that they are marred by inaccuracies, inconsisten-

cies and other kinds of careless writing; Miss Powell, in the space of one page, gets her heroine's great-grandmother mixed up with her great-great-grandmother; she uses "phenomena" as if it were singular, she mistakes the meaning of "perquisites"; and she is addicted to such usages as "imbecility" and "normalcy." These errors might not be important; Scott Fitzgerald in his best work sometimes misused words even more seriously. But her carelessness extends also to the organic life of the story. Miss Powell has a way of resorting, in the latter parts of her novels, to violent and sudden incidents that she needs for the machinery of the action but has not taken the trouble to make plausible; and in the case of this latest novel, these incidents—the death of the grandfather from walking into a third rail and the killing off of another character by an abortion— are particularly unconvincing, owing to the fact that the rest of the narrative seems to run pretty close to experience. Miss Powell has simply not allowed herself time to smooth these gashes and hummocks out. And the whole book, as I say, gives the impression of being merely an all-but-final draft which represents the stage at which the writer has got all his material down but has not yet done the sculptural rehandling which is to bring out its self-consistent contours and set it in a permanent pose.

Powell was devastated. "If Bunny's review had been offset by a powerful, favorable one the book would have gotten off," she wrote in her diary on November 28, her forty-eighth birthday. "As it is, it is very discouraging to have someone (who actually has told me I'm infinitely better than John Marquand and equal to Sinclair Lewis at his best) do me so much genuine damage. I have enough damage done me already, merely by the desire to write and my pleasure in people and strange angles of life rather than the English-class models."

In fact, the book "got off" relatively well *despite* Wilson's
review. By 1951, *My Home Is Far Away* had sold almost 6,500 copies,
probably more than any of Powell's other books to date except *A Time
to Be Born*. Three years after being reissued in 1995 (along with the
first publication of her diaries), it had sold many more copies than
any other Powell novel—twenty thousand and counting fast, with no
end in sight.

Released just as World War II was beginning to wind down,
the book was dedicated to Powell's cousin Jack—John Franklin
Sherman—who was then an army sergeant stationed in Europe.
Sherman, an elegant, highly intelligent man then in his early thirties, with a warm and fanciful sense of humor, was the son of
Hattie Sherman's brother Jay. Powell had known him since he was
a baby; when Jojo was four months old, she had likened her son's
"shy, wistful, little smile" to the one she remembered from Jack's
infancy.

After Sherman's mother died, in 1926, he had gone to live with
Orpha May Steinbrueck in Shelby, and there he had stayed, gradually
becoming a successful local businessman and then an educator. With
the exception of his years of army service, Jack Sherman supported
and took care of Auntie May for the last thirty years of her life; later
he would become Jojo's guardian as well. The correspondence
between the cousins is voluminous—dating from 1931 until three
weeks before Powell's death—and virtually every letter is suffused
with humor and affection.

Typically, Powell made no comment whatsoever about the end
of the war in the pages of her diary. She had her own battles to
fight—for her writing and for Jojo. He had become increasingly disturbed at the Gladwyne Colony, and Powell started taking him to a
psychiatrist in New York for treatment with insulin shock therapy.
The results were promising; Powell perceived a new "emotional
poise and localization" in her son, who now "seemed to be aware of

what he was feeling, instead of bewildered and apt to get himself worked up on a totally unrelated matter."

Powell herself was taking a good deal of medication—in her words, a "strange combination of gland, appetite and Benzedrine vitamin pills." She quickly dropped twenty pounds but found that she simultaneously lost all interest in work. "If I don't write for five years I may make quite a name for myself and if I can stop for ten I may give Katherine Ann [Porter] and Dorothy Parker a run for their money," she joked to Edmund Wilson, with whom she had begun to make up.

When she visited Ohio in the early summer of 1945, she found the experience uncannily similar to stepping into a scene from *My Home Is Far Away.* "Both my sisters met me with a car and that unlimited gas that the Middlewesterners always seem to wangle," she wrote to Max Perkins. The three women stopped by their old homes in Shelby and Mount Gilead; Powell inquired about her stepmother, and Phyllis told her for the first time about the grisly exhumation and reburial of their half-sister Emily Helen Powell.*

Powell was impressed by the wealth she saw in Cleveland—"the miles and miles of private homes as big as our public libraries, the beautiful country clubs, the glorification of material conveniences, the vast invincible Magazine Public that in New York we can thank God forget." She was neither sorry to have come nor sorry to leave when it was time to board the train for New York:

> I was glad to get my background into a fluid state again. . . . I
> caught the language again quickly and the familiar combination
> of open hearts and closed minds that represents so much of the
> country except in New York where we have closed hearts first,

---

* *There is no evidence to suggest that Sabra Powell ever read—or even knew about—*My Home Is Far Away; *one can only imagine what her reaction might have been to Powell's magnificent act of revenge.*

and minds so open that carrier pigeons can fly straight through
without leaving a message. Having been reminded again that
New York is no part of America, I still feel safer here—at least
we can write or paint here without the *Woman's Home Companion* breathing on our necks.

She took another trip that autumn, driving down to Florida
with Margaret De Silver. "Expensive due to five overnights, but very
instructive since I realized how cheap and well-fed the rest of U.S. is
and how much better the service and quality and prices," she wrote
home to Joe. "We haven't realized how steep New York has been getting." Powell and De Silver visited the painter Alexander Brook in
Savannah; Esther Andrews came up to meet them in Miami, and then
the three continued down to Key West, where Powell stayed first
with Andrews and Chambers and then in Pauline Hemingway's
house. While there, she worked on a never-finished sequel to *My
Home Is Far Away* and on the manuscript that would develop into *The
Locusts Have No King*.

By the summer of 1946, she had progressed sufficiently on the
latter to jot down some preliminary thoughts: "Offhand, I would
describe it as a follow-up of *A Time to Be Born*, which dealt with New
York in the beginning follies of war. This book deals with the more
desperate follies of post-war Manhattan—the exaggerated drive to
perdition of a nation now conditioned to destruction."

That fall was an unhappy time for her. Crushed by the death of
her little cat, Perkins, in September, Powell was inspired to write in
her diary one of the most loving farewell tributes to a pet ever
recorded. Later the same month, her doctors decided that she
needed a hysterectomy, a more commonplace operation then than it
is today. As usual, Powell was oddly delighted to be in a hospital.
"This is a wonderful place and I'm glad I have any excuse to be here,"
she wrote to Max Perkins. With her signature bluntness, she informed friends that she had just been "spayed."

The following June, Max Perkins died suddenly, and Powell sent a sorrowful note to his assistant, Irma Wyckoff, acknowledging the "millions of other people's tribulations that Max went through emotionally besides his own—if he ever had time for his own." She continued, "I do think we all exhausted him. Fighting the new kind of publishing exhausted him and the new kind of author exhausted him. But I don't know what we'll do without him."

Privately, however, Powell had had decidedly mixed feelings about her editor. After only two meetings with his successor, John Hall Wheelock, she confided to her diary that she now felt closer to him than she ever had to any other editor, including Perkins. In a much franker eulogy than that sent to Wyckoff, she noted:

> Max was an admirable institution and of unquestioned integrity—even his enemies admitted it—but toward the last I had my private opinion that the word "integrity" so universally applied to any businessman means that he has never done anything to jeopardize the firm's money. . . . He always put a book's financial possibilities before anything else. His good judgment (primarily appraisal) lay in his strength to dismiss a manuscript of sheer artistic merit instead of plunging and employing his talents to persuade backing. How strange that his financial caution and his labor over such trashy works as Taylor Caldwell, Marcia Davenport, etc., should have given him the reputation for high artistic courage.

She particularly disliked Davenport's fiction, with its determinedly glamorous mixture of elite society and unbridled passions. Powell thought the popular author a "perfect cesspool of gentility of the grossest order" and always referred to her best-seller *East Side, West Side* as *East Side, East Side*.

The autumn of 1947 comprised yet another series of disasters. On September 12, John Dos Passos and his wife, Katy, planned to take a leisurely trip from Cape Cod to a Connecticut inn. Late in the afternoon, while driving on Route 28 near Wareham, Massachusetts, Dos Passos, squinting into the sunset, failed to notice a pickup truck parked on an angle, with its tailgate protruding into the road. There was a collision, and the top of the car was sheared off. Katy Smith Dos Passos died instantly; John Dos Passos suffered facial lacerations and lost his right eye.

Powell wrote to her friend immediately: "I am thinking about you all the time and I find two things to be glad about. One, that you are a writer so that agony is of service to you, cruel as our work is—and another, that you have physical pain to dull the unbearable other kind."

Thanks to Margaret De Silver's generosity, Powell was able to travel the next week to Boston, where she paid a long visit to Dos Passos in Massachusetts General Hospital. "He was reading *Great Expectations*!!!" she wrote to Sara Murphy. She wandered around Beacon Hill and believed she had discovered the secret of the Bostonian character: "Family home, dignified profession, whorehouses, taverns and churches, all in half a block."

Powell had not known Katy Dos Passos especially well, but she was uncommonly moved by her passing and composed a meditation after a Sunday walk through the Boston Public Garden:

A lawn bloomed on this gray lovely day with blue morning glories and I heard hidden organ music coming from the still green earth and trees and the great houses themselves as if all this was a gravely joyous welcome to a sweet, much-loved lady ghost, telling her to have no fear—here was an august ancient company, honored not doomed by death, and here was joy everlasting, a prize she was deemed fit to win. The wind carried off and then brought back the fragments of distant church music and there seemed a delicate consolation in remembering that she was an odd, fey creature, never to be wholly known or even guessed. Living, she had the quality of a lost legend, someone whose essence could not be captured, mercurial from imp to child to sphinx—as if, even when alive, she had been a visiting Soul.

Only two months later, it would be time for John Dos Passos to come to Powell's aid, after a routine visit from Jojo turned into a nightmare.

Jojo had arrived from Gladwyne on November 22; Powell noted that he was looking well and ambitiously trying to think of a way to earn some money of his own. The early part of the visit seems to have been uneventful; the family probably went out to dinner together (the Grand Ticino on Thompson Street was a favorite), and Jojo likely spent much of his free time playing the piano, reading through his books, listening to records, and studying his maps—his usual at-home activities.

However, on November 28—Powell's birthday—something went horribly wrong. We will probably never know exactly what happened, but the memories of Powell's surviving family members, augmented by some cryptic entries in her own diary, suggest that Jojo, now a full-grown man of twenty-six, lost his temper with his mother and beat her badly.

"Evidently life gets incredibly more terrifying," Powell wrote immediately after the incident. "The childish 'foolish' fears of the bogeyman waiting in the dark are sounder than any hope. Beaten—head bashed—knocked down—and the monster face at last revealed was my birthday present today."

By December 5, Powell was already dissembling, referring to the event as an "accident." She recorded, "Stunned and frightened, Dos got me doctor, neurologist. Head no better." The following day, she was admitted to St. Luke's Hospital, where she had given birth to Jojo in 1921. Her doctors told her that above and beyond her primary complaint, she was in a perilous nervous condition—"my veins flat, my reactions bad, rock-bottom point of fatigue"——that would keep her in the hospital for more than two weeks.

Jojo had long been capable of violent actions, but in the past these had almost invariably been directed against himself. Although he would continue to live at home at least part-time until 1954, the need for a certain caution in day-to-day relations now became obvious. After this outburst, the Goushas no longer rented their beloved summer cottage on Long Island; it was too remote, and therefore too risky. Powell's love for Jojo never wavered, and that love was reciprocated. Still, for many years, she could never feel entirely at ease with her only child.

CHAPTER EIGHT

Dreams and Destroyers

❧

*Humor's an anesthetic, that's all, laughing gas while
your guts are jerked out, your honor sold.*

DAWN POWELL, 1937

NINETEEN FORTY-SEVEN WAS one of the worst years in
Powell's life. And yet, clinging to her work as if to some profound
and desperately needed psychological buoy, Powell managed to summon one of her funniest and most penetrating satires, *The Locusts
Have No King*, from her misery. The effort seems to have exhausted
her—this would prove to be her last published novel for six years, a
much longer interregnum than she had ever permitted herself
before—but she finished the job, and finished it in style.

Like many of her previous books, *The Locusts Have No King* had
its origins in a diary entry. In January 1943, Powell had scribbled
down some notes toward a study of those people she called the
"Destroyers—that cruel, unhappy ever-dissatisfied group who feed

on frustrations (Dorothy Parker, Wolcott Gibbs, [playwright and humorist] Arthur Kober, etc.)":

> They have perverted their rather infantile ambitions into destruction of others' ambitions and happiness. If people are in love, they must mar it with laughter; if people are laughing, they must stop it with "Your slip is showing." They are in a permanent prep school where they perpetually haze each other. They destroy their own happiness by being ashamed of whatever brings it; they want to be loved but are unloving; they want to destroy but be themselves saved.

She mulled over several possible titles for the "Destroyers" book, among them *Prudentius Psychomachia* and *O Strange New War.* (Her rejected titles were not always so dreadful—at the same time, she was toying with the idea of writing a "masculine" novel to be called *Promiscuity Recollected in Senility.*) Her final choice was taken from the biblical book of Proverbs: "The locusts have no king, yet go they forth all of them by bands." In January 1946, she completed the impressionistic sixth chapter, "Moonlight on Rubberleg Square," out of which the rest of the story would evolve. Rubberleg Square is a mythical, mystical location in Greenwich Village, where the "real night does not begin . . . till [the] stroke of twelve, the moment after all decisions have been made and abandoned":

> The reformed citizens who have cautiously stayed home reading four-dollar books that instruct as well as entertain, and have even gone to bed because tomorrow is a big day at the office, suddenly rear up in their sheets, throw on their clothes once more, and dash out for one night-cap to ward off wagon-pride. Couples who have braved Broadway to attend a solemn play concerning injustice out of town are smitten with an irresistible craving for the proximity of barflies, wastrels, crooks.

The artist's model who has been doing uptown nightclubs in her room-mate's mink has had as much splendour as her Irish blood and whiskey content can endure and has escaped in a taxicab to the Florida bar downtown where her amazing hair-do and evening clothes make a gratifying glow in the dingy room and her amorous whim is satisfied by a genial merchant mariner more than it would have been by the elderly broker who was her dinner host. Here, on Rubberleg Square, the four dark streets suddenly come to life with running feet. "BAR," in red or blue neon lights, glows in any direction as if it was all one will-o'-the-wisp, same bar, same Bill, Hank, Jim, Al pushing Same-agains across the same counter.

As it is in *Turn, Magic Wheel*, New York City is the central figure in *The Locusts Have No King*. However, Manhattan had changed in the dozen years between the two books. Powell specifically intended her new work to reflect the postwar ambience: the return of the soldiers, the shortage of apartments, the changed circumstances and different challenges of peacetime. This book would be, she asserted, a "Hogarthian record of the follies of our day."

It was an unsettled and solemn moment, for the resolution of World War II could hardly be called decisive. All but immediately, the Soviet Union had begun to absorb countries in Eastern Europe under the guise of "protective occupation," with the result that only months after V-J day, a fresh conflict seemed not only inevitable but imminent. Moreover, there existed a terrible new weapon, the atomic bomb, which would soon be succeeded by even more deadly armaments. Powell, who was often oblivious to international events, found herself riveted with horrified fascination to the radio broadcasts of the atomic tests in the South Pacific. Atypically—and somewhat incredibly—she wondered in her diary why the United States (which she called an "increasingly bigoted, money-mad, culture-hating nation") was so reluctant to share its nuclear secrets with

Stalin's Soviet Union, which she described as a "nation that dangerously prizes art and culture and brains."

An overriding anxiety over the possibility of immediate annihi-
lation haunts *The Locusts Have No King*, with the terror at last made
explicit on its final page. The story closes with its two most attractive
characters, Frederick and Lyle—both of whom have spent much of
the novel in the arms of other lovers—reconciled at last and listening to the same broadcast of the Bikini bomb tests that had so pan-
icked Powell: "Frederick was full of fear, too. He went over to Lyle
and held her tightly. In a world of destruction one must hold fast to
whatever fragments of love are left, for sometimes a mosaic can be
more beautiful than an unbroken pattern."

It is a sober, realistic, but intrinsically romantic conclusion—
the lovers against the world; *The Locusts Have No King* may be read as
a quest for stability within a civilization that had suddenly come to
seem heedless and impermanent. Powell's own domestic philoso-
phies had grown more traditional with the onset of middle age. "The
moral of the story is that love must be guarded against the Destroyers and that fidelity is romantic," she wrote as she was finishing the
book. "Even unasked and unrequited, it is the great true romance,
more compensatory and personally enriching than revengeful flur-
ries and escapades which momentarily stroke the pride but only
curdle the memory of what was pure and genuine in the true love."
The lesson of the novel, she stated, was simple: "Cling to whatever
is fine."

Such serious concerns inform but never interfere with Powell's
usual comic frolics among the Manhattan intelligentsia. The hero,
Frederick Olliver, is a medieval scholar who lives alone in the West
Village, eking out a marginal existence teaching courses at the
"League for Cultural Foundation" (Powell's jibe at the New School
for Social Research). After Olliver's most recent book becomes an
unexpected hit, he is tapped for the editorship of an idiotic humor
magazine called *Haw* (Marcia Willard receives an issue of this same

mythical journal in *My Home Is Far Away*). Inducted into the literary elite (he meets Dennis Orphen at one drunken party), his head neatly turned, Frederick abandons his patrician, married lover, Lyle Gaynor, and becomes enamored of a dizzy, ferociously ambitious, and sexually omnivorous young airhead named Dodo, who in turn leaves *him* for a newer and more prominent "genius." And so Frederick and Lyle are left alone, and amid the whirl of uncertainty about the future of the world, they do indeed cling to "something fine": one another.

In January 1948, Powell sent the manuscript to Edmund Wilson, requesting a promotional blurb for the dust jacket—one of the many literary favors Wilson habitually refused to grant, even to his best friends. "It would be fatal for me to make an exception for Dawn," he wrote decisively to John Wheelock, adding that he wouldn't have been able to offer much praise anyway, as he found the book inconsistent and unpolished (some of the same complaints he had voiced about *My Home Is Far Away*). He did, however, compile a list of typographical errors and narrative implausibilities for Powell's correction.

Eager to find a publisher in England, Powell wrote one of her most charming and illuminating letters to Michael Sadleir at Constable:

> The theme, as you so perspicaciously gathered from the Biblical title, deals with the disease of destruction sweeping through our times—no leader is needed, each person is out to destroy whatever valuable or beautiful thing life has. The moral is that in an age of destruction one must cling to whatever remnants of love, friendship, or hope above and beyond reason that one has, for the enemy is all around, ready to snatch it. You will see that I refer to the enemy not as Fascism, Communism, Mammon or anything but the plague of destructivism—inherent in human nature but released in magnified potency since the war.

My novels are based on the fantastic designs made by real
human beings earnestly laboring to maladjust themselves to
fate. There is no principle for them to prove—they may dis-
obey the law of gravity as they please. My characters are not
slaves to an author's propaganda. I give them their heads. They
furnish their own nooses.

Despite this pitch, Sadleir turned down *The Locusts Have No King*
(as he had *My Home Is Far Away*); the book would not be published in
England until W. H. Allen brought it out in the mid-1950s. Sadleir
wrote a gentle letter of rejection to Powell, expressing his doubts
that depleted, impoverished postwar Britain would appreciate her
new novel: "The state of society which it scarifies would be particularly antipathetic to a bankrupt nation living on short commons and,
unreasonable though such a prejudice may be, it is one which a publisher must take into account."

Privately, however, Sadleir simply didn't think *The Locusts Have
No King* was very good. It was "too long for its content," he told
Wheelock. "Her real brilliance is clogged by a lot of general exag-
geration, which toward the end of the book makes really rather
tedious reading."

There is still debate about the novel's merits. Some readers,
even those otherwise well disposed to Powell's work, will agree with
Sadleir that it is too wordy for what it has to say; others would rank
it among the very finest of her books. Both assessments are valid:
Locusts is indeed somewhat overextended, but so are many other
unquestionably great comedies (one thinks immediately of the
Richard Strauss/Hugo von Hofmannsthal opera *Der Rosenkavalier*, or
a romping, gigantic epic such as *Tristram Shandy*). We forgive such
longeurs, and forgive them happily, because the inspired moments are
so rewarding. And the best parts of this book rank with the most
trenchant and insightful writing Powell ever did; only in *A Time to Be*

Born, perhaps, does the author so persuasively balance the same mixture of giddy wit and high seriousness that we find in *The Locusts Have No King*.

Alice S. Morris in the *New York Times* began her review with one of the most sensible and acute paragraphs printed about Powell during her lifetime:

> If the art of satire at Miss Powell's hand is less baleful, knife-edged and glittering than when Mr. Evelyn Waugh puts his hand to it, it is equally relevant and more humane. In *The Locusts Have No King*, Miss Powell pins down her locusts—some New York barflies, bigwigs and gadabouts—with drastic precision, but never without pity. . . . The combination of a waspish sense of satire with a human sense of pathos results in a novel that is highly entertaining and curiously touching.

Orville Prescott, long-standing chief book critic of the *Times*, particularly liked the character of Dodo: "Miss Powell roasts her to a lovely golden brown," he wrote. "Only a woman writer, and a cruel one, could paint so fiendish a portrait of a completely unbearable woman." Although it emphasized the stereotype of Powell's "cruelty," Prescott's overall evaluation was basically positive.

Lewis Gannett, a friend since the Goushas' first days in the Village, was now the book critic for the *New York Herald Tribune*. Like Prescott, he found the novel amusing but brutal:

> There is a bitter aftertaste in the sparkling liqueur of Dawn Powell's prose. At once mercilessly catty and ruefully impish, her story of a Latin scholar lost in the bars and garrets and duplex apartments of Manhattan sometimes approaches the comic strip in its broad satire, is rescued by biting wit and almost stumbles into tears at the end.

In the *Nation*, Diana Trilling wrote about *The Locusts Have No King* rather as she had about *A Time to Be Born*. She instantly acknowledged Powell's "great intelligence and fiercely courageous wit" but objected to the "discrepancy between the power of mind revealed on every page of her novel and the insignificance of the human beings upon whom she directs her excellent intelligence":

> A shabbier crowd of hangers-on and bar flies it would be hard to find. Not a single individual among them, either positively or negatively, either by the nature of his ambition or the distance of his fall from glory, suggests any human ideal which justifies a writer bothering with the human race at all.

Powell shrugged off such commentary; it was old news to her by now. "Gist of criticisms (Diana Trilling, etc.) of my novel is if they had my automobile they wouldn't visit my folks, they'd visit *theirs*," she grumbled in some disgust.

The Locusts Have No King was issued in April 1948. The sales were initially promising—some four thousand copies in the first month—but they leveled off thereafter, for a total of only 4,949 copies sold, substantially fewer than *My Home Is Far Away*, and just slightly more than half the sales of *A Time to Be Born* six years earlier. With the exception of *Angels on Toast*, *The Locusts Have No King* was Powell's poorest seller for Scribner's; its relative failure must have especially rankled, given that her publisher had recently upped her advance to $1,500 per novel.

As always, the money came and went, spent on Jojo's care, on his nurse, Louise Lee, on drinks and dinners at Manhattan's finest restaurants, and on the couple's living quarters, complete with Marie Jeffers, their full-time maid. There was always enough money for luxuries, it seems, but urgent bills often went unpaid. Powell loved the prestige of a large apartment at a good address, and 35 East

Ninth Street was a doorman building located only a minute's walk from Washington Square.

Although she disliked the perpetual darkness of their duplex, she was delighted with her sunny workroom on the roof of the building, where she could tend a garden in the spring and watch the snow fall over the Village in the winter. She cared little for modern "conveniences"; once, when one of her nieces paid a visit, she was startled to find that the knobs on the antiquated Gousha radio had long since fallen off and that Dawn was reduced to turning the dial with a kitchen knife.

"Although it seems that my beloved city is being pulled down around my ears, our own lives seem singularly untouched by progress," she wrote in response to a questionnaire about her work in the early 1950s. "I have never had an automobile, Mixmaster, Bendix, a television set or pressure cooker and have the same two maids we had twenty-five years ago, the same ignorance of mechanics and games, even many of the same friends. However, I like progressive jazz, modern music, radio crime programs, night disk jockeys and the United Nations Building."

A rapprochement with Joe began as their forties came to a close; from this time he starts to reappear frequently in Powell's diary and in her letters. By now an obvious and debilitated alcoholic, he would nonetheless remain a successful advertising executive until he turned sixty-seven and reached mandatory retirement age. Cornell, the firm he had joined in the 1920s, had metamorphosed into the enormously profitable Geyer, Cornell, Newell Agency. Will Lee Doyle, who worked with Gousha as a rookie adman in the late 1940s, would still remember him vividly in 1996:

Joe was one of a wide variety of characters who amused and fascinated me when I joined the agency on my first post-war job. It was something like joining an opera troupe because egos were stand-outs and a raffish, good-natured sophistication reigned at all levels. . . . I recall that when he said something offhandedly witty, I cracked back, "Touché, Mr. Gousha!" He scowled at this impertinent sass, and his breathing was somewhere between a gasp and a whistle, close to asthmatic. His paunch was substantial, his face and hair ruddy. The expression around his eyes and mouth was one of disgust for the day's routine frustrations. A rebel was within, I'd say, held in check by a pretty good paycheck, plus the convivial lunches.

While Doyle believed that "Joe's lunchtime imbibing surely assuaged his anxieties," he added that he never saw the older man "all-out drunk or even tipsy." Indeed, real inebriation was evidently saved for the evening, when Joe would eat at Tony's (once his favorite speakeasy, now a legitimate establishment) on West Forty-sixth Street, or at the Blue Ribbon, a German restaurant off Times Square that would survive into the 1970s, and occasionally at such New York landmarks as "21" or Tavern on the Green.

In March 1948, Powell traveled to Florida and then on to Haiti with Margaret De Silver, at De Silver's expense. The Miami-to-Port-au-Prince portion of the voyage may have been Dawn's first airplane trip, and in any event, it made an enormous impact on her: five years later, she would remember that flight as one of the peak experiences of her life. "First awe and ecstasy of Nature I ever experienced," she decided. "The look down at the transparent blue waters to the bottom of the ocean and little submarine variations of waters and hills giving different colors and geometric designs as mathematical as if measured by a formal abstractionist, as brilliant in color and form as if God had hung from Heaven by his heels to paint this."

In Port-au-Prince, she stayed at the Hotel Olofsson, which was popular with Hemingway, Dos Passos, and other colleagues. From there, she sent back some amused and definitely unconventional tourist-wife reports to Joe: "Beer bad and very high—fifty cents a bottle—and in the clip house the girls are told to order it for their sailors as they are told to order champagne other places. The leading whorehouse is called the Square Deal Joint."

Forgoing the Long Island refuge, the Goushas spent most of the summer of 1948 in town; Powell made brief excursions to Gerald and Sara Murphy's home and to see Margaret De Silver on Cape Cod. Back in Manhattan, on July 20, she came across one of those sudden, shockingly public tragedies that every longtime urban resident will occasionally encounter. While out for a walk, she saw the corpse of a young black girl, crushed by a city bus at the intersection of Fifth Avenue and Fourteenth Street, lying "sweetly . . . gay in five o'clock, after-work, date clothes." In her diary, she wrote about this unfortunate stranger and her random death with sorrow and empathy.

Powell's moods fluctuated wildly from moment to moment, day to day. Lack of money was often a major factor in her despair. On August 1, for example, stretching the truth only slightly, she complained that she was now in much the same position she had been in at the age of twelve—"unable to have haircut, soda pop—ridiculous at my age; ridiculous to be unable to help anyone, to repay a kindness, buy a jar of cold cream, to have to ask always."

The next day found her in a markedly different frame of mind, for she had sold a short story and was suddenly flush. "At this point, [the Brandt Agency] telephoned. *Today's Woman* had bought 'Devil's Grip' story for $900. Immediately the town looked finer than ever, and the prospects ahead for August even finer."

Powell switched agents in October, having felt a vague but not clearly defined need for some kind of change in her professional life. "Can we get a Hollywood divorce and still be frightfully, frightfully good friends?" her letter to Carl Brandt began. "I mean, hold hands in nightclubs and gaze deep into each other's pocketbooks for the photographers?"

She signed with Ivan van Auw at the dynamic and aggressive

new MCA conglomerate, which promised to give her the promotional buildup she thought she deserved. She would stay at MCA for less than two years, however, before returning to the Brandt Agency, where she would remain for the rest of her life. It was not a change of *agent* she had wanted, she would realize by then—it was a change of *publisher*. Increasingly, Scribner's seemed oblivious to her career.*

In April 1949, Powell went into the hospital for surgery on her chest and was surprised and relieved when the mysterious growth she had lived with for twenty years was extracted and explained as a "teratoma." It was a brutal operation, five hours long and involving three transfusions and a period of recovery in an oxygen tent. Powell later graphically told her sisters that her doctor had been in her chest cavity "up to his shoulders."

"Here is the family scandal I must now reveal," her letter continued:

> This here cyst (dermoid) or terra toma [*sic*] is a *twin*. That is, it is my own frustrated twin, a type of cyst that occurs (not very often) in the chest or other sections—even the head of a man or woman. It is made up of parts of various things—hair, teeth, sometimes an eye or a jawbone. It lives off your heart and lung and is "benign"—unless it gets overgrown and shoves out the organs you need as mine started to do. It was as large as a grapefruit and had cut off all but ⅓ of my lung space so it was about ready to shove me out.
>
> I had nine broken ribs before and probably Terry [the teratoma] would keep cracking them if I let him. I was very glad on hearing of my twin that he hadn't popped out of my chest during a formal dinner party, me in my strapless and him grabbing my martini. I rather thought he'd come out saying "O.K.

---

* *She was particularly unhappy with the marketing department, whose inane "happy-go-lucky" ad campaign was only its worst offense.*

Louis, drop the gun." Anyway, I breathe wonderfully as if I never breathed before.

In fact, the teratoma—the term is derived from the Greek word for "monster"—is now classified as nothing more than a large tumor, usually attached to the heart; such growths have nothing to do with failed twins. But Powell would believe this more dramatic explanation for the rest of her life.

As it happened, Dawn's sister Mabel was experiencing serious health problems of her own. Because she was a Christian Scientist, she resisted seeing a doctor for as long as she could, but by the middle of 1949, it was obvious to her friends and family that she was gravely ill and probably dying. She finally capitulated and agreed to go in for some tests, which revealed advanced uterine cancer that had metastasized throughout her body. She underwent treatment—almost half a century later, her niece Phyllis Poccia would marvel at the gallantry with which she faced her last months—but on October 26, 1949, Mabel Powell Pocock died at a hospital near her home in Cleveland Heights, at the age of fifty-four.

Powell traveled out to Ohio for the funeral—a lavish affair at the Pocock home, where Mabel lay in state—and would later base the most macabre (and one of the best) of her short stories, "The Glads," on the gathering. But she never memorialized her sister in any diaries or letters that have come to light. As she herself had suggested in *Come Back to Sorrento*, some feelings may simply be too enormous to face.

And so her diary for that day reads: "Mabel died at 9:50. Yesterday morning I was waked by dream. . . ." There the entry breaks off. Similarly, on the railway journey home from the funeral, she dashed off an amusing—and entirely beside-the-point—postcard to her sister Phyllis, a bright and silly sketch about the complications of urinating in a private sleeping compartment once the bed has been pulled down over the toilet. Only in the final sentence does she let on that something terrible had happened: "The trip seems like a bad dream," Powell wrote, as if as an afterthought. And with that, the subject was closed.

The three sisters who had survived so much together were now parted at last. Whatever youthful resentment Dawn may have felt toward her older sister, Mabel had been one of only two other people besides herself who had known and shared the full horror of her childhood. In a reflection of her early literary bent and her love for Alexandre Dumas, the young Dawn had often regarded the three Powell sisters as the Three Musketeers—and certainly they had been forced to fight some daunting psychological battles together. Now one musketeer was gone, along with a huge amount of Powell's own history. She never explicitly elaborated on her grief, but she did add the date of Mabel's death to the list of anniversaries, usually sorrowful, that she observed privately every year. Soon thereafter, Mabel would begin visiting her in her dreams.

Poor Phyllis initially bore the brunt of Dawn's response to their sister's passing. "Odd thing about a death in the family," Powell wrote in her diary on November 17. "The values shift and become topsy-turvy; truth long-lost emerges or is, until some other death, submerged. Mabel gone; suddenly Phyllis—hitherto seen as anti-Mabel or everything I chose to imagine—has the eccentricities I used to fashion on Mabel.*

In a nostalgic mood, Powell went back to her planned sequel to *My Home Is Far Away*, provisionally entitled *Marcia;* she would work on it occasionally, though with dwindling enthusiasm, for the rest of her years. The eighty double-spaced typewritten pages (and hundreds of pages of notes) that have survived indicate that this book would been more overtly fictional than *My Home Is Far Away* and that it would have

---

* *In fact, the bond between Dawn and Phyllis was far too sturdy to be so easily ruptured. Although Phyllis was a devoted, deeply traditional midwestern wife and mother, she was proud of her ever-so-slightly notorious sister in far-off Greenwich Village; the two spoke on the telephone or corresponded as often as twice a week.*

had the Dawn/Marcia character moving to Cleveland—a city that Powell enjoyed and visited throughout her life but never actually resided in.

Marcia was Powell's principal project during her monthlong residency at the MacDowell Colony, a prestigious, by-invitation-only working retreat for composers, writers, and artists, established near Peterborough, New Hampshire, as a memorial to the American composer Edward MacDowell (best remembered today for piano miniatures such as "To a Wild Rose"). She arrived there in June 1949 and was assigned to the Helen Wood Studio, a full mile from the main house, where breakfast and dinner were served at fixed and, for Powell, uncommonly early hours. "The sheer shock of three or four miles' walk every day will doubtless wear off and leave my mind a poetic blank suitable for composition," she wrote to Joe.

The whole purpose of the MacDowell Colony—the isolation it provided for intensive, undisturbed work—was lost on Powell. She called it a "weird set-up of rubbing your nose in whatever you're doing day and night with no change of scene or pace or face." She objected to the "politely veiled law of appearing at whatever reading or concert some egotistical colonist announces for evening." The environment itself she found "singularly graceless, foodless and cheerless," and she missed her Village watering holes:

> There was a cocktail party but the eager inmates had drunk it all up in twenty-five minutes. However, everyone patronizes the local package store and it's glug-glug-glug in the privacy of the studios and it's glug-glug-glug in the bedrooms by the moon. There is complete freedom—no overseeing—and any-one seems able to disappear in a gutter for days with no reproach. I have a pint of rye on hand for medicinal reasons. You learn to be very stingy very soon and drink alone in the dark, so I am told—not for moral reasons but to keep the thirsty pack from snatching it.

"Did you know MacDowell was off his rocker up here the last few years?" she informed Joe.

> There is a bird all over the place supposed to have inspired "To a Wild Rose" as it sings [the] first four notes. (I *would* say it was "From the Halls of Montezuma"—until frowned on and told it was the Wild Rose bird.) Well, this bird shrieks this from every tree and bush and after MacDowell had written the song (and very likely taught the bird to plug it) he wanted to do more profound work but the damn bird kept dinging away at his old popular hit till the poor man cracked. My theory is that Mrs. MacDowell started this place after his death to see how many other artists would be driven nuts by it, too.

As might be imagined, Powell did very little work at the MacDowell Colony.

Indeed, no matter where she set pen to paper, *Marcia* simply refused to take off. "When I look over this novel I enjoy it but get no further—lucifying past chapters, whittling really," she wrote in January 1950, securely back in New York. "Some kind of outside support is really needed to give me confidence. If I cannot write—if that pleasure is crushed out of me—then I might as well have been finished off by my operation."

Little outside support was forthcoming, but Powell did find the inspiration for a new—and completely unrelated—novel only a few days later, during a weekend at Gerald and Sara Murphy's home in Snedens Landing. She picked up a copy of Sir William Maxwell's edition of *The Creevey Papers* and was exhilarated—"especially at Mrs. Creevey's letters to her husband from Bath in which she refers to 'that Wicked Pavilion'—the place everyone enjoys till after midnight, drinking so they cannot get up till noon, and then with heads."

She likened this "Wicked Pavilion" to her beloved Café

Lafayette (then under threat by the new owners of the lot on which it sat) and began to fashion the outline of a book around it. "Delighted with new novel—*so far*—as it seems to have already been written in my head waiting for the title (and focal point of the Lafayette) to release it," she wrote, exulting, for one brief moment, in her gifts:

> How wonderful to feel it again—the wheel beneath the hand, the chariot leave the ground. Even though there will be the certain colossally depressed days one is happy over that initial sense of power over the instrument.

Soon enough, however, it would become clear that Powell was experiencing her first extended period of writer's block. After a promising beginning, the *Wicked Pavilion* project was moving along slowly; *Marcia*, for its part, was tentatively shelved. She tackled *The Brooklyn Widow* once again but made no further progress on that elusive play. And she even found it impossible to dash off a children's book about cats ("thirty-five pages or ten thousand words," she told herself encouragingly) that she planned to submit for the Julia Ellsworth Ford juvenile prize.

This last idea, which she referred to as *Yow*, would join *Marcia* and *The Brooklyn Widow* in the category of unfinished projects that would obsess her to the end, albeit never quite enough to induce her to actually sit down and get them written. The notes she made toward it are charming and only enhance one's regret that her sole venture into children's literature was never completed: "Tom, the delicatessen cat on strike around Department of Health which forbade cats in delicatessens." "Has friend, Bill (or Mac), grocery cat, expense account . . . Mac says how about having a quick one (mouse)?" "Two leggers like anybody who feeds them, have no real affection. Like cows because they feed them; like mothers because they feed them. Change affection according to who feeds them. At least we're better than humans who kill for no reason."*

In the early summer of 1950, Powell had an unexpected—and predictably disagreeable—reunion with an old rival. Sue Lawson visited New York and arrived unannounced at Margaret De Silver's apartment, where she saw Dawn for the first time in many years. As had so often happened in the old days, the evening culminated in a fight, with Lawson's choking De Silver and Powell's attempting to pull her off—and receiving a "sock in the face" as the reward for her efforts. "I gave her a good kick personally and pushed her in a chair where she sat with insane blazing eyes, face distorted with hate," Powell wrote to Edmund Wilson. "Evidently strain of standing by while her husband is a martyr has filled her with an understandable hatred of everybody else in the world" (Jack Lawson had recently been jailed for contempt after publicly denouncing, from the witness stand, the HUAC investigation of purported Communist subversion in Hollywood). There is no evidence that Powell saw or communicated with either of the Lawsons thereafter.

De Silver left New York shortly after this rambunctious night for her vacation home on Cape Cod, where Powell kept her apprised of goings-on in the city in a string of amusing letters. Edmund Wilson's wife Elena's prime achievement, Dawn reported, was "deirascibilitizing as well as rejuvenating the Bard"; she herself had helped Jacques LeClercq find "summer tail" by introducing him to her friend Mary Grand ("She flung herself and all two hundred pounds at tiny Jacques and said WHO is this adorable man?"); Louise

---

* Although Yow never proceeded much beyond these snatches, the concept would remain a favorite, and the author would return to the book many times, however fleetingly. In the final months of her life, painfully aware of her diminishing strength, Powell would attempt to work on her last novel, which she called Summer Rose; on a long short story, "Aunt Hannah from Pike's Peak"; and on an essay for the New York Times. Failing on all fronts, she would at last go back to Yow. "God, how wonderful if I could get some writing done," she would exclaim on July 18, 1965, shortly before she died. "If, for instance, I could knock off the cat book just for fun." It is the last of her works mentioned in her diary.

Lee had taken some leave and so was no longer hanging the family laundry out the windows of 35 East Ninth Street ("Louise has always been a defender of the right of Old Rags to Get the Sun").

Powell enjoyed making such playful sport of her acquaintances and could never quite comprehend why people found her unsparing conversation shocking. "Lunch with Dos," she noted in her diary on one occasion, "and I gave what I considered a cheery talk on New York gossip and gaiety at end of which Dos said 'Good God, Dawn, you make my hair stand on end.'"

Aware of Powell's domestic problems and her continuing inability to settle down to serious work, De Silver surprised her frustrated and impoverished friend with a round-trip ticket to France on the luxurious ocean liner *Ile de France*. Powell arranged to leave on October 14. "I have a great deal to thank you for—immeasurable, in fact," she wrote to De Silver. "It is so rare that gifts of money are tied up with those fabulosities—the gift to the soul."

She devoted much of the rest of the summer to preparing for her voyage. "What I wish to do is to know my own country as well as possible before traveling," she said, "since I am always so bored by foreigners, however intellectual, who are limited in knowledge of their own country." She collected suggestions from such friends as novelist and editor George Davis, with whom she had worked at *Mademoiselle:* "Get in touch with someone you know so they can get you out of whatever place you go first and don't like." Esther Andrews's advice was more sweeping: "Go to Venice *at once.*"

Before her departure, Powell wrote a long letter to her editor at Scribner's, John Hall Wheelock, describing the plan for her new novel, which she had already definitely named *The Wicked Pavilion*:

> Reading the gossipy letters of French ladies and all the letters in the *Creevey Papers,* it struck me how sad it was that the vivid realness of the life as described by these ordinary letter-writers—the customs, the town talk, the scandal, the financial

and personal problems of a Londoner or Parisian—was never really done in a novel. . . . I felt compelled to do my own favorite city the service the old letter-writers did for their times. I know New York very well and am still exploring it— walking around the water's edge from Battery to Throgs Neck, under its bridges and God knows in and out of dozens of levels of society.

She also provided a (much less specific) report on *Marcia.* "The sequel to *My Home Is Far Away,* which you saw in part, has undergone considerable revision and may get done first," she said. "As I told you, the death of my sister last year paralyzed that background for me in a curious way, and it only became workable a short while ago, but the novel will be a very good one and may detach itself from my personal feelings at an ocean's distance."

Exhausted, depressed, and painfully conscious of her own mortality, Powell looked upon Paris as something of a last hope. The self-proclaimed "permanent visitor" was so gloomy that her thoughts were not directed toward the excitement of her upcoming ocean voyage, or even any touristy anticipations she had of her first sight of Europe. Instead, on the day she sailed, she jotted down a brief, autumnal meditation on lost time:

> The reason friends in late middle-age appear inadequate is that one expects them to give back one's youth—everything one once had with them—and one charges them with the lack that is in oneself, for even if they could give, your container is now a sieve and can hold no gifts for long.

Crossing the Atlantic that October, she shared a cabin on the *Ile de France* with a "Boston spinster roommate . . . shocked at immorality everywhere but crazy to find it."* Although she enjoyed the

---

* *She would later incorporate this acquaintance into a short story entitled "The Pilgrim."*

gourmet meals on board ("splendid filet mignons and a specially good cheese"), she was laid low by seasickness for much of the crossing and continued to be nauseated for some time after the ship docked in France.

In Paris, Powell checked into the Hotel Lutetia, unaware that only five years before, it had been a notorious center for collaborators with the German occupation. Several of her Parisian friends were unhappy that she had decided to stay there, but she reasoned that the war was now over, and the hotel's ownership had changed. Besides, it was reasonably priced and centrally located on the Left Bank, and the staff was courteous and helpful (it remains a popular establishment today). Initially, she was delighted with the prospect of a strange city in which she might hibernate:

> I have seen nobody and have not tried to. I celebrate my loneliness and this is a wonderful city to be alone in. . . . I mean it is so overwhelming that to have somebody with you trying to talk about how Elsie has her hair fixed now or what kind of car your wife likes best would be just like an interruption while reading the most galloping mystery.

Such insular privacy soon lost its appeal, though (as it always did for Powell), and she contacted her old friend Eugene Jolas, now the editor of the avant-garde journal *transition*. Jolas turned up promptly at the Lutetia, "very distinguished and faunish (stout faunish) and much gray hair." She told Joe, "This is my first human contact and I am very pleased."

She liked the beauty, antiquity, and unfamiliar environment of Paris but didn't much care for the French: "God, what terrifying women—vultures behind cash registers wherever you turn, bleak, veiled avarice and hate." She was afraid to drink in the bistros for fear that she might "smile at the busboy or laugh out loud and get arrested as this town is not one to encourage democratic good nature." All in all, Powell thought that France needed a "good shot of rye" to make it merrier—"an American Legion convention, let's say."

Through Jolas and his wife, Maria, Powell had passing encounters with Samuel Beckett (who took the trio drinking one night on the Champs-Elysées), Simone de Beauvoir ("a Carol Hill [Brandt] type, only with a French mean look"), and Jean-Paul Sartre ("a very tiny, sandy, little jockey type who seems very keen, interested and much nicer than I thought"). On one occasion, she offended the Francophile Jolas by suggesting that the lionized Sartre was essentially another "commercial enterprise like cornflakes or Shirley Temple"—because, she said, restaurants, hotels, magazines, theaters, and real estate all thrived on his approval. "This view was not—as he held —the stupid view of America toward France but my own," she told Edmund Wilson. To Joe, she described Jolas as "neuro, thinking everything I say represents American lack of reverence for Racine." Nonetheless, their twenty-five-year friendship survived her visit intact, and Powell would be saddened to learn of Jolas's death shortly thereafter.

"You can live very cheaply in Paris," she wrote in her diary, amending the cliché with the disclaimer "but it's no pleasure." Still, she learned the bus lines, climbed to the top of the cathedral of Notre Dame, went to hear her old friend Libby Holman sing in a nightclub ("a baffling amount of folk songs to do with lost babies, etc., but enough 'I'm a Bad Woman and How I Love It!' to get bravos"), and made notes about the radically different culture she was warily observing—rather like a latter-day American Mrs. Trollope come to dissect the Old World. "French frown on Pernod but actually it is their wines that kill," she wrote. "The most moralizing people in the world drink quarts of wine—the way country people kill themselves eating pies and cakes, healthy because they raise it and they save money. After a couple of quarts, *one* Pernod and what a cluck-cluck goes on."

Whatever writing she did on this trip was mostly contained in the lengthy letters she sent back to Joe, Wilson, De Silver, Phyllis, and Jack Sherman. She would make use of her letters to Joe, in particular, in the novel she was to publish in 1957, *A Cage for Lovers*. As Christmas approached, she reported to her sister that the "Xmas spirit was comparatively quiet except for church bells which don't go ding ding but one very alarming bong bong bong very fast."

It is unlikely that even under the best of circumstances, Powell would have remained in France for very long; she was too accustomed to the swift pace and easy informality of New York. As it happened, she had chosen an especially terrifying season to cut herself off from friends, family, and her familiar milieu.

The Korean War had begun the preceding summer but appeared to be winding down quickly. However, just as Powell was settling into the Lutetia, the People's Republic of China, then newly Communist and considered the wildest of wild cards, entered the fray. This had ominous implications: China had recently signed a friendship accord with the Soviet Union, which was already known to possess nuclear weapons. The United Nations forces were routed and forced to retreat below the thirty-eighth parallel. In the winter of 1950, it seemed to many that a full-fledged global war was in the making; in hindsight, the world was closer to nuclear conflict than at any other time prior to the Cuban missile crisis of 1962.

"French elated at our Korean defeats," she wrote to Joe. "If direct war, word is that Russians would be in Paris overnight. . . . People have asked me where I intend to go when the big putsch comes."

By the middle of December, Powell was already planning her escape. Passage was evidently not available on the *Ile de France*, and the tickets she had been given by De Silver were nontransferable. So she wired Scribner's to request funding for an immediate return voyage, a request that was granted. "Things too shaky to anticipate being isolated here," she told Phyllis.

With her departure date set for early January, Powell crossed the English Channel and paid her first and only visit to London. She stayed near Piccadilly, at Brown's Hotel in Albermarle Street, then less well maintained, less baronial, and less costly than it is today. She found the English people a salutary change from the French, endowed with "matchless charm" and the wry wit that she believed was "strictly a British invention."

Powell had always dreamed of seeing London, and her mood was elevated by her brief stay there—of which, unfortunately, she left very few recorded impressions. She arrived back in New York on the S.S. *DeGrasse* on January 25, 1951. Glad to be home—she would never again take such a lengthy or ambitious leave—she was especially pleased by the improvement she noted in Jojo. "His best period so far," she wrote in March, having detected a new maturity in his comprehension and behavior.

She had done almost no writing in Europe, and when she took inventory of her progress on *The Wicked Pavilion*, she grew alarmed: "Novel began in January 1950—and it seems to me steadily worked on but actually only a little done." On July 29, she estimated that she had completed only fourteen pages in a year and a half.

Panic now set in—along with another self-described "suicidal period"—and she decided to change some of her professional associations. She dropped MCA and returned to the Brandt Agency. She set rigid work hours for herself and became enormously cross when they were violated. And finally, she decided to leave Scribner's.

There had been tension in her relations with the publishing house for some time, stemming mostly from a project that she had been championing for at least a dozen years but that Scribner's had shown no enthusiasm for whatsoever. Powell had been publishing short stories since 1919 and had long wanted to put together a collection; indeed, as early as 1940, she had offered to assemble an anthology of her work for Max Perkins. In general, volumes of short stories sold poorly, and Scribner's had consistently made it clear that it was not interested in producing such a book. Once more she pitched the idea, and once more she was turned down; this time, however, Powell took the rejection personally. "My feeling is that I need the confidence of a book coming out to make the novel good," she insisted.

On September 2, 1951, she wrote a warm but firm letter to John Wheelock, severing her ties with Scribner's and emphasizing her unhappiness about the impasse over her short stories. Houghton Mifflin was only too happy to sign her up—and the very first project was to be her cherished story collection.

It was Rosalind Baker Wilson—Edmund Wilson's eldest daughter—who brought Powell to Houghton Mifflin, a Boston-based house with a distinguished history. By 1951, Wilson was in her late twenties; funny, unpretentious, warmhearted, and a skillful editor, she lived on Louisburg Square on Beacon Hill, within walking distance of the company's offices at Two Park Street. Powell admired the younger woman enormously and empathized with the tribulations she must have experienced growing up with her distinguished and imperious father.

She placed Rosalind in the same league as her cousin Jack, whom she described as a "person who had such responsibilities and adult demands for understanding in youth that he carries the yearning for a childhood through life"—in other words, somebody like Powell herself. "In their masquerade as wide-eyed youth," she continued, "such people acquire a great deal more knowledge and human background than more openly cynical adults do—and this feeds into their work, giving Rosalind's writing a depth and compassion and brilliance."

For her part, Wilson considered Powell "certainly the wittiest person I have ever known, with a rapid-fire running commentary." She thought Powell at least as funny as Dorothy Parker, but she felt that her humor was more difficult to encapsulate in a mere quotation because she created full, detailed situations rather than bons mots. Their friendship would endure until Powell's death.

New contract signed, Powell sat down to read and evaluate the hundreds of stories she had written over the years. The result would be a slim volume of eighteen stories—some of them quite short indeed—called *Sunday, Monday and Always*. Published in June 1952, the collection is uneven. Powell continually fought off a tendency to overwrite, and she seems to have found this clipped, tautly controlled genre restrictive. Much of her best writing always went into inspired digressions from her plots, and such a method was not naturally suited to the traditional short-story form, which has room for few (if any) meanderings. She was herself aware of the shortcomings that marred many of her stories, which overlaid, she thought, an "excellent real treatment of character and dialogue on a structure of contrived, exaggerated and strained story." Moreover, a majority of these pieces were written—usually hurriedly—for no reason other than financial necessity, further compromising their quality.

The stories she culled for *Sunday, Monday and Always* are undoubtedly among her best. None of the early—and voluminous—work she did for such magazines as *Snappy Stories* or *College Humor* is included; indeed, the first entry is "Such a Pretty Day," which the *New Yorker* had published in 1933, a full decade and a half after she began to sell her fiction. ("Such a Pretty Day" is one of only five stories the *New Yorker* ever purchased from Powell; over the years, she received enough rejection slips from Katherine White, the magazine's fiction editor, to paper a small room.) Later inclusions came from such sources as *Collier's*, *Mademoiselle*, *Cosmopolitan*, and *Story*.

For many readers, the finest stories in the book are the ones that had not yet seen print—particularly "The Roof," with its unflinching portrait of an old, ailing man whom nobody wants, and "The Glads," an intricate, acerbic preparation for a grisly surprise ending. But these were not the sort of stories that were sought out by magazine editors: love interest was minimal, there were no happy endings, and Powell was just as contemptuous of determined "up-lifters" as H. L. Mencken had been. "The Roof," for example (which was written as "Troupial Bird"), had been turned down by *Harper's*, *Harper's Bazaar*, the *New Yorker*, *Today's Woman*, and *Mademoiselle*, among others, before it finally appeared in *Sunday, Monday and Always.*

It was Powell's dark, mordant attitude toward the world that rankled editors and many readers—and she knew it. "The Secret of My Failure," Powell headed a 1956 diary entry. "Just thought why I don't sell stories to popular magazines. All have subtitles—'Last time Gary saw Cindy she was a gawky child; now she was a beautiful woman. . . .' I can't help writing, 'Last time Fatso saw Myrt she was a desirable woman; now she was an old bag.'"

The reviews of *Sunday, Monday and Always* were excellent in their way, though many critics used the occasion to praise Powell's work in general rather than to laud these particular stories. Going down the list of eighteen selections in the *New York Times*, Orville Prescott checked off "seven as excellent, six as good and only five as ordinary"—not an especially impressive tally for thirty-five years' work. Prescott did, however, make note of the author's "sort of pity-ing insight": "Miss Powell actually seems to feel sincerely sorry for several of her frustrated, disappointed and unhappy characters."

Malcolm Cowley, an old friend who would subsequently become Powell's editor at Viking, wrote an appreciative review in the *New York Post* but begged, in the final line, for "more relief from these creeps, drips, jerks, phonies, fussbudgets, finaglers and fuddy-duddies."

The *Saturday Review* cheered Powell's ability to be "entertaining without becoming trivial." Moreover, "beneath their facades of bore-dom and suavity, her people are naïve, provincial and essentially rather decent human beings," the article, by William Peden, contin-ued. "The author seldom flogs or flays them. She likes them and is kind to them."

Finally, in the *New York Times Book Review*, then as now a related but semiautonomous entity within the larger newspaper, John Nerber called Powell a "satirist of great distinction," whose "pen is always double-edged; the savageness of her portrait is always balanced by the implication that the likeness is from life, and what a pity it is that life can be so dreadful. It is one of Miss Powell's triumphs that, somehow, unobtrusively, the warmth of her pity comes through."

The book apparently sold moderately well for such an anthology (probably about two thousand copies, after returns), and the author received a congratulatory letter from Paul Brooks, Houghton Mifflin's senior editor. It was an auspicious start for her new association.

As Powell had hoped, her momentum on *The Wicked Pavilion* had picked up again just around the time she knew her short-story collection would be published. She blamed *My Home Is Far Away* and her abortive work on *Marcia* for her miserable progress: "Each new day's labor seems to draw more blood instead of resuscitating it," she wrote.

> This began in *My Home Is Far Away,* when I was burning myself fishing live coals from what should have been a dead bonfire. By the time I had seared my soul, dressing my old wounds in new bandages—unrelieved, unilluminating, yet disguised—I had done myself the favor of taking the joy out of writing. Since then, all has been uphill with emotions spent on live situations and an increasing need to substitute ferocity of word thrust for feeling. By this time simple feeling in my writing has ended up in simple pain for me.

The opportunity to convey again her beloved New York was the key to her revitalization. "I am New York—this minute—now," she had written. "I know more about it than anyone—not historically but momentarily." One night, at the Hotel Lafayette, she had run into the writer Glenway Wescott, whom she knew only slightly but who told her she was immortalizing New York as Balzac had Paris. "It illumined my whole disorder," she said.

"Never forget geography," Powell wrote as she settled down to work on her new novel again. "New York is heroine. Make the city live so that reader walking about town thinks—here is the Fifth Avenue Hotel, where so and so came." By the middle of 1952, she was working steadily on *The Wicked Pavilion*; she would now be able to summon the strength to persist through the book.

In the meantime, she was also becoming involved in political activity for the first time since her youthful, halfhearted endeavors for the suffragist cause. Delighted by the easy humor and patrician intelligence of Adlai Stevenson, she joined a group of "Volunteers for Stevenson" and spent much of her free time campaigning on his behalf. She was deeply disgusted by the current crop of Republicans, who acted, she said, "as if America had no future and no hopes." She detested Joseph McCarthy and his spurious anti-Communist crusade, though her distrust of communism—and especially of most Communists—remained unwavering: "Thinking of Josie Herbst, Max Gorelik, Jack Lawson, etc. . . . . All these people in their earlier days were completely opportunistic, wanting money and able to butter up anybody for it." She particularly disliked Lillian Hellman, whom she considered a talentless self-promoter.

As she grew older, Powell found herself increasingly attracted to the company of younger people, and in these years she made a number of new such friends, among them Esther Andrews's affluent nephew Thomas Wanning, who became a favorite drinking partner, and Peter Martin, the love child of the anarchist Carlo Tresca and Bina Flynn, a sister of the American Communist leader Elizabeth Gurley Flynn. An editor and writer, Martin would eventually help establish two legendary bookshops, City Lights in San Francisco and the New Yorker on the Upper West Side of Manhattan.

Another friend Powell made in the early 1950s would later play an essential part in the revival of interest in her work; this was the young author Gore Vidal, whom she met through John Latouche. Vidal and Powell did not see one another often, but their meetings were always affectionate and mutually admiring. Powell pronounced Vidal a "genuine novelist—power at the wheel, a rich, regal, original mind with unlimited treasures and the serene generosity of one who knows he will come into more and more. Something of Disraeli—a high, patrician, Solomon-like judgment and philosophic power, with wit, poetry and music. Not to be fit in any fashion, but will outlive them all, like the great ones."

Vidal would repay these compliments in a 1987 article for the *New York Review of Books*. Writing at a time when Powell had been almost entirely forgotten, he called her "our best comic novelist" (an appraisal he would adjust to "our best midcentury novelist" for the *New Yorker* ten years later). The effect of Vidal's evaluation cannot be overstated; shortly after the piece appeared, Powell's major novels began to be reprinted, and eventually most of her best work was made available, some books for the first time in fifty years.

Powell's acquisition of such bright new acquaintances counteracted a number of personal losses she suffered during the same years. In October 1951, Virginia, the daughter born to Roy and Sabra Powell in 1916, died of cancer. After referring to the dead woman as a "delicate, sweet little thing bearing full brunt of my stepmother's nerve-wracking, nervous devotion," Powell realized that she didn't even know her half-sister's married name.

That name had been Virginia McLaughlin since 1937, and its owner had indeed been crushed down and harassed by Sabra for much of her life. Virginia's son, Richard McLaughlin, recalled that when his parents moved the twenty miles west from Oberlin to Norwalk, Ohio, "at least in part to get away from Sabra," only a few days elapsed before his maternal grandmother purchased a house two doors down the street and promptly moved in. Sabra herself would die in Norwalk in 1956.

The sudden death of her old friend Niles Spencer, in early 1952, moved Powell to near silence, her usual response to the most piercing tragedies. "Niles died," she wrote in her diary. "Cannot bear to think about this." So she didn't—at least not in any form that has been preserved, for the diary entry breaks off there. However, a couple of days later, she found herself wondering if the fact that she had been writing about the death of an artist (in *The Wicked Pavilion*) had somehow prefigured Spencer's demise. Powell had few mystical beliefs, but she was firmly convinced that she was gifted with a certain prescience—that her fiction often predicted events that were soon to happen to people she knew.

Although Powell was never especially close to Dylan Thomas, she spent enough time with him during his New York jaunts to be captivated by his legendary charm; moreover, she thought his poetry arresting, original, and musical. She was shocked and saddened when Thomas died at St. Vincent's Hospital in November 1953, having suffered a notorious "gross insult to the brain" after an exhaustive drinking session at Greenwich Village's White Horse Tavern.

As family and friends passed away, Powell also remarked disturbing changes in her city; she said she was no longer so fond of it as before because it was now "full of Americans." There exists a candid photograph of Powell that was shot around this time, probably on Sixth Avenue (which had lately—and futilely—been rechristened "Avenue of the Americas"). It is not one of her best likenesses: the photograph is slightly out of focus, and Powell is at her heaviest—170 pounds or more—standing on the street with a neutral expression on her face.

And yet she seems a fascinating fixed point, motionless within a riot of activity—the gigantic, unprecedentedly affluent New York making itself over with uncommon industry. One of the many cheaply made, cramped, and very expensive postwar apartment buildings is rising behind her (this was the era when Village developers made sure to give their monstrosities pompous and pseudo-arty names),while older brownstones stand precariously (and temporarily) off to her side. If the Village was "still the Village, after all," as Powell had proclaimed in 1918, it was now an altered version of itself. Necessarily, Powell, too, had changed; she had moved to New York just before her twenty-second birthday, a high-spirited, pixielike country girl out to conquer worlds. Now she was almost sixty, and a beaten-down, harried, and sorrowful sixty at that.

The New York Landmarks Preservation Commission would begin to come into its power only in the 1960s, too late to save the Hotel Lafayette and the Hotel Brevoort (both of which would qualify today as untouchable Manhattan treasures) and their neighbors on the block bounded by East Eighth and Ninth Streets, Fifth Avenue, and University Place—all unceremoniously demolished in the early 1950s. Powell paid scant attention to the actual destruction in her diary—"Lafayette is down," she noted on August 24, 1953—but she photographed the wreckage and would immortalize her longtime salon in *The Wicked Pavilion*.

It was in 1951 that Powell first began to be haunted by long, detailed, sometimes sentimental, sometimes macabre dreams about loved ones from her past. "I am exhausted by another night with the dead," she wrote on May 23. "As a matter of fact I have spent more time with the dead than with the quick, for as soon as I pop off to sleep there is my grandmother (dead since 1922) waiting or my father (1926) or my mother (1903) or my grandfather (1902) waiting with a picnic basket and I'm off for a shore dinner with the stiffs."

These dreams, she said, were "never dramatic or plot dreams (which would help me out in my work)"; instead, they were "usually outings and exclusively family except when some death in the newspapers the day before brings in a stranger such as Niles Spencer, Julie Garfield [the actor better known as John Garfield], or sometimes my own son, always four years old.*

---

* For whatever it is worth, Jojo turned four in 1925, the year his parents discovered how deeply disturbed he was and also the year that Whither, Powell's disowned first novel, was published.

The dreams persisted, and Powell began a sketch that she entitled, with typical bluntness, "Out with the Stiffs." She would work on it slowly, with no particular impetus to finish up, for the better part of a decade. In 1957, she would declare that if she ever wrote an autobiography—"horrible idea," she appended immediately—it should open with this piece.

Eventually, "Out with the Stiffs" would evolve into "A Lesson for Runaways" and then into "What Are You Doing in My Dreams?" under which title it would be published in *Vogue* in 1963. "It is as if the day I left Ohio I split in two at the crossroads, and went up both roads, half of me by day in New York and the other half by night with the dead in long-ago Ohio," she wrote. "How tired you can be in the morning after a night with the dead!"

These dreams were not only a new font of literary inspiration (despite what she decried as their lack of plot) but also, Powell believed, some sort of genuine communication with people she had loved: "Feel that much is being done by dreams now—as if the other D.P. is now working with me to get done all the things once started. In night I wake up and realize work is being done by my night self."

It was a curious and exhilarating experience for her, that sensations summoned from death should now be affirming her life. "I feel there is a sudden rush of utterly undeserved luck and attention weaving toward me and I must be braced not to be bowled over," she wrote on February 17, 1953. "Also, I know that my dead are all pitching together with me to hurry my work so I can join them. They arrange my ideas, give me stories, fill me with a long-ago mind, and I seem to be availing myself of their help."

CHAPTER NINE

The Collapse

~≈~

We have about sixty cents between us, and Post check doesn't come.

DAWN POWELL, 1958

POWELL COMPLETED *The Wicked Pavilion* in February 1954. For all the anxious effort she expended on it, all its fits and starts, the novel flows wonderfully well, and it has remained among the most popular of her New York books.

There are good reasons for that popularity. The wit is gentler here—and for many, easier to take—than in most of her earlier satires. The narrative is suffused with nostalgia for the Greenwich Village Powell remembered, and particularly for the old Lafayette (here called the Café Julien), where much of the action is set. The characters, however silly their delusions, are warm and fully fleshed out, the writing is careful (*too* careful, Powell fretted as she read through the galley proofs), and the story engages our sympathy from the beginning. As in *Turn, Magic Wheel*, we hear a great deal about one central figure long before we meet him, but when the artist known only as Marius (likely a bow to the aesthetician Walter Pater and his sole novel, *Marius the Epicurean*) appears toward the conclusion of *The Wicked Pavilion,* there is nothing anticlimactic about him.

The Wicked Pavilion is one of the few Powell novels that seem to grow organically out of their story, rather than dancing merrily around it. Nonetheless, there are several familiar figures in the narrative, notably the ghastly Okie from *Turn, Magic Wheel*, an "indefatigable, omnipresent, indestructible publisher, refugee from half a dozen bankruptcies, perennial Extra Man at the best dinners, relentless raconteur, and known far and wide as The Bore That Walks Like A Man."

Another oldtimer, Dennis Orphen, stands outside the action. He functions as a sort of fictional bookend, beginning *The Wicked Pavilion* with several paragraphs of reportage on the state of New York City in A.D. 1948 and then, almost three hundred pages later, bringing the novel to a close in a similar manner. Excepting a few passing references along the way, this is Orphen's lone contribution to the book. The mood he establishes is both vivid and bleak:

> There was nothing unusual about that New York winter of 1948 for the unusual was now the usual. Elderly ladies died of starvation in shabby hotels leaving boxes full of rags and hundred-dollar bills; bands of children robbed and raped through the city streets, lovers could find no beds, hamburgers were forty cents at lunch counters, truck drivers demanded double wages to properly educate their young in the starving high-class professions; aged spinsters, brides and mothers were shot by demented youths, frightened girls screamed for help in the night while police, in pairs for safety's sake, pinned tickets on parked automobiles. Citizens harassed by Internal Revenue hounds jumped out of windows for want of forty dollars, fam-

ilies on relief bought bigger television sets to match the new time-bought furniture. The Friendly Loan Agent, the Smiling Banker, the Laughing Financial Aid lurked in dark alleys to terrorize the innocent; baby sitters received a dollar an hour with torture concessions; universities dynamited acres of historic mansions and playgrounds to build halls for teaching history and child psychology. Men of education were allowed to make enough at their jobs to defray the cost of going to an office; parents were able, by patriotic investment in the world's largest munitions plant, to send their sons to the fine college next door to it, though time and labor would have been saved by whizzing the sons direct from home to factory to have their heads blown off at once.

Against this grim background, Powell launches immediately into a portrait of the Julien on a slow night in February 1948. Settling down to a dinner of pork chops and beer, Rick Prescott wonders why he keeps coming back to the run-down, overpriced, and not especially hospitable café. He asks his waiter to explain the spot's continuing appeal to a certain group of people:

> Philippe gave this question some judicious thought.
> "They come because they have always come here," he said.
> "Why did they come here the first time, then?"
> "Nobody ever comes to the Julien for the first time."

In short, the Julien is a hangout—an insular, convivial, cliquish spot that just somehow *happened,* a place where everybody has her own corner to command, his own role to play in the unspoken hierarchy. On this particular evening, Rick has come to the Julien in search of a lost love, Ellenora Carsdale, with whom he had a disquieting but exhilarating affair. The circle of characters also includes Jerry Dulaine (one of Powell's voracious women on the make) and

Elsie Hookley (a rebellious transplanted Boston matron), who live in the same apartment house and enjoy a bemused, improbable friendship. But Powell's main concern is with sending up yet another Manhattan Bohemia: this time the art world is in for the same treatment given the theatrical world in *The Happy Island* and the literary world in *Turn, Magic Wheel* and *The Locusts Have No King.*

Powell had always had a number of artist friends, including Reginald Marsh (who would provide the dust-jacket illustration for *The Wicked Pavilion*), Alexander Brook, Peggy Bacon, Peter Blume, Stuart Davis, Loren MacIver, and the much-lamented Niles Spencer. By the early 1950s, with the Lafayette on the verge of demolition, she had begun to frequent the Cedar Bar on Eighth Street, soon to become the epicenter for the lubrications of the Abstract Expressionist movement. She was well prepared to turn her satirist's gaze on the visionaries and the frauds, the serious scholars and the pretentious hangers-on (the preposterous Okie, no less, has a "theory about Marius' final use of white"), the avaricious dealers and gallery owners, the mercurial ascent and crash of reputations.

With this object in mind, Powell weaves much of her story around two less-than-successful painters, Dalzell Sloane and Ben Forrester, who are suddenly hot commodities because of their past association with the dear departed Marius, whose fame—and prices—have shot through the roof. As the novel proceeds, Dalzell and Ben begin to create forged masterpieces in the style of Marius, and matters grow more and more complicated right up to the surprisingly moving resolution.

Despite Dennis Orphen's depressive prologue and the concluding demolition of the Café Julien, *The Wicked Pavilion* is suffused with an autumnal warmth; Powell's passion for New York is clearly undimmed. How many adopted New Yorkers will not recognize some part of their younger selves in this description of Rick Prescott's initial walk through midtown?

It was the first time he'd ever been in New York, the city of his dreams, the first time he'd worn his officer's uniform, the first time he'd been drunk on champagne. New York loved him as it loved no other young man, and he embraced the city, impulsively discarding everything he had hitherto cherished of his Michigan boyhood loyalties. In Radio City Gardens he looked up at the colossal Prometheus commanding the city's very heart and thought, Me! He wandered up and down in a kind of smiling daze, slipped away from the buddies and home-town friends supervising his departure and strolled happily down Fifth Avenue, finding all faces beautiful and wondrously kind, the lacy fragility of the city trees incomparably superior to his huge native forests. Under the giant diesel hum of street and harbor traffic he caught the sweet music of danger, the voices of deathless love and magic adventure.

Much as Manhattan may have changed in the years since these words were written, such epiphanies remain both frequent and timeless.

Published in the early fall of 1954, *The Wicked Pavilion* would rank with *A Time to Be Born* as Powell's best-selling book during her lifetime, with a total print run of nine thousand.* It was certainly among her grandest successes. This was her only novel to make the *New York Times* best-seller list (even if only for one week, that of October 17, 1954); moreover, it was reviewed on the front page of the *New York Herald Tribune*. It is true that Powell never received the attention she deserved during her lifetime, but contrary to legend, she was never a completely neglected author, and this was one of her better moments.

In his book column for the *Times,* Charles Poore drew comparisons with Thackeray: "This is Miss Powell's *Vanity Fair* of a resolutely

---

* *Tracking down exact figures for Powell's sales and returns at Houghton Mifflin has proved impossible.*

uprooted generation that has had so many homes it can only call
home now an oasis of the gourmets stared at by flitting trippers and
presided over by totemic waiters. It is a modern morality play, a
chronicle written with a kind of furious compassion, savage grace
and style, wit and ribald laughter."

Frederic Morton, writing in the same paper, liked the book but
seemed intent on converting Powell into some sort of moral crusader, a role for which she was distinctly unsuited. "What appears
most fundamentally lacking is the sense of outrage which serves as
engine to even the most sophisticated satirist," Morton argued.
"Miss Powell does not possess the pure indignation that moves Evelyn Waugh to his absurdities and forced Orwell into his haunting
contortions. Her verbal equipment is probably unsurpassed among
writers of her genre—but she views the antics of humanity with too
surgical a calm."

Powell had an important champion in the successful English
novelist and playwright J. B. Priestley, who wrote about her new
book in the London Sunday *Times.* "I never miss anything Dawn Powell writes," he said.

> [*The Wicked Pavilion*] is not her best work but it will serve. I
> mention it because she has not been published over here, I
> think, for some time, and I wish her earlier novels could be
> reissued (Penguin—forward!). Many readers who would enjoy
> her sardonic wit and ingenious plotting have probably been
> misled by her name, which suggests ultra-romantic magazine
> serials. Her fiction is about as much like them as *asperges vinai-
> grettes* is like a chocolate sundae.*

Back in America, Brendan Gill recommended *The Wicked Pavilion* in the *New Yorker:* "If what you hope for in a novel is that, witty and

---

* For her part, Powell thought her name conjured up the image of an unsuccessful stripper.

yet serious, it will depict interesting people stumbling into and struggling out of interesting dilemmas and yet will neither break your heart nor leave you in a state of post-soap-operative shock, you are advised to try *The Wicked Pavilion*," he wrote. "Miss Powell is witty and serious and her outlook is neither Kafka-black nor Rinso-white."

The author herself was pleased with the novel and claimed to miss working on it when it was done. "As a writer you live the lives of your characters so intently and for such a long time—years, usually—that it's a great relief to get [a book] published and go back to living your own life for a little while, at least till the next novel starts crowding you," she stated for the Houghton Mifflin publicity department. "But *The Wicked Pavilion* was different—I think because it was so contemporary that every day something more happens that belongs in it. It's too late, of course—it can't go on running like a TV serial. What I wanted to do in this book especially was to make the characters live so that their lives could extend beyond the limits of the book and I may have succeeded too well for my own peace of mind."

That "peace of mind" was threatened anyway, for Jojo had taken a sharp turn for the worse. His life had been proceeding without undue disturbance at the Gladwyne Colony in Pennsylvania, where he worked in a hospital gift shop and enthusiastically took part in the daily religious services. He was permitted to pay regular visits home, where his beloved Louise Lee awaited him, sometimes in company with the young man she had raised as her son, Bobby Morrison, whom Jojo considered his best friend.

The routine had been shattered, however, on May 14, 1954, when Lee, while working at the Goushas' apartment, suffered a severe stroke and collapsed to the floor, unconscious. The tiny Powell somehow managed to load the substantial Louise into a shopping cart and push her the half mile to St. Vincent's Hospital—a surreal image. There Louise lay, partially paralyzed, for more than a month, with Powell footing all of her medical bills. Eventually, she was moved to a home in Perth Amboy, New Jersey, where she made a modest recovery, but she would never regain sufficient strength to resume her duties with Jojo.

This was the first time Powell's son had lost somebody so dear to him, and he did not take it well. He grew obsessed with the absent "Deesie"—where was she? why couldn't he see her? when was she coming back?—and in his desperation, he ran away from the Gladwyne Colony once too often. The Gladwyne administrators, fed up with Jojo's tantrums (and, most likely, with the Gousha family's chronically delinquent payment), let it be known that his welcome at the colony had come to an end.

Jojo thus came home to live at 35 East Ninth Street, where there was nobody but his mother and father to look after him; like most autistic persons, he did not make friends easily, and a fitting substitute for Louise could not be found. At first Powell was happy with his presence and confident that she could accomplish more with Jojo at home alone than she had ever been able to do when Louise was there with him. "Adversity has its advantages," she said.

On July 29, though, everything fell apart. "He got slowly worked up over 'Will Deesie never come back?'" Powell wrote to her sister Phyllis, "and then this worked out into an obsession about wanting to be black, and repeating this over and over with other angles till I had to face the fact that it would get worse and what form would it take—?

"I know we alone cannot handle the case even if we did nothing else," she continued,

> nor if we had two permanent attendants for him, as his nervous energy is terrific, more or less feeding on others' to nourish itself so everybody around is a wreck by night when he will say innocently "I enjoyed the sail today and the walk and now let's take a bus ride over New York before playing parchesi and read-

ing Mark Twain!" *Every* day! And never knowing when a criticism or sharp word from somebody may set him off into either hysterics, tantrums or black-outs.

Realizing that she and Joe could no longer afford a private institution, Powell set her sights on placing Jojo in a public hospital, Creedmore, operated by the City of New York. There was a catch, however: her son would first have to undergo two weeks of observation at Bellevue Hospital in midtown Manhattan. Powell was initially impressed with Bellevue; there were more young people than at Gladwyne, and the facility offered some experimental courses in art and music therapy. But Jojo tried to break out before his two weeks were up, and he was then confined to a restricted ward. Powell visited him and could scarcely choke back her tears when he told her, "Mother, if you weren't sick when you came in this place, you would be when you got out."

It was ultimately decided that Jojo was too disturbed to live at the relatively low-security Creedmore, and he was transferred instead to the Manhattan State Hospital on Ward's Island, beneath the Triboro Bridge near East 125th Street. Travelers to New York routinely pass the hospital on their way in from the Queens airports: Manhattan State consists primarily of three tall, tan, monumentally ugly brick buildings with metal grates covering the windows. A more forbidding environment would be difficult to imagine. This would be Jojo's home for the next dozen years—indeed, until long after his parents had both died, at which point he became a ward of New York State.

Initially, Powell detested Manhattan State and everything about it. She bewailed the Spartan, prison cell–like living quarters, and what she termed the "lostness of having no treasure chest of one's own, no place for private letters, a handkerchief, etc." She was disappointed to find that Jojo had taken up cigarette smoking ("Mother, it's the only pleasure I have," was his pitiful rejoinder). He had been

prescribed Thorazine, a powerful antipsychotic medication and de-
pressant that kept him in a continuous near-stupor. There was even
some discussion of performing a prefrontal lobotomy, then a not-
uncommon operation; only the passionate intervention of John Dos
Passos, who implored the Goushas not to let the medical establishment use Jojo as a guinea pig, dissuaded Dawn and Joe from giving
the go-ahead.

Fortunately, not long before, autism had been recognized as a
distinct psychological condition, and serious research had begun into
its causes and treatment. A young doctor affiliated with Manhattan
State, Howard Zucker, found Jojo of enormous interest and worked
with him privately. In 1996, Zucker, who remembered their association vividly, sat with me for an interview. A conscientious physician,
he would not violate the confidentiality of his doctor-patient relationship with the still-living Jojo, but within carefully delineated
boundaries, he was both eloquent and helpful.

"I found some striking similarities between the boy and his
mother," Zucker said. "I've now read through the diaries [which had
just been published] and it seems to me that both of them were subject to vast mood swings. Both of them had problems controlling
their anger. Both of them had phenomenal memories—Joe could
recite whole pages of Dickens by heart. And both of them had a tendency toward wordplay and a disposition to make fun of things.

"For example," he continued, "religion was terribly important
to Joe"—Zucker never called him Jojo—"and yet he wrote his own
Christmas carols that had some of his mother's sarcasm. I remember
one called 'Hokum, All Ye Faithful.'"

Zucker was impressed by the hopes that Powell invested in her
son. "So many of the parents of troubled children are either disturbed themselves or, if not, give up on their children very early on,"
he explained. "I always had the sense that Powell was deeply interested and absolutely sincere in her concern for Joe."

For her part, Powell considered Zucker something of a miracle worker. "We noticed a new advance in Jojo's control," she wrote to him in early 1957, after an extended outpatient visit.

> He was much more assured of his own importance. He referred to "*my* apartment," "*my* home," "*my* friend" instead of "the" or "our." The lack of medication (and quiet) seemed to have made him more sensible about commonplace things and aware of personalities around him, too, telling anecdotes about other patients or repeating what they had said. He seemed relaxed and confident of your belief in him.

"Several patients had told him the reason he had his vomiting spells was the manner he smoked—gulping and swallowing—so he informed me he wasn't going to smoke all weekend," she continued.

> He seems finally assured that his home is his—he sleeps late, bathes and shaves himself, gets himself coffee or whatever he wants, makes tea and brings it in for both of us when he likes, makes the beds and, without any fuss, adapts himself increasingly to the family habits and routines. He reads for long periods instead of glancing over something, and went to considerable trouble fishing out articles on Manhattan State in some newspapers, which he pored over with great interest.

Her experience with Dr. Zucker changed Powell's opinion of Manhattan State—and for that matter, of public hospitals in general. "There is always a chance in a rotating staff of a state institution (rather than a private one) of a new drug, a sympathetic doctor or companion," she wrote. Zucker concurred with Powell's analysis: "At the time I was seeing Joe, experimentation with medication was more advanced in state hospitals than in private ones, which were uncertain and unready to take a chance," he said.

Still, there was one ward in the facility where life was markedly more hellish than anything at such elite institutions as Gladwyne or Seagirt. When Jojo was at his angriest—and almost anything could trigger him—he would be removed to a ward known as M-5. "This was where the most disturbed patients were aggregated in an effort to better control them," Zucker recalled. "Such a place is wild and disturbing in itself. Everybody who is there is in a period of real upset, and it is an extremely stimulating experience to have a lot of other upset people around you all expressing that upset at the same time. I should think the situation has improved since then, but public hospitals still have problems dealing with a large number of deeply upset people." To judge from Powell's diaries and letters, Jojo was confined in M-5 for a few days at least once or twice a year.

Even after Zucker left the hospital, in the late 1950s, he continued to visit Jojo whenever he could. "I felt badly about breaking off the relationship, because in my mind he needed that sort of steadiness," he said. "We corresponded every Christmastime—his upset periods usually came around Christmas, Easter, or his birthday. Finally, in 1986, he sent me a letter, and for the first time he was angry at me and he demanded that I visit him right away. Well, I was unable to visit him at that time, and I never heard from him again."

As Louise Lee recovered from her stroke, Powell would occasionally travel with Jojo to New Jersey, where they found his old nurse calmly on the mend, "obviously pleased to have people at her beck and call instead of vice versa." (Powell went on here to make the unique, baffling—and of course stunningly incorrect—statement that "Negroes don't have to pay taxes. They enjoy rights and also feudal privileges.") In time, Louise would move to a religious nursing home in her native Boston, where she would die in 1960. The ever-loyal Jojo would still be talking of her in the 1990s.

Powell became a prolific free-lance writer again in the mid-1950s. On skimming through the tawdry, sensationalist pages of the current incarnation of the *New York Post*, a reader may have difficulty imagining that this was once a serious newspaper, with an unusually distinguished book column (James T. Farrell, Malcolm Cowley, and others of their stature were regular contributors to its pages). Powell, who had written for the *Post* intermittently back in the 1920s, now returned to the paper to earn some additional money.

Roughly a hundred of Powell's reviews have been identified (the *Post* has never been indexed), and for the most part they make for depressing reading. There are some amusing remarks along the way, to be sure, and it is interesting to read her responses to this or that important (or not-so-important) book when it was new; but as a daily book critic, Powell—who could be so wonderfully astute and perceptive when writing about a work that intrigued her in a letter or a diary—was little more than a talented hack. Sifting through these terse, necessarily formulaic notices, we can almost hear her meter ticking. We sense her impatience to finish up what she considered scut work, and to return to her true calling.

She enjoyed much of what she covered, from the first collection of cartoons by Jules Feiffer through *Short Stories from Russia Today* to analyses of the murder trials of Sam Sheppard and Lizzie Borden (both of whom she believed to be innocent). But she often lapsed into the lamest journalese to express her pleasure. Louis Kronenberger's *A Month of Sundays,* for example, was a "brilliant literary feat—in fact, a godsend!" and Allen Churchill's *The Improper Bohemians* "should provide enough kindling for a fine weekend." She closed an otherwise thoughtful appraisal of *The Living Novel,* a symposium edited by Granville Hicks, with the bland summation, "It's a good show, all told."

Other reviews were more mixed. John O'Hara's *Ourselves to Know* was greeted with grudging praise; Powell recognized a pro but didn't much like the book itself. She thought Mary McCarthy's *The Oasis* (complete with a picture of the "pretty author evidently reclining on the other end of Truman Capote's couch") opened superbly but ended up "magisterially dull." She appended some personal recollections to her critiques of biographies of Robert

Benchley and Dylan Thomas, and savaged *Beloved Infidel*, Sheilah Graham's first memoir of F. Scott Fitzgerald.

Powell seemed particularly interested in the more celebrated women writers then working in France. Of Nathalie Sarraute's *The Planetarium,* she said that the author's "jeweled wisdom gives depth and new illumination to ancient truths of human behavior." But she thought very little of Françoise Sagan and actively disliked Simone de Beauvoir's *America Day by Day,* which she considered a classic example of European arrogance: "Americans don't agree on which are America's great writers, old or new, she complains, and though Mme. de Beauvoir grants that differences of opinion do occasionally exist in her own country, that, after all, is France." De Beauvoir's modern-day America "seems more remote than Mrs. Trollope's of the 1830s," Powell summarized, adding that Trollope was a "far keener and more independent observer."

She recommended two biographies by her old friend Charles Norman, of Ezra Pound and e. e. cummings. This was an odd and touching payback: thirty years before, Norman had published one of the few welcoming reviews of her first novel, *Whither*, in these same pages. She was an early admirer of Edward Gorey ("Mr. Gorey's humor is not sick; it is merely fatal") and wrote appreciatively of Randall Jarrell's *Pictures from an Institution* and Harvey Swados's *Nights in the Gardens of Brooklyn.* She was willing to allow herself to be unexpectedly carried away (one mark of a mature critic), as she was by *The Waters of the End*, the first—and, it seems, only—novel by a young American writer named Charles Ingle, whom she placed on a level with Henry Green, Malcolm Lowry, Djuna Barnes, and Glenway Wescott.

Like many readers since, Powell was both fascinated and perplexed by *The Recognitions*, the gigantic, almost impossibly erudite first novel by William Gaddis. "Mr. Gaddis has wit and a vast fund of information, assets that tend to cancel each other out," she wrote. "The reader scampering to catch the ever-defaulting hero in his many guises through bordellos and monasteries is exasperated by Author Gaddis as Ancient Mariner, waylaying him with lectures on the Church Fathers, the Anti-Christ Descartes or the *Book of the Dead.*"

It is not surprising that the agnostic Powell, who gave hardly a thought to religion of any kind, should have become frustrated at Gaddis's obsessive and often mocking allusions to saints, relics, and church history; his irreverence horrified believers and delighted "fallen" Catholics, but it had little relevance to Powell's concerns. She must have been at least intrigued by the publication of another major book about artists who made their living through forgery; the hustlers and poseurs in *The Recognitions* are not so dissimilar from those in *The Wicked Pavilion.* Reading both books back to back, one gets the distinct impression that Gaddis and Powell attended the same parties and merely reported them differently.

In addition to her work for the *Post,* Powell adapted two stories for television, one a vastly expanded version of "You Should Have Brought Your Mink" (a tiny vignette collected in *Sunday, Monday and Always*) and the other an unidentified episode for the television program "Studio One." Neither seems actually to have been telecast. She also agreed to cut, revise, and rewrite *Angels on Toast* for a mass-market pulp paperback published by Fawcett Gold Medal. She spent two months on this dubious project, beginning in August 1955 and turning in the finished book, now titled *A Man's Affair,* on October 13.

A Man's Affair need not long detain us. It was written in great haste and entirely for money (of which Powell saw only about five hundred dollars; Scribner's collected much of her thousand-dollar fee to recoup her twenty-year-old advance). In no way does it improve upon her initial conception—quite the reverse, in fact: the "new" version is sketchy and sloppy, with little of the slapdash energy that makes the original *Angels on Toast* so appealing. Powell was apparently pressured by her editors to "sex it up"—a pressure she resisted. "This push-button sex doesn't work except for undersexed readers," she reflected. "Most exciting thing is the longing—a caveman pounce often paralyzes the response in a female. Explicit sex can freeze."

A more significant project was the brief, uncharacteristic novel Powell was writing for Houghton Mifflin, eventually to be published as *A Cage for Lovers*. She had begun to sketch what she called a "nurse story" in February 1955, as her "personal rebellion" against the proposed sequel to *My Home Is Far Away*. She worked on *A Cage for Lovers* during a month at Yaddo, an invitational artists' retreat near Saratoga Springs, New York, that she found much more congenial than the MacDowell Colony. By July 5 she could report with satisfaction that she was already up to page 60. "'Marcia' was a much better book but for sheer limbering up I need this one," she wrote in her diary. "So far I do not feel anything distinguished or gay about it, certainly nothing funny, but I did want to pacify a public that seems to regard wit—especially if it sounds original or spontaneous—as immoral."

Indeed, *A Cage for Lovers* is almost unrelievedly solemn. A latter-day reader occasionally has the sensation that Powell was deliberately suppressing any tendency whatsoever toward humor (rather the same sense one has while watching Woody Allen's similarly atypical film *Interiors*). Rightly or wrongly, however, Powell was fully conscious of what she was doing. "There is no wit or humor in this story, so it may be successful," she wrote in April 1956, when the novel was about half finished. "Waugh, Huxley, Thurber—none were really able to make a decent living until they lost their sense of humor and practically their ability to feel."

The story itself is relatively uneventful. Christine Drummond, the young charge of a wealthy dowager named Miss Lesley Patterson, finds herself suffocated by the jealous affection of her benefactor and by the near-constant attention she demands. Escaping, she flees to Paris, where she discovers just how tough it is to get by without the financial and emotional coddling to which she has grown accustomed. Eventually, Miss Lesley has a stroke, Christine feels compelled to return to her, and the book comes to an end.

Powell herself provided a fair summary of the psychological drama underlying *A Cage for Lovers* when she wrote to Rosalind Wilson, her editor, "The story actually describes what happened when a girl said—as so many of us say most of our lives—'What am I doing here?'":

> She has been living other people's lives—first her mother's, and then Miss Lesley Patterson's, until she can scarcely tell what sort of person she is. It is basically the story of an impulsive, warm young woman, detoured but not corrupted by her quick affections, escaping to find her own special destiny. The search for herself is as suspenseful as if the quarry were her enemy.

She tried on a number of titles—among them *Bridesmaid*, *Lady in Waiting*, *Wedding Dress*, *Shadow of Love*, and *The Ways of Love*—that were better suited for popular pulp romance fiction than for the intricate psychological study she had planned. Finally settling on *A Cage for Lovers*, she handed in a first draft to Houghton Mifflin on March 12, 1957.

Powell's publisher had been uncommonly supportive of her during the creation of *A Cage for Lovers*, even going so far as to put her up in the Ritz-Carlton Hotel, overlooking the Boston Public Garden, for a week of intensive work in the summer of 1956. But while Rosalind Wilson was enthusiastic about the finished book, others at the firm were less pleased, and Powell was persuaded to cut several key scenes, rearrange others, and remove much of the Parisian detail she had been storing up since her visit to France in 1950. (It was suggested to her that the powers-that-be at Houghton Mifflin were concerned that it might "turn into another Paris Left Bank sort of book.")

And so it is difficult to evaluate *A Cage for Lovers* because, according to Powell, the finished product really wasn't hers. As published, it is her shortest novel by far, at barely forty-five thousand words. Most of her friends were confused and disappointed by it, with the notable exception of Edmund Wilson, who thought *Cage* a "masterly performance" with "French-type purity of style and sense of classical form." Unfortunately, he wrote these words in private correspondence rather than for print.

Although Powell would later claim that the novel had been ruined in the editing process, she held Rosalind Wilson blameless for the company's meddling, according to a diary entry from 1964. She in fact planned to bequeath all rights to the book to her Houghton editor. We may never know exactly what Powell intended with this minor, unusual, but sporadically eloquent and haunting book: though the manuscript existed as late as 1992, it has now apparently vanished.* Should an original typescript ever be found and published, it may be necessary to revise our opinion of *A Cage for Lovers*.

The reviews were few and concise, usually vaguely favorable but nothing more. After describing Powell as a "professional writer" (high praise for somebody who had already published fourteen novels!), Lenard Kaufman, in the *New York Times Book Review,* asserted that her books had "structure, purpose and meaning." In *A Cage for Lovers,* she was "saying very clearly that love—all love—is a trap," he continued, "and she states her case convincingly. One does wish, however, that she had declined the temptation, at the end, to tie up all the ribbons into a package that is just a little too neat, a little too pat. It detracts from the basic vitality of her book."

On the author's home turf, the *New York Post*, Martha Mac-Gregor began her article with an encomium on Powell's work in general: "She is not imitative, nor has she imitators. . . . The trademark of her work is her wit, which is genuinely funny, sometimes extremely unkind and never merely clever. . . . No one can beat her at the penetrating sentence which sizes up a person or a situation in

---

* *The strange case of Powell's private papers is examined in the epilogue.*

one shrewd comment." However, she went on gingerly to suggest that this new book "does not display her special talent for satire with the fireworks of some of her novels."

Mary Ross, who had begun reviewing Powell's work in the *New York Herald Tribune* with *The Bride's House* in 1929, was allotted only a four-inch column for her latest critique (this despite the fact that just three years earlier, *The Wicked Pavilion* had been splashed over the front page of the Sunday book section). "This is not a simple tale but a novel in substance," Ross wrote, "its apparent simplicity reflecting a high degree of sophistication. Offbeat, so to speak, it serves, among other things, as an eloquent reminder of some of the tribulations of youth."

Maurice Dolbier, a writer for the *Herald Tribune,* interviewed Powell shortly after the publication of *A Cage for Lovers.* "I remember the day only in an alcoholic haze," he said in 1993.

> Back then, the publicity departments at publishing houses kept well-stocked bars as part of doing business, and we drank most of the afternoon. I had interviewed Ayn Rand just the day before and I'd begun by asking her what she thought was the principal function of the novelist in the twentieth century. This greatly excited Rand and she went on for about an hour— about communism and capitalism, on the superiority of Plato to Aristotle, even throwing in some extended commentary about Rachmaninoff, as I recall.
>
> Well! I decided to start off by asking Dawn the same question—what did *she* think was the principal function of the novelist in the twentieth century? And she said, "Oh, that's easy— to keep out of everyone's way." I liked her straight off.

Dolbier and Powell became friends after this and saw one another fairly regularly, most often at meetings of the international writers' advocacy group, PEN. At one point she requested that he come by and interview her again, confiding, "I've changed my entire childhood since I saw you last."

She told Dolbier that *Dance Night* was her favorite among her novels; *A Cage for Lovers,* she said, was merely a "good book." But she defended the new novel in her diaries:

> Still convinced that it is a delicate, skillful dissection of Inherited Money Complacency. Like a dope addict, Miss Lesley wants to see others depend on it so she can constantly see its superiority to all human qualities or contentments proved. Take away the really limitless rewards of human qualities and emotions and make these fortunate people depend, like herself, on the solid, steady assurance of stocks and bonds—then let them try to get those and see who is boss.

A Cage for Lovers sold poorly—well under its initial press run of four thousand copies—and has not been generally available since the 1960s. Yet it has always exerted a curious fascination for actors and filmmakers. Immediately after its publication, the actress Anne Baxter phoned Powell to inquire about stage and movie rights, and in 1981, long after Powell's death, some serious interest was expressed in turning *A Cage for Lovers* into a movie. In the end, nothing came of either project.

Eventually, Powell developed a calm perspective on this unsuccessful detour: "I regard *Cage for Lovers* as a vacation from myself—a sabbatical from which I return to self, renewed."

Powell's social life was a major component in her renewal. It sometimes seems that she met every celebrated person in New York at least once; reading through her diaries, one regularly comes across entries noting such things as "Bobby Lewis's wonderful party for Lena Horne with Peggy Fears, Marlene Dietrich, Gloria Vanderbilt, Truman Capote, Tennessee Williams." But she was no snob, and she got along just as well with people she met on buses and subways or in stores, restaurants, and bars.

Her intimates, however, were few and carefully chosen. Coby Gilman was still among them, of course, though he had become such a sloppy and constant drunkard that Powell often tired of him, once going so far as to pour a tureen of hot soup over his head in full view of some horrified onlookers. This was not an isolated incident: as Powell aged and her life grew ever more difficult, she increasingly allowed the ferocious internal furies so often described in her diaries to surface and explode. At these times, her behavior could be abrupt, caustic, and even brutal.

She remained especially close to John Dos Passos, Edmund Wilson, Gerald and Sara Murphy, and—mostly through letters—Esther Andrews. Canby Chambers would die in 1958, and Andrews herself would begin to suffer from what was likely Alzheimer's disease; she would die in 1962.

Andrews Wanning, Esther Andrews's nephew and later an English professor, occasionally joined his brother Tommy and Powell at the Cedar Bar. "The decor was very undistinguished—poor marble-topped tables all over the place," he would recall in 1994. "But all the artists were there and so was Dawn, almost every night. Her favorite companion was a taxi driver who would get off his shift at midnight and come in for a nightcap. Dawn loved to talk with him in a somewhat philosophic vein—sharing thoughts about life and politics and one thing or another. She found him interesting. As a rule, the artists themselves were simply not that brilliant to talk to."

The crowd at the Cedar might include Jackson Pollock, Willem de Kooning, Robert De Niro Sr., and Franz Kline (of whom Powell was especially fond). She much enjoyed the myriad sexual intrigues of the tavern: the array of young women so eager to sleep with lauded artists and thus prove themselves "Villagers," and the artists themselves only too happy to cooperate. She would incorporate some of the Cedar scene into her last book, *The Golden Spur*.

"When she had the right amount of booze in her, she was the funniest woman I ever knew," Wanning said. "Cold sober, I never found her that funny—and when she had had too much to drink she wasn't funny at all. She got rather obstreperous and tossed herself around."

Powell saw a good deal of the poet and editor Lloyd Frankenberg and his wife, the artist Loren MacIver, near neighbors of hers and Joe's in the Village and friends of many years' standing. "Joe was a very retiring man, who kept pretty much to himself," MacIver remembered in 1993, "but Dawn was genuinely sweet, and so terribly concerned about her son. I like the phrase 'detained in childhood' to describe Jojo.

"As for her wit, I thought it was mostly honest and goodhearted, even rather kindly," she continued. "When she had somebody on a pin, you always had the sense that she had him there only to inspect him, to learn something about him—and about herself. You *knew* she would eventually let him go."

Powell still remained in touch with some chums from her early youth—mainly Lake Erie girls such as Eleanor Farnham and, until her death in 1958, Charlotte Johnson—and resumed a correspondence with her first New York roommate, Katherine Vedder, now known as K. V. Busch and running a realty company in Biloxi, Mississippi. She made some new friends, too. Monroe Stearns, a teacher, writer, and editor, was among the closest of these, a man of such sincerity and charm that he even won over the reclusive Joseph Gousha, to become one of the few people Dawn and Joe regularly saw together.

They first met through Coby, who had translated several French novels for Prentice-Hall, where Stearns was working. Stearns shared

Powell's passion for the work of Charles Dickens, whom they both thought grossly misunderstood. She once proposed that the two of them collaborate on an unconventional sort of Dickens reader:

> The dowdy and soppy aspects of Dickens have been drummed into us for so long that the sheer wit and brilliance of many passages has been neglected. I don't mean the jolly Pickwickish sort of thing but the kind of wit that later became peculiarly Bright Young Englishman wit—the Noël Coward school. The reason for the durability of these bubbles is that they are actually not superficial or mere smart fizz but are genuine champagne from the very best grapes and the very best-manured soil.

This was one of two editorial projects that particularly appealed to Powell at the time; she also wanted to gather together a volume of foreign impressions of the United States, incorporating the work of Dickens, the Trollopes, de Tocqueville, and others. Neither idea would ever come to fruition.

Powell still enjoyed the company of handsome young men, and her interest in them was not always platonic. Her editor from *Mademoiselle* days, the novelist George Davis, had recently died, and his nephew Peter, a student at Miami University in Ohio, came to visit her one evening in 1959 with the intention of gathering reminiscences for a biography he planned to write of his uncle. Powell was then acting as caretaker for Margaret De Silver's apartment (her friend was away for the summer), and she invited him up for supper.

The moment Peter Davis arrived, Powell made him a large gin drink. "I didn't want to seem ungracious, but I'm allergic to gin, so I waited for the right opportunity and then poured it out," he recounted in 1997. Powell immediately refilled his glass, made some hamburgers stuffed with cottage cheese—which "fell apart while she was cooking them but still tasted delicious"—and then brought out a collection of pornographic art. "She seemed intent on my looking at the pictures closely, and she watched my reactions as I did so," Davis said. "I had the distinct impression she was waiting for me to make a pass at her, and she made it very clear she didn't want me to leave. But I was twenty-three years old and fairly innocent, and a little anxious, and I just didn't have any sexual interest in her. She was terribly nice, however—a wonderful raconteur." For her part, Powell was moved by the young man's devoted interest in his "near-famous" uncle: "That night, as we drank gin and ate hamburgers, a George was recreated of such magnificence and genius that it is a wonder he could ever have stayed dead."

She was also unusually impressed by a young English art historian and curator named Bryan Robertson, whom she met while he was on a tour of American museums and galleries. "He finds me a combination of the Queen Mother and Mae West, God forbid," she wrote. "He is probably the most charming, honest young fellow I ever met—even on second meeting."

Robertson had called her on impulse. "Her books had just begun to come out in England and she was very well reviewed in the British press," he would explain in 1997. "I had read *The Wicked Pavilion* and had been especially taken by *My Home Is Far Away*. We had a mutual friend in common, Robert Coates, who suggested I ring her up the next time I was in New York. So I did."

They ate at a Longchamps Restaurant near Powell's apartment. "The first time it was just the two of us, but I later came to know Joe and Coby as well," Robertson said. "Coby was charming, very likeable, harmless, a little clouded but not really befuddled. I saw him as the licensed jester, the courtier—somebody to open bottles, say gentlemanly things, and cue jokes for Dawn."

Robertson discerned two definite and contradictory strains in Powell's personality. On the one hand, "she was very independent and self-possessed for her time, rather amazingly so—keeping her own name, paying her way, doing her thing, and taking an assertive, almost masculine attitude toward sex."

And yet on the other hand, she also had a "near-Edwardian sense of propriety," Robertson found. "Like a number of important authors in this century—F. Scott Fitzgerald and Ford Madox Ford come to mind—she believed in chivalry, gallantry, and a traditional code of good behavior. I can imagine her having a one-night stand with somebody—so long as that was all it would ever be—but never having a second relationship, not while Joe was alive. That would have been out of line."

Another younger friend, this one female, was Russia Luca Hughes, an educator who was for many years a research assistant to psychologist Kenneth Clark. Powell was especially partial to Hughes's children, Morgan and Neill. "I think she really enjoyed Neill most of all," Hughes said in 1995. "They would have long, intricate, and fascinating conversations together. It was a special bond."

Then there was Peter Martin's radiantly beautiful "California blond" girlfriend Jacqueline Miller (later Jacqueline Miller Rice), who would become Powell's executor. Her fulfillment of those duties will come in for some criticism, but there can be no doubt that she was a devoted, generous, and almost worshipful companion to Powell during the latter's lifetime. The older woman reciprocated her affection: she was intrigued by Rice's beaming good health and exuberant vitality, and she enjoyed vicariously her complicated love life.

Frances Keene, too, spent a great deal of time with Powell in the mid-1950s. "She was very demonstrative," Keene said in 1994.

> After she'd met you once, she would always embrace you. I knew her best during a time when she wanted nobody else in the family to drink but herself. And so she hid her drinking from Joe. She'd pour her martinis into a small water glass and

sometimes hide them behind a wall of books. Once I came
across some long-forgotten drink and she said, "Oh, dear, that
must be two or three months old." But I never saw her drunk; I
saw her, shall we say, *enhanced*?

"Dawn had a real genius—natural, constantly welling," Keene
added. "A breeze would go by and trigger all these thoughts and
associations in her. She was interested in everything." A typical visit
might begin with a walk through the Village.

> We'd start off on East Ninth Street and walk down to Washing-
> ton Square because she loved the Arch so much. And then we'd
> often stop in for a milkshake on Eighth Street—many people
> who drink are fond of milkshakes because they're nourishing
> but still liquid. Then, after a while, she'd say, "I'm feeling a lit-
> tle tired—let's go in and have a drink." And then she'd bring
> the liquor out of the bookcase.

Keene knew few others in Powell's circle. "She had the habit of
making you feel that you were the only person she could talk to—
which of course wasn't true. But we liked to believe it.

"Her writing was her bulwark against the chaos and tragedy of
her life," Keene believed. "Everything stopped for her when she was
writing. She'd say, 'I'm sorry, I'm working now,' and everybody
would go home. That was it."

Powell would require that bulwark increasingly, for 1957 ended in
calamity. Jojo was again on Ward M-5 at Manhattan State Hospital;
forbidden a pass to spend Christmas at home, he had cut his wrists.
"Saw him and really was shattered by the monstrous madmen there
this time," Powell wrote after a cheerless visit on December 24.

That same month, the sixty-seven-year-old Joe was informed

that he was being "retired" from his advertising agency as of New Year's, and that he would receive no further salary after the end of January 1958. In addition to the complete and total collapse of the regular family finances, this also meant an end to the long-standing customs on which Joe had relied for emotional stability: the escape to a midtown office for seven or eight hours a day, and the boozy company-subsidized lunches. On January 2, Powell reported that the newly housebound Joe was already in an "alcoholic hostile frenzy"; he would remain that way for most of the next few months.

The Goushas now had no economic security whatsoever—no savings, no income. Powell made some halfhearted attempts to secure an editing job at a magazine or publishing house, without success. The bills began to pile up, the phone was turned off, and merchants discontinued their credit; demand letters arrived daily, and a number of lawsuits were threatened. But there was nothing they could do about any of it, so after a while, the numbed Powell simply stopped opening her mail.

To exacerbate matters, 35 East Ninth Street, which had been home to the Goushas since 1942, was in the process of being converted into a cooperative building; under the law then in effect, tenants who declined to buy their apartments were required to vacate. It was against this chaotic and threatening background that Powell on March 19 started her fifteenth—and final—novel, *The Golden Spur*. Somehow she found the energy to complete ten thousand words by the end of April.

An enduring myth about Powell's life (one unfortunately perpetuated by the present writer in prior books) has it that the sixty-one-year-old author and her husband were legally evicted from their home and put out on the streets. In fact, no record of such an eviction has been located in the New York City archives, nor did Powell herself suggest anything of the sort in surviving letters or diaries.

Still, what *did* happen was hardly less tragic and disruptive. The Goushas had been told of the planned transition from rental to co-op in the summer of 1957 and immediately realized they would no longer be able to remain in their apartment. Powell made some inquiries into other living quarters as Joe's retirement approached, but once his salary stopped and the money ran out, the aging and impoverished pair seem simply to have accepted their fate, paying little (if any) rent as the conversion proceeded. The landlords finally brought suit against them, and the Goushas moved out hurriedly at the end of October 1958, by which point they were indeed probably only one step ahead of the sheriff.

Jacqueline Rice remembers the shrunken, disconsolate Powell sitting alone on some boxes piled up on the sidewalk outside 35 East Ninth Street. There, she waited quietly for the movers to arrive, watching some of her insufficiently secured papers fly away in the autumn wind—papers that may have been letters from Malcolm Lowry, Hemingway, or Dos Passos, or pages from the manuscripts of *Turn, Magic Wheel* or *My Home Is Far Away*, both of which now survive only in part. They might have been anything at all.

The list of materials Powell put into storage makes for poignant reading. In addition to "three straight chairs, one large dirty rug, three small dirty rugs," her possessions included complete sets of the journals *Secession* and *transition,* first editions by Hemingway and John Dos Passos (most of them autographed), and her writing desk. Once, "we didn't have money, TV or cars and some thought that we were poor but we were rich because we had our books," Powell reflected despairingly in her diary. Now those volumes were crated and inaccessible at Ellinger Fireproof Storage, a warehouse facility on Hudson Street.

At a stage in her life when she should have been feted and honored as one of America's great writers, Dawn Powell was homeless, forced to seek shelter in a series of seedy residential hotels. The Goushas moved first to the Hotel Irving, at 26 Gramercy Park, a place neither of them found adequate: the hot water rarely functioned, and the hotel prohibited pets, so they had to board their cat,

Fagin, at a veterinarian's office. Three weeks later, Dawn and Joe (and Fagin) moved to the Madison Square Hotel, which would be their home for the rest of the winter.

The Madison Square Hotel, demolished in the 1970s, was located at 35 Madison Avenue, near the corner of East Twenty-sixth Street. "The halls reek of old people," Powell wrote.

> The elevator and lobby smell of brown envelopes (Unemploy-
> ment and Social Security checks), perfumed disinfectants, san-
> itized mold; the walls shake down powdered dust of ages and
> the trucks pound through the streets. The Socially Secure hob-
> ble and limp and waddle and creep through the Stanford White
> lobby and fall into place on the sofas or in their own wheel-
> chairs in the lobby where they watch everybody in and out.

The cramped quarters necessitated a renewed intimacy between the couple, which, probably to their mutual surprise, both partners found fulfilling. They were now closer than they had been in decades, cooking most meals in their rooms, strolling through lower Manhattan together, and enjoying one another's company. "When he has been home, we have gotten acquainted really," Powell reflected about her husband.

Not even such reduced circumstances could crush her curios-ity. She took an unspoiled, almost childlike delight in learning the secrets of a new home, a new neighborhood: the view from her bay window, through which she could glimpse the East River; the "inde-fatigable industry" with which a nearby skyscraper was decorated with angels and Christmas trees for the holiday season; and "the excitement at 9 A.M. of watching city come awake, people go to work."

Friends looked after them when they could. Monroe Stearns had Dawn and Joe over for Thanksgiving dinner, Lloyd Frankenburg and Loren MacIver invited them to a party for the harpsichordist

Rosalyn Tureck, and Frances Keene attempted to interest St. Martin's Press in a prospective volume of Powell's critical writings. Gore Vidal, too, cheered her by recounting a lecture he had given at Harvard during the course of which he called her "America's only satirist."

Nobody in the extended Gousha, Powell, or Sherman families was informed about the extent of Powell's financial desperation ("We have about sixty cents between us and *Post* check doesn't come," she wrote one awful day). Its revelation, with the publication of Powell's diaries in 1995, came as a deep and sorrowful shock to surviving nieces and cousins, all of whom agreed that funds could have been raised to bail out their far-off, much-loved relative. Powell's pride—in her work, in her reputation, and over what she still regarded as a precarious escape from the Midwest—prevented her from asking for a handout from the folks back home.

In May 1959, the Goushas left the Madison Square Hotel and sublet an apartment at 23 Bank Street from the biographer Katherine Anthony. It was a full four rooms, Powell exulted, "beyond belief perfect," but the arrangement was good for only four months. When that period expired, Margaret De Silver took the couple in to her own home at 130 West Twelfth Street, and it is likely that they camped out in other places as well.

This nomadic existence continued until February 1960, when Powell found a stuffy, dark, and rather dismal flat for $135 a month—"A wing chopped off from a ten room apartment," she told her sister—buried within one of the Village's handsomest buildings, 43 Fifth Avenue. It had been almost a year and a half since the Goushas had last had their own place; Powell was now able to liberate most of her materials from the warehouse and move them into their new home.

It was Margaret De Silver who had finally rescued them. "Money from Margaret saves all," Powell wrote in her diary on

Dawn Powell. *(Bertrand de Geofrey)*

ABOVE: Esther Andrews.
(Collection Elizabeth Harries)

ABOVE RIGHT: John Dos Passos.
(John Mills, Jr.)

RIGHT: Ernest Hemingway. *(Helen Breaker)*

ABOVE: Dorothy Parker.
(Associated Press)

CENTER: Edmund Wilson.
(Sylvia Salmi)

ABOVE RIGHT: Margaret De
Silver. *(Sylvia Salmi, Collection*
Jacqueline Miller Rice)

RIGHT: Coburn Gilman.
(Collection Tim Page)

The last photograph of the three sisters: Dawn Powell, Phyllis Cook, and Mabel Pocock, probably taken about 1945. *(Collection Tim Page)*

Dawn Powell in the 1950s—in the studio and on the street. *(Collection Tim Page)*

Joseph Gousha in the 1950s, leaving his favorite bar and restaurant, Tony's, on West Forty-sixth Street in New York. *(Collection Tim Page)*

A joke that almost worked: Dawn Powell and an unidentified friend in a photo booth. *(Collection Tim Page)*

May 20, 1964: Powell receives the American Institute of Arts and Letters' Marjorie Peabody Waite Award for lifetime achievement, presented by her longtime friend Malcolm Cowley. *(Collection Tim Page)*

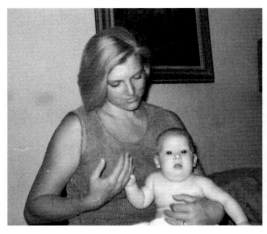

Jacqueline Miller Rice—a close friend who would become Powell's executrix—and her baby, Hilary Dawn Rice, at Powell's apartment in the summer of 1965.

(Carol Warstler)

Novelist and close friend Hannah Green in 1995. *(John Wesley)*

Probably the last photo of
Dawn Powell, taken in the
summer of 1965 in the penthouse
at 95 Christopher Street.
(Carol Warstler)

Coburn Gilman reading on the
balcony of Powell's last apartment.
(Collection Jacqueline Miller Rice)

Joseph Gousha Jr. ("Jojo") during an
outing in 1992. *(Jack Sherman)*

Jack Sherman in 1998 on the site of the
Shelby Junction Depot. *(David G. Kanzeg)*

August 2, 1959. The amount of the gift (and the manner in which it was administered) remain unclear, but De Silver was a woman of enormous means, and somehow she ensured that the Goushas would never again suffer such grave financial troubles. The generous, warmhearted De Silver now became the writer's true patron.

In September 1959, Orpha May Steinbrueck died, at the age of ninety; she was buried with her sisters and her daughter in Shelby's Oakland Cemetery. As was her habit, Powell recorded virtually nothing about the passing of one of the most important influences on her life. Still, the death undoubtedly affected her enormously—Orpha May had been mother, father, role model, and teacher to the young Dawn—and brought her even closer to Jack Sherman, who, along with his sister Rita, had lived with and lovingly tended to Auntie May in her declining years.

One of Powell's nieces, Phyllis's daughter Carol Warstler, visited New York with her family around this time. According to a letter Powell sent to De Silver, Warstler declined an invitation to come to the Gousha apartment with an improbable excuse: "I'd just love to, Aunt Dawn, only we've planned to take a tour of Greenwich Village and just won't have time to see you."

"I was so startled to think I almost prevented them from seeing mysterious Greenwich Village that I didn't think to say, as [Thomas] Wanning suggested, 'but dearie, your Auntie Dawn IS Greenwich Village,'" Powell wrote. For her part, Carol Warstler disputes Powell's version of the story: "Aunt Dawn was a writer, and writers elaborate," she said with a sigh in 1997. "We were in town for five days, I was on the phone with her every day—sometimes several times a day—and the Sunday morning visit that we in fact had with Aunt Dawn and Uncle Joe had been planned before we left Ohio."

In any event, it was a good yarn—and there could be no doubt that the "permanent visitor" was now a permanent fixture within the Village. Books such as Allen Churchill's *The Improper Bohemians* (which Powell herself had reviewed for the *Post*), a solid, nostalgic history of the neighborhood and its creative past, touted her continued residency; the *New York Times Magazine* photographed her browsing in a supposedly "typical" Village antique store; and *Life* magazine came close to commissioning a first-person story about Dawn Powell's Greenwich Village, going so far as to photograph her in coffeehouses throughout the neighborhood around Bleecker Street.

But if Greenwich Village was indeed a "state of mind" (as John Reed insisted early in the century), minds could change—and the Village had. Although Powell was intrigued by the "beatniks" she saw on the street and had probably herself smoked marijuana, she had no sympathy with the burgeoning drug culture. "These dopesters are feeble little squares," she wrote after seeing the Living Theater production of Jack Gelber's *The Connection*. "These are the people whose life is dope and getting it; there is no tragedy here any more than there is in cats waiting for mice. That's their life and it's too bad when no mice show up."

Similarly, and for much the same reason, she disliked the new wave of little magazines, such as *Evergreen Review,* that had started to appear in the late 1950s, calling them "pure poison." "Stories all concern marijuana (gage or pot), dope, heroin, sickness," she grumbled in her diary.

After serving as a juror for a literary prize awarded at Barnard College (one of her copanelists was Bernard Malamud), she had mixed opinions on the quality of the submissions. On the one hand, she told Jack Sherman, the students seemed to write fluently— "more so than in my day when there were just two or three of us in a class who could put a sentence together." But on the other hand, she was displeased by what she perceived as the influence of Freud and psychoanalysis. "They write in the first person a lot, and remember sexy moments from their childhood and faraway first lays when they were a rather bored ten or eleven. In fact they seem self-absorbed, sex-obsessed, oblivious to all surroundings and people."

Edmund Wilson was another to whom she complained about the emphasis on sex in much modern fiction:

> The difference between the boy and girl sex writers is that the girls are more reckless, and throw themselves naked in some fencecorner near their husband's office or outside the sheriff's home, because they are FREE, see—and no sneakiness about it. Also they talk about their ways of performance and their contraceptives all the time. REVOLTING.

"Let's bring back the gay old hypocrisies and the pleasure of black sin framed in white lies," she continued. "And I wish nice girls would go back to their ferneries and start blushing behind their fans."

As Powell grew older, her fundamental conservatism and an underlying cranky obstinancy that had long been part of her nature increasingly asserted themselves. But her tastes were unpredictable, and she was in no sense closed-minded. For example, she enjoyed some of the rock and roll that had begun to dominate Village juke-boxes and was delighted when the novelty hit "The Chipmunk Song" replaced more saccharine arrangements of Christmas carols on the radio. And she loved the barbed, irreverent, slightly surreal humor of *Mad* magazine. Over *Mad*'s forty-five-year history, its demographics have remained pretty much unchanged; the magazine has always appealed most strongly to preteen and teenage boys. Powell may then have been its oldest (and almost certainly its most distinguished) woman fan.

In March 1960, she returned to Yaddo, this time for a stay of almost two months. She made a number of new acquaintances there—including the Chinese-American composer Chou Wen-Chung, the

Canadian novelist Adele Wiseman, and the model, designer, artist, and writer Pati Hill—and renewed her old acquaintance with John Cheever.

But her closest friend at Yaddo was Hannah Green. A fellow Ohioan (from Glendale, a spacious, affluent suburb of Cincinnati), the lanky, affectionate Green was then in her middle thirties and already at work on *The Dead of the House*, a slim, intensely poetic and beautifully crafted novel of childhood that would be published in 1972 and reissued, to enormous acclaim, just prior to the author's death, in 1996.

"I was at Yaddo for quite a while that year," Green would recall in 1993. "There were only a few of us in the main house—it felt like one big long winter sleep-over—and one day we got the word that Dawn Powell would soon be joining us. Nobody knew anything about her—how old she was, where she lived, what she had done— just nothing at all, as was the policy at Yaddo." Green remembered her first impression of Powell's "adorable face with beautiful black eyes and dyed reddish-brown hair, cut short and very soft, like a twenties bob." It was obvious to her that Powell was in poor physical and emotional health, yet the older woman retained an enchanting, childlike purity, Green thought.

"We became the house rebels," she continued.

> Dawn prized a quick, mischievous intelligence. She did not suf-
> fer fools gladly, and she couldn't stand hypocrisy. I found out
> later that there were a lot of people who didn't like Dawn
> because she'd laid them low for their pretensions. But I never
> saw that happen. Oh, she might tell a funny story that would
> make somebody look a little ridiculous, but her wit really
> wasn't hostile—it was sportive. She wasn't like John Cheever,
> for example, to whom I took a dislike after he said Dawn held
> her hands like a woodchuck.

"Dawn helped me summon the courage to move to New York," Green explained.

> I had been at Stanford and then I was sort of an arts-colony bum for about a year and a half while I was beginning to work on *The Dead of the House*. And Dawn told me I simply had to move to New York and there was nothing more to be said about it. Looking back on it now, that was pretty exciting—being introduced to Greenwich Village by Dawn Powell! She took me all around—to the Cedar, to parties, to the shops, everywhere. Because of my connection to Dawn and the people she knew, my first New York job was working as an assistant to Matthew Josephson, and my first New York apartment was a sublet from Harold Rosenberg.

Powell left Yaddo unexpectedly in late April after a severe nosebleed required that she be rushed to the Saratoga Springs hospital in the early-morning hours by Cheever and another fellow colonist, Lore Groszman (a writer now better known as Lore Segal). She went back to Manhattan by train later in the week and was probably just as glad to get home. "Anytime Dawn goes away, no matter how much she wants to go, she's miserable until she smells the sidewalks of New York once again," Joe Gousha later told Hannah.

Less than a week after Powell returned to New York, however, it was Joe who had to be hospitalized. Awakening on the morning of May 4 in excruciating pain, he was taken by ambulance to St. Vincent's, where he was diagnosed with rectal cancer. X-ray therapy was begun immediately, followed by a colostomy to reduce pressure on the malignant zone, but the cancer was a serious one, and these were merely stop-gap measures; he was informed that he would have to have a major—and life-threatening—operation before long.

In June, Powell traveled to her alma mater, Lake Erie College, to accept an honorary doctorate, the only academic acknowledgment she would ever receive. The honor had come about through her friendship with a young English professor named William Peterson, who had taken an interest in her work when he arrived at the college. Through Peterson's advocacy, she was formally recognized by the school that had meant so much to her. After the ceremony, she drove around the Cleveland waterfront with Jack Sherman and Eleanor Farnham before sitting down to a meal at the elegant Hotel Cleveland on Public Square.

Upon her return to New York, she realized that some of the most valuable material that she had put in storage had inexplicably disappeared; missing were several first editions and paintings by Luis Quintinilla and Reginald Marsh. "Discovery that the only things I have are what I have given away," she wrote glumly in her diary. Her immediate family offered little consolation: Jojo was confined to the violent ward again, and Joe was in an increasingly morbid mood. Under such circumstances, it was hard for her even to think, so it is no wonder that she found it difficult to make any headway on *The Golden Spur*. "Don't care if they turn it down completely," she confessed on July 31.

Joe's surgery took place on August 5. He survived the operation and seemed at first to be recuperating quickly, but complications set in before the week was out. On August 15, he was placed on the critical list and all but given up for dead. To widespread amazement, he held on, however barely. "Joe gasping and getting intravenous—surrounded by nurses, interns and too weak to eat or move," Powell noted.

In late September, Joe regained his powers of communication. "Joe improved mightily," Powell recorded. "Mind returns. Says he feels like Falstaff's awakening." He remained in the hospital, however, too weak to go home, and in November had to undergo a skin-grafting surgery. "In afternoon he was 'floating on air' from anesthetic still and very gay," wrote his wife. "Said operation was 'amusing.' No longer could say something was 'no skin off his ass.'"

"Would you say off-hand that 1960 has been cooked up by enemy operators?" Powell asked her sister Phyllis in a letter sent at the end of the year. It wasn't until January 1961 that husband and wife were reunited at 43 Fifth Avenue. Joe had lost a great deal of weight, shriveling from a hefty two hundred pounds down to 142, but he had made what all considered to be a miraculous recovery. Since there were no funds to cover home care, Powell now had the responsibility of looking after him: "Joe goes out once or twice a day," she reported to Phyllis. "He does have to make a whole career of changing his bandages, soaking twice a day an hour at a time, and every other day there is blood all over the place and I have to keep soaking and cleaning the stuff—sheets, underwear, etc.—before sending to laundry and frankly the smell makes it impossible to have anyone come in who doesn't know."

She went on to describe a routine day: "Get up, cook, wash dishes, make beds, rush to get chapter ready and then take up for two o'clock appointment uptown, rush back and do book review for *Post*, rush to deliver THAT myself downtown, back to pick up stuff for supper, swig a drink and fall asleep." The following morning, the cycle would begin all over again. She was sixty-four years old.

Fatigue shadowed her social life. In February 1961, she spent the evening with Edmund Wilson, dining at the Princeton Club and taking in a performance of Edward Albee's *American Dream*, which she found "extraordinarily fresh." "Bunny and I, determined to be less than our sleepy age, afterward knew we wanted a drink but were hardly able to sit up and stay awake," Powell recorded in her diary. "Our feet with one accord strolled into Liquor Store where we each selected pints of rye, strolled out into cab and tore to our separate beds where we could drop our clothes, put nipple on bottle and slurp the whole thing down at ease."

On May 4, Powell entered Mount Sinai Hospital to be treated for exhaustion and anemia. She was apparently then informed that she, too, might be suffering from cancer, and her doctors urged her to have a small growth removed. Instead, she checked herself out and promised to come back in June for surgery. She never did.

"Jack Sherman wrote of Auntie May's way of looking her problems straight in the eye," Powell wrote in her diary on January 16, 1962. "But my belief is she solved them by looking straight past them so they never had a chance to scare her." Certainly, this was the way Powell had been running her own life for many years. But there would be no way to look past the cataclysm that was fast approaching.

On February 8, Joe was rushed to St. Vincent's. The battle was lost; Powell, obviously in shock, wrote paralyzed, aching banalities in her diary: "Dr. Edlich—lovely, intelligent, kind doctor. Nice cops—ambulance—St. Vincent's. Poor Joe in pain and Hannah came with me. Nice entrance woman at St. Vincent's."

Joseph Roebuck Gousha died at St. Vincent's at around two-thirty in the afternoon on February 14, 1962. "Typical of that loving golden Leo lad to die on Valentine's Day," Powell wrote. She found herself musing on something Joe had said when he regretted needing care: "Every girl should know that in her wedding vows she is promising to look after a sick old man." But she also decided that the "reality" of a situation often stood in the way of what she termed the "Truth": "Joe's poor pained body in bed hid the real Joe—jaunty, etc.—and now he is freed."

The faithful Monroe Stearns, who had himself recently lost his wife, helped arrange for Joe's cremation at St. Michael's Cemetery in Queens. Powell, who believed that death was an absolute conclusion to life and living, never claimed Joe's ashes, which would finally be buried in a mass grave on the grounds of St. Michael's some thirty years later.

This did not mean that she forgot her husband; far from it. "Must guard against the curious form death takes," she wrote in her diary on February 22. "The bereaved suddenly must *hate* someone as if that person has to be punished for still being alive. I find myself schizing around hating, loving, etc., to fill in the strange numbness." Nonetheless, she undoubtedly also felt some sad relief that the ordeal had ended: "I do know I could not have gone on in my desperate duties much more, and for a year or two or more have often stopped in the street with my bundles and wondered if I was about to drop dead."

Whatever one may make of their marriage, with all of its self-destructive behavior, its drunken infidelities, and its other obvious imperfections, Dawn and Joe had remained devoted companions from that first walk on Staten Island, when they were both bright and beautiful newcomers to the city and anything seemed possible. Now they were parted forever, and Powell wrote an unusual, yet touching and appropriate, memorial tribute in her diary:

> Someone asked me about the long marriage to Joe—forty-two years—and I reflected that he was the only person in the world I found it always a kick to run into on the street.
>
> As for his death, this is a curious thing to say but after forty-two years of life together—much of it precarious and crushing—we have been through worse disasters together, and I'm sure Joe would feel the same way about me.

The End

❧

How alone we all are.

"I AM REALLY FASCINATED by the aging process, even if the victim is me," Powell wrote to Phyllis a few months after Joe's death.

"Somebody told me humans age like trees," she continued. "One seems to be about forty for eight or ten years and then almost overnight teeth and hair and all age and you are fifty for about ten years, then with a big clank like a rusty chain you're sixty and so on." She signed the letter "Dawn (Age 80)."

Powell would never recover from Joe's passing; it was a mortal, if not yet fatal, wound. She resumed her work, saw friends, brought playing cards, cigarettes, and candy to Jojo at Manhattan State, and cashed monthly checks for $97.50, her insurance benefits as a widow. But Joe dominated her thoughts. On February 28, she bought herself a red rose to commemorate the anniversary of their first date at the Claremont Inn; it became an annual custom she would observe for what remained of her life. She found herself frequenting Joe's favorite restaurants—particularly the Blue Ribbon off Times Square—and reflecting upon his "complete passion for restaurant eating—whether he had clothes or not."

Eventually, Joe joined the rest of Powell's dead in her dreams:

> Very vivid and shaking. I was in my bed on the street next to the Wanamaker building, and he came and sat on the bed—saying it was more than he could stand, our separation. There were tears in his eyes and I held his hand and tried to console him but people were passing by on the street, staring at us.
>
> In the morning I was sick and shook up—the first chipping off of the ice barricade I built up in last few months when he was already gone. "I'm no good to you or myself or anybody anymore," he cried out one day in December. "I'm no help to you." I said he was—that I couldn't work or live without him to turn to. It is true that things do not have much meaning.

Jojo took Joe's death relatively calmly, though his questions were many. "He wanted me to be sure and frame all the snapshots of Daddy," Powell wrote. "He would like to have a motion picture made of Daddy's whole life. He would also like records of Daddy's voice." Once, Jojo asked whether there were many bars in Heaven. He hoped so, he said, because his father had liked them so much.

Just as Powell got back to serious work on *The Golden Spur,* she received some more disturbing news: Margaret De Silver was hopelessly ill with an intestinal ailment that closely resembled the cancer that had killed Joe. "Last year a radium or X-ray job burned her (they forgot her) and infected itself later," Powell explained to her nieces Alice Hoover and Carol Warstler. "All of us thought her doctors and hospitals were killing her—and I still think so. The only reason I'm alive is that I walked out of Mt. Sinai Hospital and refused to let them operate."

Margaret died on June 1. Powell was at her bedside, holding her hand, stroking her head, and repeating the words "Don't be afraid" again and again in a soft, consoling voice. "Margaret—gasping and sucking in life like Joe—dying about 12," she recorded. "Beautiful East River view—serene and lovely as all settings for death, orphans, tragedy are, and why the turmoil of city is less scary."

Jacqueline Rice was with Powell when Margaret died; indeed, the two had by now become virtually inseparable. "She has a Murphy marvelous trait," Powell wrote to Gerald and Sara Murphy about her younger friend:

> She wants to make everybody comfortable, unworried, beautiful, fulfilled, fed, loved and gay. I think this trait has loused her two or three great loves—as Lover Boy doesn't want to share the wealth. Usually he (whoever he is) is alarmed to find himself worshipped, overwhelmed with love and protection—I've had to fend off this gorgeous forest fire of affection, too, but should always have thanked my stars for it.

"Even when I'm tired of her, the mere sight of that radiant blonde happy puss of hers is refreshing," she told Jack Sherman.

Throughout the devastation of the previous four years, Powell had attempted to work on *The Golden Spur* whenever possible. Her old friend Malcolm Cowley had brought her to a new publisher, Viking Press, in 1958, after the editing debacle of *A Cage for Lovers* made her continued association with Houghton Mifflin impossible. Cowley now served as her senior editor. He told Powell that he thought she had always written two types of novels, satirical and sentimental, and made it clear that Viking preferred her satire. She would receive two thousand dollars for the new book—half upon signing and the other half on completion. It was the largest advance she had received for a book in twenty years, though it was still less than the twenty-five hundred apiece she had earned for *Turn, Magic Wheel* and *The Happy Island.*

Powell never believed that Cowley liked the resulting book very much. "In looking over Malcolm's comments on *Spur* and recalling his dubiousness at conference, I sense negative reaction," she had written in 1959. "With deep, sentimental nostalgia for his old Village days, he is disappointed that my Village is not what he imagined and he is cross about it." Whether or not her suspicion was correct, the two never allowed the natural tensions of the editing process to interfere with their friendship, and Cowley and his wife, Muriel, would prove enormously supportive of Powell in her few remaining years.

The manuscript was finished in mid-1962, at which point it was passed on to another senior editor, Helen Taylor, with whom the author clashed immediately. Powell explained to Cowley that she was so "exhausted by three years of drawing an iron curtain between my personal problems and the acrobatic necessities of a comic novel that I was not ready to be challenged ten to twenty times per page on every quip, every reference, every character's reaction, and frequently on character's expenditures."

Powell ignored Taylor's revisions and insisted that the book be published exactly as written. "The business of literal editing is dangerous," she decided, and launched into an impromptu parody:

1. "Who was that lady I seen you with last night?"
2. "That was no lady that was my wife."

Copy note—"Seen" change to "saw." Or if "seen" is kept, questioner is obviously coarse type and would not say "lady" but "broad."

1. "Who was that broad I seen you with last night?" *Specify place here. Wouldn't he have encountered several females in a large city during one evening?*

1. "Who was that lady (*or broad*) I saw (*or seen*) you with last night on the corner of 60th Street and Central Park West?"
   2. "That lady was my wife"—*or . . .*

Had Powell deliberately planned *The Golden Spur* as a last testament, it couldn't have been a much more thorough or appropriate summation of her life's work. It is filled with her recurrent topics—Ohio, New York, young provincials and worldly sophisticates, fleabag hotels and Park Avenue splendor, innocence and experience—and she is especially acute when writing of those points where all these elements intersect. It is the most encyclopedic of her books, filled with long and sometimes vastly entertaining digressions on Greenwich Village history, literary politics, aesthetics, sexual politics, and many other subjects.

And yet Powell relays a clear, direct story, one of her most perfect, in *The Golden Spur*. A young man named Jonathan Jaimison, from Silver City, Ohio, has learned that his real father was not the person who raised him from childhood but rather a shadowy figure in Greenwich Village with whom his long-deceased mother once had an affair. So Jonathan, who has always felt himself to be something of an exile in Ohio, comes to New York in search of his true father and, by extension, his own roots. He checks into a hotel that sounds as if it were modeled upon the Madison Square, and goes to the bar where his mother was once a fixture, the Golden Spur—helpfully described to him as a place where everybody comes "until they can afford not to."

This is a book about the new Village—the 1960s Village in its germinal form—written by a celebrant from an earlier era. The

Washington Square portrayed here is filled with beatniks, berets, muscular lesbians, sinister children, derelicts, and, of course, preoccupied New Yorkers going about their business. A hungry Jonathan asks after the nearest coffee shop:

> A benign, white-haired old gentleman, wide-brimmed black hat on lap, black ribbons fluttering from his spectacles, sat on a bench reading a paperback copy of *The Dance of Life*. Reassured by the title, Jonathan coughed to get his attention.
>
> "Could you tell me where I can get a cup of coffee here?" he asked.
>
> Without looking up from his reading, the gentleman reached in his pocket and handed out a quarter before turning a page. Jonathan stared at the coin in his palm.
>
> "Thank you, sir," he said. "Thank you very much."
>
> How strange New Yorkers were, he marveled, but he would get used to their ways.

Above all, *The Golden Spur* is about impermanence—the fleeting glory and sorrow of changing times. *The Wicked Pavilion* concludes with the destruction of the Hotel Lafayette/Café Julien; here again, within the first few pages, we are witness to the demolition of a New York landmark, this time the old John Wanamaker store near Astor Place:

> "Can you tell me if there's something special about this particular wrecking to bring out such a crowd?" Jonathan asked.
>
> The gentleman snorted. "Of course I can tell you. In the first place this was a splendid old landmark and people like to see the old order blown up. Then there is the curious dirt and uproar which are the vitamins of New York, and of course the secret hope that the street will cave in and swallow us all up."

Jonathan meets several potential candidates for his biological paternity: the successful writer Alvine Harshawe (another Andrew Callingham type), the famous painter Hugow, and the lawyer George Terrence (with whose daughter he has an affair). All are intrigued and stimulated by the possibility that they may have fathered this handsome and decent young man. After many false turns, he discovers the identity of his father: he was a certain Major Wedburn, who died the very day of Jonathan's arrival in New York. By now, however, the young man is caught up in the whirl of present-day Manhattan. He abandons his obsession with the past, accepts his part in the continuum, allows himself to fall in love, and is ready to go on with his life—an ending in the sunniest C major.

Considering Powell's own physical and emotional state, it seems almost incredible that she should have been able to carry off such a cheery and affirmative work. She was not a traditional romantic by any means ("The truth had no part in love anyway, except for the truth of finding each other at the right moment," she observes), but her affection for her young characters and her confidence in the life they have ahead of them in New York come through. The city was the "only place where people with nothing behind them but their wits can be and do everything," she had told Jack Sherman in a 1931 letter—and despite everything she had been through, she still believed that.

The Golden Spur was published on October 5, 1962. If it did not receive the sort of banner treatment that had been accorded *The Wicked Pavilion,* neither was it ignored, like *A Cage for Lovers.* Most of the reviews were respectful and understanding, if rarely as well placed as an author might have wished. It was greeted as a good book, a serious book, but hardly a "big" book in the contemporary realm of blockbuster best-sellers.

In the *New York Times Book Review,* Morris Gilbert wrote that Powell had been for years "whipping up successive human comedies of the most fastidious disenchantment." Her "comic spirit is a mordant one; her knowingness is proverbially satanic," he continued. "In *The Golden Spur* she is again at her most outrageous and again goes swinging on her patented Ohio–New York pendulum—a thoroughly familiar one for her, a native of little Shelby, Ohio and a habitué of the metropolis."

His most astute comments were saved for the last lines of his review: "There are new notes—more than a trace of nostalgia for other Village days, and an occasional distinctly autumnal coloration in the human landscape. But the author's pyrotechnical wickedness is still guaranteed to satisfy."

Lewis Terwilliger, writing in the soon-to-be-shuttered *New York Herald Tribune*, thought that Powell, despite her background in "wide-eyed Ohio," had a wonderful "Manhattan talent for seeing through everybody and enjoying them thoroughly in the process." In this new novel, "she chaperones Jonathan through the mazes of Manhattan on a search as deftly plotted as a good mystery story," he wrote. "There's a bit of philosophy in it too—something about that search for identity which is the essence of coming of age."

Her friend Robert Payne titled his notice for the *Saturday Review* "Parsifal in the Village." "All true comedy is a morality play and deadpan Jonathan-Parsifal is essentially a moral figure, with the weight of the universe twirling about his little finger. But what is chiefly important is the zest, the spendthrift wit, the wild and joyful improvisations at which Dawn Powell is a virtuoso."

Finally, Edmund Wilson decided to write about Powell's work for the first time since his mixed review of *My Home Is Far Away* nearly destroyed their friendship. The resulting article, which appeared in the November 17, 1962, issue of the *New Yorker*, was by far the lengthiest and most probing critical piece written about Powell during her lifetime.

"Why is it that the novels of Miss Dawn Powell are so much less

well known than they deserve to be?" Wilson's two-thousand-word
study began. He went on to offer a few possible answers:

> This is, I believe, partly due to her complete indifference to
> publicity. She rarely goes to publishers' lunches or has pub-
> lishers' parties given her; she declines to play the great lady of
> letters, and she does not encourage interviews or the appear-
> ance of her photograph on book jackets. No effort has been
> made to glamorize her, and it would be hopeless to try to glam-
> orize her novels. For in these novels—another reason that they
> have not been more popular—she does nothing to stimulate
> feminine daydreams. The woman reader can find no comfort in
> identifying herself with Miss Powell's heroines. The women
> who appear in her stories are likely to be as sordid and absurd
> as the men. There are no love scenes that will rouse you or
> melt you.

Then he proceeded to the heart of the matter:

> Love is not Miss Powell's theme. Her real theme is the provin-
> cial in New York who has come on from the Middle West and
> acclimated himself (or herself) to the city and made himself a
> permanent place there, without, however, losing his fascinated
> sense of an alien and anarchic society. Like Miss Powell, who
> was born in Ohio, these immigrants find themselves vividly
> aware of elements of Manhattan life that the native of New York
> takes for granted, since he has usually no very intimate experi-
> ence of anything else to contrast with them. To such recent
> arrivals in town, the New Yorkers seem giddy and unreliable,
> their activities confused and often pointless; yet once the trans-
> plantation has taken root, they may enjoy in the very amorality
> of this life a certain relaxation and freedom, a certain convivial

comfort in the assurance that, whatever you do, no one—though lovers and spouses may occasionally make themselves disagreeable—is really going to call you to account. Such a world has great comic possibilities if one has enjoyed it on its own terms and yet observed it from a point of view that does not quite accept these terms as normal, and Miss Powell has exploited these possibilities with a wit, a gift of comic invention and an individual accent that make her books unlike all others. The mind, the personality behind them, with all its sophistication, is very stout and self-sustaining, strong in Middle Western common sense, capable of toughness and brusqueness; yet a fairyland strain of Welsh fantasy instills into everything she writes a kind of kaleidoscopic liveliness that renders even her hardheadedness elusive.

It was perfect, it was poetry, it was Powell all over—somebody at last *understood*. Wilson called her novels "among the most amusing being written, and in this respect quite on a level with those of Anthony Powell, Evelyn Waugh and Muriel Spark."

An exhilarated Powell grabbed up as many copies of the magazine as she could afford and sent them off to her friends and family. "Here is important *New Yorker* piece," she told Phyllis. "I mean one that sells books since Wilson is the world's greatest critic."

And certainly such a review *should* have sold books—but sadly, it didn't: *The Golden Spur* may not even have recouped the advance Viking paid for it. The press has changed hands since the novel was published, and nobody working there in 1997 could determine how many copies had been sold or even how many had been printed. We do know that by March 1963, Powell had yet to earn out $604 of her $2,000 advance. "Ah, success!" she wrote sarcastically to Dos Passos. "I should have [the royalty statement] framed for my jealous friends."

The Golden Spur was dedicated to Margaret De Silver, as Powell had promised her dying friend that it would be. For a time, it seemed as if Powell were going to lose not only Joe and Margaret in 1962, but her only surviving sister as well. In her diary, she wrote only two words about the malady: "Phyllis sick." In fact, Phyllis Powell Cook was desperately and mysteriously ill, and thought to be dying. Powell poured her sorrow and compassion not into her diary but into a series of letters to two of Phyllis's daughters, Carol Warstler and Alice Hoover.

"It is terribly disheartening I know to wake up every morning hoping the whole deal is a bad dream and that a miracle has happened," she told Alice. "The thing is that sometimes the miracle *does* happen and you forget all the bad weeks." Remarkably, such a "miracle" actually occurred: Phyllis suddenly regained her health and was released from the hospital in early 1963. She would live for another twenty-two years.

Even during this trying period, there were some bright moments. Powell was invited to dinner by the celebrated New York social leader, philanthropist, and sometime author Brooke Astor ("Why?" Powell scribbled in her journal. "Does she think we writers should band together?"). Despite her skepticism, a modest, mutually appreciative friendship seems to have ensued, though the ninety-year-old Astor would have no memory of Powell in 1996.

More significant was Powell's last chance for a Broadway production. She was approached by Charles Strouse and Lee Adams, creators of the stage hit *Bye, Bye Birdie* and the soon-to-be-produced *Golden Boy*, who were looking for a new project. They had both read and admired *The Golden Spur*, and they told Powell they thought her book would make a terrific musical comedy.

Several meetings followed, and Powell came to like both men enormously. "You will not be surprised to know that one of them— Lee Adams—is an Ohio State graduate from Mansfield," she told Phyllis. "About thirty-four and very intelligent and quick and talented. Hearing of my Shelby background he was very startled and explained to the producer, 'Listen, compared to Dawn's home-town—mine was a metropolis!'" Powell would work on the play for much of 1963, completing at least one act.

She had also started another novel—to be called *Summer Rose*—of which only inconclusive fragments would be discovered after her death. She described the book to Carol Brandt as a "short comic dilemma involving only two figures and some absent menaces, with a New York and surrounding airports backdrop."

In March 1963, *The Golden Spur* was short-listed for the National Book Award, and Powell appeared on a CBS morning television program to discuss her work with anchorman Harry Reasoner and a fellow nominee (in the nonfiction category), historian Barbara Tuchman. Powell must have been disappointed when, a few days later, she learned that she hadn't won. But she took it philosophically and even claimed to feel a certain relief: "I have no equipment for prize-winning—no small talk, no time for idle graciousness and required public show, no clothes either or desire for front," she wrote in her journal. "I realize I have no yen for any experience (even a triumph) that blocks observation, when I am the observed instead of the observer. Time is too short to miss so many sights."

That spring, she moved to a penthouse at 95 Christopher Street, an elegant, high-rise art deco residence at the corner of Bleecker Street. She had quarreled with her landlords at 43 Fifth Avenue, who refused to let her out of her lease. But she felt she *had* to leave, whatever their objections: the Fifth Avenue apartment was too closely intertwined with the gloomiest period of her life, and besides, it was dark and cramped, while the new place was sunny and open, with panoramic views of the city. Deciding to take the risk, Dawn moved to Christopher Street.

She loved the apartment, and her mood improved immediately. Publication of *The Golden Spur* had triggered a revival of interest in her work. She sold a fine story, "The Elopers," based on Jojo's illness and his visits home, to the *Saturday Evening Post* for fifteen hundred dollars (more than she had received for the majority of her novels), and placed the memoir that had begun as "Out with the Stiffs" with *Vogue;* it was now entitled "What Are You Doing in My Dreams?" Meanwhile, *Esquire* was interested in flying her out to Hollywood to write a profile of actor James Stewart on the set of a film called *Take Her, She's Mine.* (As it turned out, Stewart was to finish shooting ahead of schedule, so the piece would be canceled.)

In late 1963, she appeared, somewhat improbably, in an *Esquire*-commissioned photograph that purported to present a reunion of the surviving members of the so-called lost generation. Although Edmund Wilson scolded her for agreeing to participate—he mistrusted the legend surrounding the 1920s and thought very little of most of the people in the picture—Powell justified it by saying she wanted to preserve her connections at the well-paying *Esquire* for future projects.

"The photograph was in fact a scream," she informed Dos Passos.

> I told them before I was not in Paris—they said this was the literary scene, 20s and 30s. So there I am, rosy and overfed, squeezed between Carl Van Vechten and Glenway Wescott, Man Ray, Marcel Duchamp (Gertrude and Alice couldn't make it), and a guard of Cowleys, Josephsons, Slater Brown, Virgil Thomson, Caresse Crosby and Kay Boyle. . . . I see Dwight Macdonald's beard wagging accusingly—"You weren't in that group"—and I will say, "Look at the record, man. The camera doesn't lie."

Knowing of Powell's travails and poor financial condition, Cowley helped arrange for her to receive the Marjorie Peabody Waite Award for lifelong achievement in literature from the American

Academy of Arts and Letters. It was presented to her in the summer of 1964, along with a check for fifteen hundred dollars, which must have been especially gratifying.

That same summer, Powell paid her last visit to Ohio. William Peterson, who had been largely responsible for her being given an honorary degree by Lake Erie in 1960, invited her out to the college again for some extended meetings with the students. She gave a lecture to the senior class. "When she began to talk, her voice, low but clear, soon claimed attention for what she was saying, not who she was," Peterson wrote in his 1996 essay "Dawn Powell Returns to Lake Erie College." He added, "Her own summary of the speech in her diary reveals her habitual irony and amused objectivity."

What Powell had written was this:

> Speech. Harold Fink, head of Fine Arts, played "Pavane for the Dead Princess," while I tried to figure out what to say. Finally told seniors not to use minds in making decisions (save them for making excuses)—experience had told me women can't get down to their real work till the man thing is settled—not for material urge or status—just possession. Own a man, but learn a trade on the side. Beware of waiting—leap before you look—you learn by leaping—if you look first you never leap. Don't wait till wisdom sets in—wisdom is ruin. Someday these happy happy days will seem pretty miserable to you. Girls cheered and were delighted. Said later it was just what they wanted to hear and what they'd been saying.

"When the talk ended, the students burst into sustained applause," Peterson recorded. "A few stood, clapping vigorously, and in a moment everyone in the auditorium had risen, welcoming and acclaiming the most distinguished writer the College had ever graduated."

From there, Powell traveled to Canton, where she visited her

sister, her nieces, and their families before going on to Shelby to see
Jack and Rita Sherman. Together, they drove through the cornfields
and small towns of central Ohio, many of which had changed only
slightly since she knew them as a child. From her bed in the Sherman
house in Shelby, she could still hear the cries of the trains roaring
through the night.

Powell was now in greater professional demand than she had
ever been. She was working with two highly successful theatrical
artists, Strouse and Adams, and their proposed musical seemed likely
to be a hit. Several movie producers were interested in obtaining
rights to *The Golden Spur*, and she was selling free-lance articles to
some of the most prestigious and high-paying magazines around. She
was dissatisfied with Viking, particularly since Cowley had moved
on from his editorial position; Carol Brandt assured her that she
could have any publisher in New York. She considered Pantheon and
Doubleday but finally went with Random House at the urging of
author and editor Morris Philipson (for whose novel *Bourgeois Anonymous* she would write an admiring blurb). The terms Brandt arranged
for her next book were splendid: $1,000 upon signing of the con-
tract, $1,000 more on delivery of the first section, $1,000 on completion, and $1,000 on publication—for a total of $4,000, by far the
largest sum she had ever received for any of her novels.

If her financial condition was much improved, her physical condition was once again worrisome. Powell had been feeling increasingly unwell since February 1964, when she had checked into St.
Luke's Hospital. The diagnosis at that time was severe anemia; she
was admitted for ten days and placed on a special diet that allowed
her only 1,200 calories per day.

When she visited Edmund Wilson's ancestral homestead in Tal-
cottville, New York, late that summer, it was obvious to her hosts
that she was ill. "She would turn quite yellow and have to lie down,"
Edmund Wilson wrote in his diary, "but then always come to at din-
nertime to have some drinks and do her best to be amusing." She

was, he said, an "old-fashioned American woman not far from the
pioneering civilization: strong-willed, stoical, plainspoken, not to be
imposed upon."

Dawn Powell learned she was mortally ill during the hot, hazy last
weeks of August 1964. Her pain had increased exponentially over the
last few months; in mid-July, she had complained to Hannah that the
agitation in her stomach made her dream of wasps and bugs squirm-
ing throughout her body. A blood test verified that she was again
suffering from anemia, with a hemoglobin measurement of 4.9.*
"Must go to hospital fast for transfusions," she wrote in her diary on
August 24. "Also intestinal something."

Her internist, Robert Solley, was away on holiday, and so Powell saw his substitute, Dr. Ben Kightlinger, in his Park Avenue office
on August 25. Kightlinger told her she had an "intestinal lump" and
recommended immediate hospitalization. Not wanting to spoil an
upcoming vacation with Jojo, she at first resisted, but a terrible night
convinced her to check into St. Luke's on August 26.

On August 28, she spent an entire day having X rays and under-
going barium treatment. Reluctant, as usual, to let any experience,
however ghastly, go to waste completely, she summed up her torment in a macabre little poem:

> *Kidneys are pink*
> *Livers are green*
> *The barium bastards*
> *Are at it again.*
> *They scream in your pipes*
> *They coil in your gripes*
> *They bubble and squeakle*

A normal hemoglobin count range is 12–16.

And bristle and fizzle

In every particulum

They haunt diverticulum

Ilium, oleum, noodle and pasta

Branchwater, Goldwater, Pepsi and Shasta . . .

The following day, Dr. Kightlinger informed her that he had
located a mysterious mass, almost certainly malignant, growing in
her ascending colon. "Must come out," she noted in her diary, following that with an uncharacteristic one-word admission: "Scared."
However, Kightlinger and Powell agreed that she would wait to talk
with Dr. Solley before any operation was scheduled.

Whatever conversation ensued with Solley seems to have confirmed Powell in her decision to let nature take its course; she
refused the operation. She wrote a letter to Gerald Murphy, another
of Solley's patients, who was himself dying of cancer: "What I love
about Dr. Solley is that he does believe we should be 'more comfortable' instead of forever trying to discipline our interiors with sword
and barium and weapons worse than the ail. He saved me again from
some swordplay—I hope—and life perks up in the sullen old bones.
(Yes, I do have bones after losing thirty-five pounds of suet.)"

When Murphy died, in October, Powell attended his funeral in
East Hampton; she thought it a "perfect small Murphy party as Gerald himself might have arranged it." Back in Manhattan again, she
attempted to make some progress on *Marcia* and on the new comic
novel she called *Summer Rose,* but her energy was depleted. "I don't
know what's wrong with me," she said to Hannah one afternoon.
Then she corrected herself. "Of course I do know. I'm dying, Hannah. Like Joe and Margaret."

" 'I'm dying'—said loudly, wildly," Hannah wrote in her diary.
But then, Green marveled, "she rises to a funny story."

Powell found some respite in humor. Once, she announced that she was going to stick her head in the typewriter: "Has anyone ever killed themselves that way?" she wondered. She had finally purchased a television set, and Hannah recalled sitting with her one day and watching a rocket launch out of Cape Canaveral. "What a boring age," Powell observed dryly as the spacecraft soared toward the heavens. On another occasion, Hannah drove up to the Cloisters, the museum of medieval art at the northern end of Manhattan, with Dawn and Jojo, who loved the place, he said, because it reminded him of ancient Rome. As they stopped to admire a painting of a man carrying the Christ child on his shoulders through the waters, Powell started to sing "Walkin' My Baby Back Home."

In November, Powell outlined the beginnings of a will. Typically, she made no mention of her few material possessions but went straight to her work. Joe's sister, Isabel, was to have all rights to *The Wicked Pavilion*, Rosalind Wilson would receive *A Cage for Lovers*, and rights to *The Golden Spur* would be split between Jack Sherman and Harry Gousha, Jr., a favorite nephew. She was undecided about *The Locusts Have No King*, but all the Ohio novels would go to Phyllis, in trust for her daughters. Unfortunately, Powell confided these decisions only to her diary, and not to an attorney; by the time she actually made out a legal will, she was too sick to care about such distinctions.

On December 11, Powell met with Lee Adams and Charles Strouse for the last time about the proposed musical comedy based on *The Golden Spur*. She told them that she did not feel well enough to continue with the project, and they suggested that everything be put on hold until she was again well. They parted on friendly terms, and Powell attended and enjoyed their current hit, *Golden Boy*.

Nineteen sixty-five was the end—a steady shriveling. Powell weighed 130 pounds on January 7 (down forty pounds from the preceding year) and was extremely frail. Nor was this her only problem: the lawyers representing 43 Fifth Avenue were actively pursuing her for back rent. They had originally asked for $1,055 but then, eager to settle their claim, offered to let her off for $500. Powell was not inclined to give them anything at all, for she had warned her landlords that she was moving out, paid for the time that she was there, and believed another tenant could easily have been found to fill the vacancy. Jojo came home for a visit and quarreled harmlessly with his mother, who in fact seemed rather proud of his obstinacy: "He was in a Gousha sarcastic dig mood," she wrote, "which is more mature, as he is getting to be."

The last work Powell completed was a nostalgic vignette about her courtship on Staten Island forty-five years earlier. The article had an unusual genesis: Powell had attended a party in January at the home of Elaine Dundy, a novelist and playwright, and had used the construction of the Verrazano-Narrows Bridge, which would soon link Staten Island with Brooklyn, as the taking-off point for a series of anecdotes about this smallest and most isolated of New York's five boroughs.

To Powell's surprise, an *Esquire* editor named Thomas Dobell who had been present at the dinner called her up the following day and asked her to put together an article about Staten Island. "Dawn said, 'I don't know what I'd say,'" Hannah wrote in her diary. "'Oh,' he said. 'Just write down everything you said last night.' Dawn said to me 'I don't know what I said. I wasn't listening to myself.'"

Esquire offered her $750, with a guarantee of $250 even if the article wasn't accepted. She finished it on March 1, noting, "Seven pages through two Ritalins and mailed Special Delivery. Greatest achievement of year and cheered me. Piece pleasant and plausible."

It is a sweet, sentimental valedictory:

Staten Island! I fell in love with it the very day I fell in love and the whole affair has the misty charm of a half-forgotten Lehar operetta. . . .

It was a Prohibition year so naturally part of the hiking equipment was a hip flask of some exquisite blend of lemonade and henbane with a zest of metal rust, but this cannot account altogether for the mysterious haze that enveloped this and all subsequent impressions of the island. First of all I found that the magic ferryboat, churning past chiming bell buoys, mud scows and ocean liners, the Statue of Liberty and little fishing boats, had transported me not to a place but to another time, say fifty years back. Even the St. George terminal, vast and bleak, perfumed with old picnic rejects, peanuts and Bull Durham tobacco, was like the old-time Midwest Junction depot with the music of foghorns and boat whistles instead of engine snorts and blasts. Once on the highway there were the dusty back roads, tangled backyards complete with burdock, lilac, berry bushes, grazing colts, abandoned toys and rusty machinery that belonged to my earliest Ohio memories.

Powell gave what would be her last print interview in early April. Entitled "Visit with a Villager," this column-length piece was published in the April 15, 1965, edition of the *Villager.* "The Village has two weeklies," she explained to Jack Sherman when she sent him a copy of the article, "this old-timer, resembling the [*Shelby*] *Globe*" and the "new *Village Voice*, a ten-cent avant-garde and political weekly with free use of four-letter words and fierce interest in local parks, schools, etc."

The *Villager* piece, written by a reporter named W. M. H. van Okker, was not especially trenchant: "Real flappers never die—neither do they fade away!" it began, going on to describe Powell's "short cut dark hair, chestnut eyes innocent of makeup . . . good-looking legs, trim ankles and feet that have danced many a Charleston." ("How do you like me being that old flapper with those fine little legs?" she asked Jack. "I should live so long for this!")

There were some factual errors, such as the surprising information that Powell had worked her "way through Mt. Holyoke College in Shelby in three years." But Powell was courteous and answered the journalist's questions straightforwardly, reiterating her belief that the "down to earth realism of the Middle West" had much in common with the best English humor. She had admired Evelyn Waugh and Aldous Huxley, she said, "until they got donnish—too academic," and continued to enjoy the work of Muriel Spark.*

"I am a realist," Powell replied when the *Villager* asked about her own fiction. "I don't like the modern abstract writing with symbols." The interview concluded with a few words about her long residency in Greenwich Village: "I am at home here. I can go out in the Village any time and find someone who speaks my language."

She became ever closer to Jackie and Hannah, who traded shifts caring for her—duties for which Powell insisted upon offering each a token payment. "Both are such efficient, willing girls," she wrote to Jack, "and both always broke so it works out." Coby came in regularly, but Powell said he became drunk after a pint of Gallo sherry— "so I have to get cross."

Jackie had recently married the painter Daniel Rice, and Powell was extremely pleased when their first daughter was born on May 2, 1965, and christened Hilary Dawn Rice. The baby was, said Powell, the "most exquisite little yellow rose of a child, elegant features, wild Irish rose."

"I adore the baby Hilary Dawn which surprises me since I am not a baby fancier," Powell wrote to Jack, who was spending the summer in Europe. Jojo happened to be home one night when the Rices stopped in for snacks and drinks. When Jackie jokingly asked tiny Hilary Dawn if she wanted a martini, Jojo spoke up sternly: "I don't think she should have a martini until she's twenty-one years old!"

---

*In her final months, she would add Brigid Brophy to her list of favored writers, and would be delighted at receiving a copy of Brophy's Two Novels, inscribed to her "with homage."

Powell composed a poem to welcome the baby, and circulated it among her friends and family:

Hilary Millery Dawn
The Rices sing hey nonny non
Of sugar and spice
And everything nice
Oh how nice of the Rices to spawn.

She continued to go out when she felt up to it and was always bemused when acquaintances complimented her on her newly svelte figure. She attended a dinner for Norman Mailer at the PEN club (which she usually referred to as the "PENIS club"), took in Marx Brothers and W. C. Fields double bills with Jojo, and grew nostalgic after a party on West End Avenue and West Seventy-fifth Street summoned up memories of her first happy days in New York, almost half a century earlier.

She wrote amusingly of a visit around this time with the recently widowed Sara Murphy, during which she mentioned that Virginia Pfeiffer and her two adopted children were now living in Mexico, not far from Pfeiffer's onetime companion Laura Archera, "the Italian girl who married Aldous Huxley."

Next thing I knew Sara had chuckles, thinking how strange for Jinny to marry Elvis Presley! Not Elvis Presley, I cried out again and again—*Aldous Huxley*—and it was her friend Laura, the one Sara never liked, remember? No, Sara never met any of Jinny's friends. In fact they never knew what became of Jinny. They heard she had gone West to live but she had gotten very strange and was adopting children all the time. Had I heard that she had married Elvis Presley?

"When I left, she asked me if I ever heard anything of Jinny Pfeiffer and I said No!"

As ever, Powell's politics resisted easy definition. She found John Dos Passos's favorable coverage of Barry Goldwater's candidacy in the *National Review* inexplicable and gleefully quoted Edmund Wilson's succinct dismissal: "too girlish for words." Yet she agreed with Dos Passos on many issues. "I am sick of Civil Rights and well-heeled 'underprivileged' types screaming for justice when writers are the worst-privileged and most underpaid and oppressed of any race," she told him. Although she liked many black people personally, she mistrusted the emerging black militancy, and the Harlem riots of 1964 put her in a rage.

Yet as early as May 1965, she had taken a decidedly "liberal" position on the Vietnam War, probably the single most divisive issue of the 1960s. "To American Academy," she wrote in her diary on May 19. "Lewis Mumford gave jolt to occasion and I realized I had gotten as chicken as the rest of America because what he said—we had no more right in Vietnam than Russia had in Cuba—was true but I did not think he should use his position to declaim this. Later I saw the only way to accomplish anything is by 'abusing' your position."

Still, Powell's English friend Bryan Robertson was probably close to the mark when he described her as being a sort of "libertarian conservative" in the years when he knew her. It is tempting but pointless to speculate as to just how she would have reacted to the social changes that were to sweep over the United States—and the world—in the next few years.

In August, Powell saw her sister Phyllis, who drove to New York with her daughter Carol Warstler and other members of the family. "It was obvious that Aunt Dawn was very ill and that was the main reason we went out," Warstler remembered. "Mother stayed with her about a week while the rest of us went to the World's Fair and visited with friends in Connecticut."

Powell was determined to let nothing spoil what she knew would be her final reunion with her beloved baby sister, the person to whom she had told her germinal stories more than sixty years earlier. "Aunt Dawn put on a really good face and was pretty much her usual cheerful self—smiling and joking," Carol Warstler recalled. Powell had paid for Jackie to rent a Volkswagen, and the three of them drove around the city, visited Jojo at Manhattan State, and ate some good meals in Village restaurants.

Before the family returned to Ohio, Carol took two snapshots of Dawn in her living room at 95 Christopher Street; they are the last known photographs of her, and among the very few that were taken with color film. The better of the pair shows Powell sitting in a red floral armchair, next to one of her overflowing bookshelves. She looks pensive and careworn, half buried within a dress that is now several sizes too large for her. But there is no mistaking the intelligence and determination in her face: she is not yet ready, in this snapshot, to give up the fight.

That same month, she sat for an interview with Robert H. Hethmon, a professor at UCLA who was pursuing a study of the Group Theatre. Fortunately, he brought along a tape recorder ("a heavy old Wollensak I lugged all over Manhattan," Hethmon said in 1997), thus providing us with the only recording of Powell's voice known to exist. In an era when pocket cassette recorders may be had for thirty dollars and any given television program will be videotaped by many thousands of viewers, it is difficult to conceive of how elusive such permanence once seemed. And so, though Powell was a regular performer on at least one weekly radio show ("Music and Manners," in 1939), was interviewed on numerous other programs, and appeared on television at least twice, only this hour-and-a-half-long conversation recorded in her apartment by a visiting stranger has survived.

It was a hot day. The windows were open, and one can hear the sounds of ambulance sirens, distant airplanes, and the exasperated honking of horns from a long-ago New York. Powell speaks slowly, dryly, precisely, in a deep, throaty voice; whenever she has said something funny, she pauses, almost imperceptibly, to see whether there will be any reaction. When Hethmon laughs, she joins in with him before proceeding with her story.

The interview is uncommonly interesting and deserves some-day to be published in its entirety (Hethmon is still at work on his massive project). Against the evidence, Powell tells her interlocutor that she was "delighted" by the critical notices for *Big Night*: "They said 'this is so powerful. . . . Miss Powell doesn't know what a script she has. . . . It's too strong for the theatre.' I was encouraged by all of that. So that very day I started a new play." Rather mischievously, she says that Stanislavsky met Stella Adler in Paris and told her that the Group had done everything wrong—that they had completely mis-understood his method.

And she speaks of Jack Lawson. "Jack and I would come out from our workout with the Group, and at that time he was making fun of the comrades and the Communist touches," she says. "I haven't caught him laughing about it since then. We stopped our friendship, because I'm such a Fascist, as you know. No, he can't stand anybody who isn't a Communist anymore. . . . That was too bad. He was so good. *Processional* was such a wonderful play."

As exhausted as Powell was, she kept up her correspondence, blast-ing Vladimir Nabokov in a letter to Edmund Wilson. She had met the Russian émigré novelist at Wilson's house and found him personally charming, but she was "wildly irritated" by his work. "The author seems motivated by a compulsion to denigrate his heroes and thus strut his own superiority, which he may not have been able to demonstrate in life so must construct these puppets to mortify and humiliate," she stated. "I disliked his dowdy translations, too—at least Constance Garnett (or was it Isabel Hapgood?) loved the whole and didn't want to stop the horses and the sleighbells just to lecture that a blur of fir trees shadowing the sky (vaguely) was really four half-grown greenish-brown specimens of Max Schlings Spruce Seedings No. 542. Who knows what the best translation is, anyway?—for the scientific exactness can be way off the true feeling."

Jack Sherman remained her most constant correspondent. "I am a great Chaucerian lover (required course in Anglo-Saxon) in spite of hating the course," she wrote. "But I really love the Greek and Latin poets. I wish I had taken more, though maybe it's the translations that give the zest. Right now I am reading my favorite Petronius in a paperback marvelous translation by one William Arrowsmith—but I am bragging as I last only about half an hour reading these days."

Powell was thrilled with Jack's decision to enroll at the University of Chicago in order to pursue a teaching degree. "I am overwhelmed with admiration for anyone in fifties able to change their life like that: new place, new regime—what will power and ambition!" she told Phyllis. She gave Sherman himself strict instructions on the way to become a writer:

A. Get started on novel before you get scared of it. . . . One advantage of the rough life you had is that it is so damn more interesting and literary than the Dull Happy Childhoods of Well Brought Up Squares.

B. Get away (I recommend N.Y.) if only for a few days when all the indecisions you are tangled in suddenly fall into focus and you can see your set-up (back and ahead).

"Start the novel (or play) and have it on the fireless cooker when you take on the teaching job or the new graduate study," she urged. "For Christ's sake don't take any teaching course which, as you know, keeps you from learning anything yourself." The best teachers, she explained, "don't follow methods but are richly informed and widely interested and interesting themselves—the difference between a doctor and a mere druggist who spoons out the advised doses."

All through that last year, Powell attempted to make some headway in her own writing, working variously on *The Brooklyn Widow*, *Summer Rose*, an essay for the *New York Times*, and *Yow*. Her diary entries from this period have the intensity of prayers: "How wonderful if I had excitement of contemporary work to wake me up—how fantastic if I could whiz through in joy and fun"; "How heavenly if I could get to work myself"; "God how wonderful if I could get some writing done—if, for instance, I could knock off the cat book just for fun."

But the turbulence in her stomach and the violent diarrhea continued unabated. Her doctors prescribed tincture of opium, which Jackie suggested be supplemented with yeast in lemonade, a home remedy that Powell found helpful. She cut out her beloved Pernod, believing it might be irritating her bowels, and switched to whiskey and milk as her "tipple"; she also developed a new, hitherto unthinkable passion for beer. "Must try to Coué myself out of this as I am in same spot as Margaret and Joe—drying up, weak, no appetite," she noted. "How alone we all are," she wrote on July 3, "even Joe with me on hand. God—how wonderful if I could get energy back and control of digestion."

Jojo arrived home for a week's vacation at the end of July, and she managed to take him to the New York World's Fair in Flushing Meadows with Bobby Morrison, the young man who had been raised by Louise Lee. "Most exhausting but worth it to get off Jojo's mind," she wrote. "Went to Pepsi-Cola show and to Schaeffer's beer garden for dried sandwiches. Then a tractor ride around the Fair with fountains—getting lost mostly and finding no glamour as people wander around in sloppy clothes and sour faces as if they were already stung and gloomy. Subway home at ten, dead tired."

On September 7, down to 105 pounds and so fatigued she could scarcely move, Powell checked herself into St. Luke's. Hannah Green remembered the fresh, sharp smell of early autumn wafting up from Morningside Park as she went to see her in the hospital. Powell's doctor suggested an emergency colostomy, which she refused: "Surgeon said okay—my right," she told Phyllis. "Said wasn't sure he could get it all anyway (so probably a series of operations, eh?)"

At the end of the month, Powell returned to 95 Christopher Street, where Jackie and Hannah continued to care for her tenderly. Most other visitors were barred. Bobby Lewis was one of the few friends permitted to call; he invited her to see the Broadway musical romance *On a Clear Day You Can See Forever*, which he had directed. Powell planned to attend but ultimately decided she was too weak to make the trip uptown.

On October 22, she sent her final letter to Jack Sherman, a cheerful combination of routine gossip and literary talk. In it Powell spoke of her admiration for Anthony Trollope and Henry Fielding ("especially his plays—terribly witty") and her small esteem for best-selling author Robert Ruark: "I got disgusted with the big conceited Hemingway imitator some years ago."

Because Dr. Solley's wife had died suddenly and he had gone out to Missouri for the funeral, Powell was left on her own for a while, "which is logical as there seems nothing anybody can do except recommend a change of laxative or something."

> Hannah cooks me a good plain supper and Jackie shows up when she can—she cleaned out my closets looking for something I could wear and found one closet full of live moths which she rapidly dispatched. I get Coby to spend the night and he makes breakfast very well now if I can keep him from getting tight by hiding bottles (at night) and I feel better knowing someone can open and shut things.

On November 6, Powell signed an uncommonly vague will prepared by one Jack Larson, a person she had earlier described to Sherman as an "excellent man who makes my income tax . . . friend and admirer of Jackie's and Dan's."

Unfortunately, the document was ineptly written, maddeningly inexact, and moreover not representative of the decisions she had made, at least as she expressed them in her letters and diaries. Larson was a certified public accountant, not a lawyer, and he was clearly out of his depth in this new assignment. "By November, Dawn was just too exhausted to care very much about her will," Jack Sherman said. "I don't think she ever really believed she was going to die anyway."

Powell made Jackie her general executor and, with Coby, her literary coexecutor. "She is *here* and nobody could get at safe deposit box or anything else otherwise," Powell explained to Jack.

A small sum of money was left to Coby. Powell's paintings, sketches, jewelry, and furs were intended for Jack Sherman and his sister, Rita, while her furniture, silverware, and china were earmarked for Jackie, and most of her other household items for Phyllis. Jojo, meanwhile, received almost nothing—only a token payment out of the net income from his mother's estate. This did not indicate any anger on Powell's part toward her son; it was simply that Jojo was now a ward of New York, and Powell had probably been advised that a sudden windfall could have disastrous consequences for him, including possible eviction from Manhattan State.

On November 8, Powell decided that she needed to go to the hospital, and Hannah and Coby summoned an ambulance. "Dawn so weak," Hannah wrote in her diary. "She could hardly raise her arms so I could put her nightgown on. When she was in the ambulance, stretched out, the white cloth over her head, Coby said 'Goodbye, Dawn,' with a sudden mustered brave cleanness."

Back in St. Luke's, she now deteriorated rapidly. Hannah recalled the "look in her eye—wild look of pain, terror, confusion of drug, the want to speak. . . . The terror of giving up the last thread of life, of connection with one's body, one's oneness, and merging into nothing. If only one believed it was infinity or heaven." Powell was semidelirious much of the time; Hannah remembered her slowly mouthing the words "snow leopard," an image of death that Ernest Hemingway had used in *The Snows of Kilimanjaro* (and that Peter Matthiesen would later explore in his own book by that name).

The night after Powell entered the hospital, a massive power failure hit the northeastern United States; it would eventually be known as the first great New York Blackout. At another time, Dawn herself might have appreciated the coincidence—the implication, somehow, that the city couldn't quite function without her bright, pulsing presence.

Jack came in from Chicago on November 13 and went directly to St. Luke's; he wrote about Powell's last hours in a letter he would post to Phyllis the following day. It is a direct, straightforward recounting of the dignified, near-Socratic death that Powell might have chosen for herself:

I am thanking God that it was possible for me to go there when I did. When I arrived at the hospital alone Saturday about 10:30 A.M., they were preparing her for the day. A new nurse was working with her and it took her about an hour. When I walked in, Dawn turned her big eyes on me. I said "Dawn, it is Jack, don't you recognize me?" She said, "yes, but for a moment I thought you were someone else." Then she said to me "you shouldn't have come" and I answered that I *had* to come. I kept holding her hand and all the while she was looking me over. Finally she said, "You look nice." Believe me, about that time I was ready to show all of New York just how emotional our family can be! All of this talking was an effort for her, but she was perfectly lucid. When I asked her how long she had been in the hospital she answered "Monday" with no hesitation. It was very obvious that she was desperately ill and not long for this earth. I spoke about a few silly things like the plane trip and finally I said the thing that I came to New York to say to her: "Don't worry, Dawn, you know that I'll look after Jojo, don't you?" And she answered "I know you will."

I know this will sound emotional and highly romantic, of which I am both, but from that moment on she seemed to start slipping away, and I do not know of one other complete sentence she spoke to anyone. Saturday evening there was no conversation with her. I later telephoned the hospital twice after I had left to check with her nurse. I had asked to stay with her there if they thought she would not live through the night. My last call was at 11:45 and the nurse told me she was just the same and she doubted if there would be any sudden turn for the worse.

Sunday morning when I got out there I knew it was the end. I was alone with her until about two with the exception of a call at the hospital by Monroe Stearns. Jackie and Bobby [Morrison] came out about two-thirty. I told the nurse I felt sure Dawn was very close to death but she would not commit herself. I talked over the phone to a doctor who was on her case as I wanted to make sure she was not in pain and to see if he would tell me anything. I was assured she was under heavy sedation. After Jackie came the nurse came back into the room with another nurse and asked us to step outside. They had hypos so we walked outside, and Jackie left to see about a form she had to fill out in the office. When the nurse came out she said to Bobby and me don't go in for a few minutes, but I did anyway. I knew that Dawn was gone then. I called a nurse passing by and she came in and in a few moments confirmed what I knew all along.

Jack gazed down at his cousin, who looked as if she were still in the midst of ferocious battle—her face drawn, her eyes open, her teeth clenched, not at all resigned. Somewhere he had read that the spirits of the newly dead may not depart the body immediately, and so he said aloud, "I love you." Remembering Dawn's own final advice to Margaret De Silver, he added, "Don't be afraid." Then—since Powell had left her body to the Cornell Medical Center and her eyes to the Eye Bank, and time was, as ever, of the essence—the hospital orderlies arrived to shuttle her remains down the hall.

Afterward

❧

HANNAH GREEN ARRIVED at St. Luke's Hospital just as Bobby Morrison, Jack Sherman, and a distraught Jackie Rice were walking toward the elevator. The news was relayed, there were hugs and tears all around, and Hannah and Jackie went out to dinner together in the Village, while Bobby returned home to Brooklyn and Jack made his gloomy way to Manhattan State Hospital.

"We finally got to Ward's Island," Jack wrote to Phyllis, "and believe me this is worse than death":

> Jojo had flipped, broken a window, torn his clothes and had been quite violent. He had been taken off his laundry job,

which he had had for eight years and then he was unable to talk
to his Mother over the phone and he sensed that something was
terribly wrong. He was in a restricted ward and it was nerve-
wracking to get to see him. He kept saying, "Is my Mother all
right? Is she like Daddy? Is she conscious? Does this mean my
days of going home are over?"

Jack consoled the orphaned Jojo as best he could, and then he
proceeded to La Guardia Airport, where he caught an evening flight
to Chicago.

In later years, Jackie Rice would bitterly regret having agreed to
become Powell's executor. By all accounts, hers was a stormy
tenure, and she fell out almost immediately with Jack and Phyllis
over the execution of the will and various matters relating to Jojo's
care. According to Jackie, most of Powell's possessions, including
many of the volumes in her substantial library, were sold to pay her
creditors; whatever the case, none of the bequeathed paintings,
sketches, furs, jewelry, or other belongings intended for the Gousha
and Sherman families ever reached them.

In the late 1960s, Jackie and her family moved to Connecticut.
There, Powell's papers were arranged, itemized, and, Jackie insists,
available to anybody who wanted to see them. She worked closely
with Matthew Josephson on the very first posthumous evaluation of
Dawn's work, which appeared in 1973 in the *Southern Review.* But her
once exuberant health had begun to fail, she suffered from chronic
depression, and she ignored other queries from scholars and filmmakers.

From 1979 through 1981, Judith Faye Pett, a doctoral student
at the University of Iowa, attempted to reach Jackie, to no avail. Pett
was at work on a dissertation about Powell's work, at a time when all
of the author's books were out of print and any interest should have

been encouraged warmly. But no reply was forthcoming. Pett included a stinging indictment in the foreword to her study:

> Dawn Powell was a prolific, professional writer. She kept records—personal diaries, unpublished manuscripts, prelimi-nary notes and plans for her novels, perhaps even letters—which are under the jurisdiction of an executrix. She also wrote many letters to friends and acquaintances in the profes-sion. Gaining access to these unpublished materials has been, in some cases, impossible. Her literary executrix, Jacqueline Miller Rice, has been unresponsive to requests for information. Mrs. Rice's refusal or inability to respond calls into question whether the role of the literary executor is to protect an author's papers *for* or *from* the interests of posterity.

Around the same time that Pett completed her dissertation—the first-ever full-length study of Dawn Powell's life and work—Gore Vidal stepped in to boost his old friend's posthumous reputa-tion. In a paragraph he contributed to a symposium on unknown writers in the Fall 1981 issue of the *Antioch Review*, he called Powell a "comic writer as good as Evelyn Waugh and better than Clemens." Six years later, he would expand this blurb into a long article entitled "Dawn Powell: The American Writer," which appeared in the *New York Review of Books* on November 5, 1987. Vidal's essay was engag-ing, perceptive, and deeply affectionate, and its publication marked the first time many younger readers (and more than a few older ones) ever heard Powell's name.

As a direct result of Vidal's prestigious championship, the Quality Paperback Book Club combined three of Powell's novels—*Angels on Toast*, *The Wicked Pavilion*, and *The Golden Spur*—into an omnibus edi-tion in 1989; each was later reissued separately in trade paperback

format by Vintage. Almost simultaneously, a small, adventurous
company named Yarrow Press brought out editions of two more
Powell novels—*The Locusts Have No King* and *A Time to Be Born*—again
in paperback. But Vintage quickly remaindered its stock, and ham-
pered by a shortage of funds and limited distribution, Yarrow folded
in 1993. Five years after the beginning of her revival, Powell was
once again completely out of print.

Here, it is necessary for the present writer to enter the story.
Throughout 1991, I was traveling regularly between New York and
California, and during one of those long plane trips, I discovered
Edmund Wilson's *New Yorker* essay on *The Golden Spur,* which had
been reprinted in a volume titled *The Bit between My Teeth.* Intrigued,
I tracked down copies of *The Wicked Pavilion* and *The Golden Spur* in
Vintage paperbacks, then found a first edition of *Turn, Magic Wheel*
for five dollars at Acres of Books, the wondrous secondhand book-
store in Long Beach, California. I decided to write an article on what
I hoped would be the Great Dawn Powell Revival for the newspaper
at which I then worked, *New York Newsday.*

As part of my research, I met Jackie Rice for drinks at a midtown Manhattan restaurant one wintry day in late 1991; I liked her
immediately. I was saddened when she informed me that none of
Powell's other friends was still living and that the author had broken
off all relations with her family long before she died, but I took these
statements at face value and proceeded with my story.

Full of flaws and misinformation though it was, the article nevertheless changed everything. A week after its publication, I was surprised to receive a telephone call from a social worker named
Michelle Borsack, who said she had read the piece to one of her
favorite patients in the hospital where she worked; his name was
Joseph R. Gousha Jr. Borsack had enjoyed the article, but she felt it
might have been stronger had I spoken with Hannah Green (who was
then living at 52 Barrow Street in New York) and Dawn's cousin Jack

Sherman in Shelby, Ohio, whose numbers she gave me. "These are the people who really take care of Jojo," she said.*

I was dumbfounded by Borsack's call and tried unsuccessfully for several weeks to reach Jackie, finally concluding, somewhat reluctantly, that our friendship had ended as suddenly as it had begun. Then, as if under a mysterious compulsion, I decided to begin tape-recording an archive of interviews about Powell that I thought might be of use to some future biographer (I had no plans to undertake the job myself at the time). I was already planning a trip to Cleveland, and the prospect of making a seventy-mile detour to meet with Jack Sherman at his home in Shelby seemed irresistible. Since 1965, I learned, Jack had served as Jojo's guardian, arranging for his needs at a series of nursing homes, visiting him twice a year, and purchasing new copies of the Bible or *David Copperfield* for him whenever yet another tantrum had reduced yet another existing copy to tatters.

As it happened, a freak snowstorm hit the Midwest the night of my visit, and I was effectively snowbound in Shelby. And so I spent the next two days talking leisurely with Jack and his sister, Rita Sherman, about their cousin. Upon hearing I was there, Carol Warstler, the oldest daughter of Phyllis Cook, drove across much of Ohio in the midst of the blizzard to contribute her own memories. I was deeply touched by the kindness and dedication of Powell's family.

At some point during our time together, Jack showed me a file of correspondence from bewildered scholars, publishers, filmmakers, and the like, all of whom had inquired about Powell's life and work, only to be ignored by Jackie Rice. By the end of our visit, a conspiracy was afoot, its goal summarized on a T-shirt my wife, Vanessa Weeks Page, had made for me: "Free Dawn Powell!"

Sherman's authority as a family member and legatee permitted

---

* *Borsack also questioned my reference to Jojo as "retarded" — a mistake that I hope has been rectified in this book.*

us to engage a copyright lawyer named Peter Skolnik, who, after reviewing the irregularities in her handling of the literary estate, threatened Jackie's lawyers with prompt legal action. In early 1994, she yielded to pressure, stepped aside as executor, and permitted the transfer of Powell's papers to Columbia University. Most of the material was in remarkably good shape, and much to her credit, Jackie had seemingly preserved all of Powell's notes and diaries, including several entries that portrayed the younger woman in a less than favorable light. Her apologies were profuse, and ultimately persuasive; she has not had an easy life. It is tempting, in the end, to agree with the assessment of Rosalind Wilson: "Jackie certainly never intended to hurt Dawn. It just happened."

There remained the question of just how to bring Powell's books to a larger audience. I felt that a collection of her best work would be the proper first step, but it seemed to me imperative that any such volume be published first in hardcover format. The five paperback reissues of the late 1980s and early 1990s had not received nearly as much media attention as they deserved; in general, paperbacks, no matter how excellent or unusual, are ignored by the larger book reviews, and I was convinced that this had contributed to the failure of the initial revival.

In late 1993, Michael Moore, an editor and partner at Steerforth Press in Vermont, visited my agent, Melanie Jackson, in New York. She asked if he was interested in Dawn Powell; he replied that he was, very much so. We subsequently met for breakfast. I mentioned my belief in the necessity of a hardcover publication, and he agreed to support such a venture, so long as future reissues might be brought out in paperback. The result was *Dawn Powell at Her Best*, a collection containing *Dance Night* and *Turn, Magic Wheel*, the novels by which Powell herself set the most store, as well as some short stories and the autobiographical vignette "What Are You Doing in My Dreams?" The book received widespread acclaim when it was issued in November 1994 and has remained a steady seller since.

By that point, we were already at work compiling the diaries. On first opening these dusty, fragile volumes at Columbia after their transfer from Jackie's house in Connecticut, I had the sure and humbling sense that a masterpiece had fallen into my hands. An abridged version was issued in 1995. Reviews appeared all over the country, most of them overwhelmingly favorable. Since then, Steerforth has continued to bring out Powell novels in handsome editions (including a reissue of *The Tenth Moon* under Dawn's original title, *Come Back to Sorrento*); in all, eleven of those books are currently available, meaning that more works by Powell are in print today than at any time during her life. The "permanent visitor" is back in our midst.

One last question still needed to be resolved. As alluded to earlier, Powell had willed her body to the Cornell Medical Center, but it was customary at the time for the hospital to return the remains to the deceased's family for eventual cremation or burial. Jack had hoped to bring Dawn back to Oakland Cemetery in Shelby, where Hattie Sherman, Dawn Gates, and Orpha May Steinbrueck already lie, and where Jojo has a plot reserved. Much of the summer of 1997 was spent attempting to track down Dawn's body and ship it home to Shelby.

A long series of communications with the New York Department of Vital Records ultimately proved fruitless, as did searches through the files of local cemeteries. Finally, just as this book was nearing completion, a document was found in the Cornell Medical Center archives. Dated May 4, 1970, almost five years after Powell's death (and the very day that the Kent State University shootings brought Ohio much unwanted national attention), the letter was from Jackie: addressed to the Cornell Department of Anatomy, it authorized the hospital to "dispose of the remains of Dawn Powell in the City Cemetery, as the family does not wish to take possession of the remains and dispose of same."

According to surviving family members, nobody in Ohio was ever presented with a choice in the matter. Jackie, who was scarcely speaking to the family by then, has defended the decision with her insistence that Dawn would have wanted to stay in New York ("She would have *hated* being in Ohio forever!"). Perhaps; in any event, sometime within the next few weeks of 1970, whatever fragments were left of Dawn Powell's body were taken to Hart Island and interred in a mass grave by Riker's Island convicts. There she is—and there she must stay.

Most of Powell's friends and family are now gone. Phyllis Cook survived her sister by twenty years, dying in 1985 in Massillon, Ohio. Coburn Gilman died of natural causes on Christmas Day, 1967. John Dos Passos died in 1970, Edmund Wilson in 1972, Sara Murphy in 1975, John Howard Lawson in 1977, Monroe Stearns in 1987, and Malcolm Cowley in 1990. Some of Powell's other friends lived long enough to give interviews but died before the completion of this book—among them Maurice Dolbier, Eleanor Farnham, Hannah Green, Frances Keene, Robert Lewis, Loren MacIver, Charles Norman, and Andrews Wanning.

In 1998, Jack Sherman was still living with his sister, Rita, a few blocks from the home he built for himself and Orpha May Steinbrueck more than sixty years ago. Until a bad fall made travel difficult for him, he would visit Jojo faithfully at least twice a year. Jojo himself has now lived longer than either of his parents and daily expresses his desire to join his mother, his father, and his cherished "Deesie" in Heaven, another home far away.

✧ NOTES ✦

Unless otherwise indicated, all quotations from Dawn Powell used within this book come from her diaries, notebooks, letters, and other papers, now housed as part of the Powell Collection at the Rare Book and Manuscript Division of Columbia University Library. Powell kept carbon copies of most of her important letters; where I know that the original copy exists in another collection, I have identified that institution. I have dated all of the letters as exactly as I can. When identifying passages from Powell's books, I have relied entirely on first editions. The only quotations I have reproduced from her diaries come from the abridged published edition, with the sole exception of her first entry in 1931. All interviews were conducted by the author unless otherwise specified.

In the source notes that follow, I have used the initials DP to identify Powell as the author of letters cited.

Prologue: Hart Island—1998

Most of the information about Hart Island comes from two long and helpful interviews with Commander Tom Antenten of the New York City Department of Correction, which administers the City Cemetery. These were supplemented by an informational flier published by the city, and by dozens of close inspections of the island made during approaches to or departures from La Guardia Airport. Confirmation of Powell's burial on Hart Island was provided in a letter dated May 4, 1970, which Jacqueline Miller Rice sent to the Cornell Medical Center. The quote "This—well, this is *me*" comes from *She Walks in Beauty*, page 227. The quotation from the *New York Times Book Review* is taken from a review published on November 26, 1995. Gore Vidal's summary of Powell's talents was published in his article "Dawn Powell: The American Writer" (*New York Review of Books*, November 5, 1987). It was the late Frances Keene who suggested that Powell was "generally considered a good novelist of the second class," in a 1994 interview. Powell's disavowal of her supposed "cynicism" may be found in her diary under the date June 16, 1948.

Chapter One: Story of a Country Girl

The chapter epigram is taken from the dust jacket for the first printing of *She Walks in Beauty;* the blurb was obviously written by Powell herself (see the bibliography for a list of Powell's works).

Other quotations from Powell's diary: "It never seemed to me . . ." (June 25, 1933); "Any barroom brawl . . ." (December 29, 1936); "Stepmother's greatest joy . . ." (January 27, 1941); "I realize more and more . . ." (February 2, 1933); "Progress is so personal . . ." (July 1, 1936); "Some people never seem to grow up . . ." (February 16, 1955); "Since sophomore college . . ." (August 15, 1932).

Quotations from Powell's letters: "No one knew who printed it . . ." (DP to Orpha May Steinbrueck, circa October 1915); "I'd send a copy to you . . ." (DP to Orpha May Steinbrueck, circa January 1915); "They aren't nearly so interesting . . ." (DP to Mabel Powell, July 13, 1918); "A summer in artistic atmosphere . . ." (ibid.); "A lot of [the suffrage work] has been among the Irish . . ." (DP to Steinbrueck and Gretchen Quiggle, July 16, 1918).

My information about Mount Gilead came from several visits to the town; long discussions with Daniel Rhodebeck, a shrewd and deeply knowledgeable local historian; and the several books on Morrow County and Ohio listed in the bibliography.

All information about the Sherman and Powell families was gleaned from family records and discussions with Jack Sherman, Carol Warstler, Richard McLaughlin, and other descendants; it was checked, whenever possible, against U.S. Census documents, real estate transfers, preserved local obituaries, and cemetery records. The Western Reserve Museum and Library, in Cleveland Heights, Ohio, was especially helpful.

There is no longer any real controversy about Dawn Powell's date of birth; as late as 1950, at least a quarter century after she began to insist she had been born in 1897, she used the 1896 date when applying for a United States passport.

Hattie Sherman died in 1903, not in 1902, as her headstone in Shelby's Oakland Cemetery would indicate (the marker was added many years later by Orpha May Steinbrueck). Information about the Stearns family was provided by Richard McLaughlin and confirmed by research in the North Olmsted city records and published histories. Memories of Sabra Stearns were provided by Carol Warstler, Phyllis Poccia, and Richard McLaughlin. Baby Emily Helen Powell is buried in the Butternut Ridge Cemetery in North Olmsted, along with Roy and Sabra Powell.

Statistics on high school attendance and college education for women were provided by the American Association of University Women. Most of the information about the character and career of Orpha May Steinbrueck comes directly from Jack Sherman, who lived with her for the better part of thirty-five years.

"There was Auntie May . . ." comes from the unpublished "Woggs" diary Powell kept in the summer of 1915. I am grateful to Sally Maier of the Shelby Historical Society for providing me with a copy of the Shelby High School yearbook, and to Lake Erie College for duplicating all the articles Powell wrote for the *Lake Erie Record.*

My interviews with Antoinette Akers, Olive Hoover Ernst, and the late Eleanor Farnham were all conducted at the McGregor Home in East Cleveland in January 1992. The quotation from Vivian Small comes from Margaret Geissman Gross's *Dancing on the Table: A History of Lake Erie College.* Information on Powell's fellow students Cornelia Wolfe, Charlotte Johnson, and Eleanor Farnham comes from both Powell's own writing and from the Lake Erie College alumni office. No last name has been found for Powell's assumed boyfriend "Ben."

Chapter Two: New York: Joe, Jojo, and Jack

The chapter epigram comes from a March 16, 1953, entry in Powell's diary. Other quotations from Powell's diary: "I want so much for my lover . . ." (June 23, 1921); "Book reviewers who have ignored my hard-fought novels . . ." (July 14, 1933); "Such a dreadful nightmare . . ." (January 1, 1934, but reported on last page of 1933 diary); "End of ten years . . ." (January 26, 1939).

Quotations from Powell's letters: "I love the farm . . ." (DP to Orpha May Steinbrueck, August 26, 1918); "Only the fact that I was a college graduate . . ." (DP to Charlotte Johnson, circa September 1918); "Dancing in the streets . . ." (DP to Charlotte Johnson, November 12, 1918); "Do you know I've lived . . ." (DP to Charlotte Johnson, December 8, 1918); "There are three stages you go through in regard to the Village . . ." (ibid.); "The boarders are sort of touchy about it . . ." (DP to Orpha May Steinbrueck, circa November 1918); "I worked all day Monday . . ." (DP to Orpha May Steinbrueck, November 23, 1919); "[Gompers] wrote personally . . ." (DP to Orpha May Steinbrueck, circa January 1920); "I would rather live here . . ." (ibid.); "But it's silly to worry . . ." (DP to Mabel Powell Pocock, late 1920 or early 1921); "I feel pretty good . . ." (DP to Mabel Powell Pocock and Phyllis Powell Cook, September 3, 1921); "The correct weight . . ." (DP to Orpha May Steinbrueck, February 15, 1923); "He pulls himself up in his bathtub . . ." (DP to Orpha May Steinbrueck, November 19, 1922); "He wears three-year-old clothes . . ." (DP to Orpha May Steinbrueck, November 21, 1923); "While we were trying to teach him . . ." (DP to Dr. Howard Zucker, February 9, 1957); "We were put in the position . . ." (ibid.); "He had sat all the pleats . . ." (DP to Joseph Gousha, June 21,

1925); "Totally unmanageable . . ." (DP to Joseph Gousha, June 25, 1925); "I have just spent two hours . . ." (DP to Joseph Gousha, June 30, 1925); "I'm very fond of him again . . ." (DP to Joseph Gousha, circa July 5, 1925); "It's funny writing away from you . . ." (DP to Joseph Gousha, March 9, 1926).

Dozens of different books—as well as my own Manhattan residence for the past twenty-two years—informed my sketch of the New York City Powell first encountered. Her early addresses are taken mostly from her correspondence with her friend Charlotte Johnson, which was returned to Powell in the 1950s. Information on the "Yeomanettes" was provided by the United States Navy.

Both the description of Powell's brief film career and the author's list of early publications are taken from a letter to Orpha May Steinbrueck dating from late 1919; it has proved impossible to track down many of the magazines Powell mentions. Information on Helen Kessel was provided by her daughter, Clare Lissfelt Meyers. Most of the information on Joseph Gousha comes from his files and scrapbooks, now part of the Dawn Powell Collection at Columbia University. Eleanor Farnham's reminiscence of Dawn and Joe was provided by the Lake Erie College archives; its date is unknown.

The quotations from Charles Norman's *Poets and People* are reprinted by permission of the author. Several clippings from the press coverage of Dawn and Joe's separate living arrangements after their marriage have survived; unfortunately, only two of them have dates: an article in the *New York Evening Journal* from January 4, 1921 ("Newlyweds Hunt Flat after Trial of Fannie Hurst's Plan") and the *Chicago News* of January 16, 1921 ("House Shortage Parts Pair").

My information on autism came from a variety of texts and encyclopedias, most of them listed in the bibliography. Dr. Morton Schwimmer and Dr. Howard Zucker were most helpful in illuminating the disorder for me. In addition to Powell's commentary in diaries and notebooks, information on Louise Lee comes from surviving members of Powell's family—especially Jack Sherman, Carol Warstler, and Phyllis Poccia—and also from an autobiographical notebook that Joseph R. Gousha, Jr., wrote in 1993. Hope Hale Davis's unpublished memoir of the young Powell was graciously provided to me by the author.

Matthew Josephson's article "Dawn Powell: A Woman of *Esprit*" was published in the Winter 1973 issue of the *Southern Review*. The quote from George Chappell comes from his book *Restaurants of New York*. Information on John Howard Lawson is derived from several doctoral dissertations, from conversations and correspondence with Lawson's biographer, Robert Hethmon, from an interview with Lawson's son, Jeffrey Lawson, and from histories of the cold war. Marjorie Howard Johnson graciously permitted me to quote from a diary kept by her father, the Cleveland-based editor and writer Nathaniel Howard. The July 17, 1928, letter from Susan Edmond Lawson to her husband was provided by the Lawson Collection in the Southern Illinois University Library in Carbondale.

Chapter Three: The Early Novels

The chapter epigram comes from a diary entry dated May 1, 1933. Other quotations from Powell's diary: "Reading *Whither* I was horrified . . ." (December 1, 1943); "Six months work . . ." (June 7, 1931); "Joe worked on novel at office . . ." (April 11, 1925); "How much sharper and better . . ." (December 1, 1934); "Female friends are the greatest hazard . . ." (March 20, 1944); "The artist who really loves people . . ." (June 16, 1948).

Quotations from *Whither*: "Around 21 or so . . ." (page 3); "Girl who was breaking off . . ." (page 5); "Truly, alcohol . . ." (page 153); "You should live down here . . ." (page 179); "Perhaps she attracted him mentally . . ." (page 295); "Healthy, good looking but very stupid . . ." (page 102); "You've got to work and write . . ." (page 291); "BABIES! The Love Perpetrators . . ." (page 64); "Thirty is really the most important age . . ." (page 107). Chapter 8 runs from page 139 to page 147.

Quoted reviews: *New York Times*, March 15, 1925; *Saturday Review of Literature*, April 18, 1925; *Literary Review*, April 11, 1925. Other review: *Boston Evening Transcript*, March 14, 1925.

Quotations from *She Walks in Beauty*: author's biography on dust jacket; "Nearly thirty . . ." (page 7); "She was a splendid woman . . ." (page 5); "For years, I have had only one desire . . ." (page 225); "She was an innocent country lass . . ." (page 14).

Edmund Wilson's statement that "Dawn was really a man" was mentioned on several occasions by his daughter, Rosalind Baker Wilson, in personal interviews.

Quoted reviews: *New York Times*, June 24, 1928; *New York Herald Tribune*, April 15, 1928; *Saturday Review of Literature*, May 12, 1928. Other reviews: *Boston Evening Transcript*, June 6, 1928; *Independent*, May 19, 1928; *Nation*, June 6, 1928; *New Republic*, May 2, 1928; *New York World*, May 6, 1928.

Quotations from *The Bride's House*: "Sophie is our blood . . ." (page 161); "It is a dreadful thing . . ." (page 202); "Lying in Jerome's arms . . ." (page 293); "Buggies and wagons . . ." (page 131).

Quoted reviews: *New York Herald Tribune*, February 24, 1929; *New York Times*, March 10, 1929; *New York Evening Post*, April 6, 1929. Other reviews: *Boston Evening Transcript*, April 20, 1929; *New Republic*, May 29, 1929; *New York World*, February 24, 1929; *Springfield* [Mass.] *Republican*, April 7, 1929.

My description of Powell's writing method comes from scrutiny of more than a dozen early loose-leaf notebooks that are currently housed at Columbia University as part of the Powell Collection.

Chapter Four: Shadow on the Heart

The chapter epigram is taken from a diary entry dated July 20, 1931. Other diary entries in this chapter: "Suddenly I thought, why that man . . ." (September 1, 1933); "Joe tight so much . . ." (February 26, 1930); "I sometimes think a writer . . ." (June 14, 1939); "I walked down Madison Avenue . . ." (May 5, 1933); "Although I set out to do a complete job . . ." (December 4, 1943); "It seems to me that ever since I finished . . ." (July 20, 1931); "Never give a guest . . ." (July 27, 1956); "No such thing as present sight . . ." (May 31, 1958); "Rich joy, which I have . . ." (April 1, 1959); "It runs along easily and solely by intuition . . ." (June 22, 1931); "How I hate the empty, silly, pointless title . . ." (May 29, 1932); "To find a public somewhere for something . . ." (April 4, 1933); "I was actually absorbed in it . . ." (March 18, 1943).

Quotations from letters: "Both Phyllis and Mabel . . ." (DP to Joseph Gousha, July 7, 1926); "He is a skeleton . . ." (DP to Joseph Gousha, circa July 5, 1926); "Every place else but New York . . ." (DP to Jack Sherman, circa June 1931); "I have, loving you . . ." (DP to Joseph Gousha, circa October 8, 1928); "I don't make beds . . ." (DP to Sara Murphy, December 14, 1949); "They thought at first my heart . . ." (DP to Mabel Powell Pocock and Phyllis Powell Cook, circa October 1929); "Telephone at bedside . . ." (ibid.); "Sort of a combination . . ." (DP to Phyllis Powell Cook, circa 1929).

For information on *Poets and People* and *All the Right Enemies*, please see the bibliography. Other data about Margaret De Silver were obtained through conversations with Frances Keene, Jacqueline Miller Rice, Jack Sherman, and Rosalind Baker Wilson, and from the many letters from De Silver in the Powell Collection. Information about Coburn Gilman was provided by Keene, Rice, Sherman, Wilson, Hannah Green, and Matthew Josephson's "Dawn Powell: A Woman of *Esprit*"; also from the alumni office at Columbia University.

Medical information on teratoma tumors was provided by Dr. Richard L. Page and Dr. Morton Schwimmer.

All information regarding Powell's publishing advances is taken from her files and her diaries, both part of the Dawn Powell Collection at Columbia. Maurice Dolbier's interview with Dawn Powell in the *Herald Tribune* was published on October 27, 1957.

Quotations from *Dance Night*: "The hell they do . . ." (page 29); "Trains whirred through the air . . ." (page 27); "Neither glad nor sorry . . ." (page 246); "Mrs. Pepper told Elsinore . . ." (page 285); "The humming of this town . . ." (page 68).

Quoted reviews: *New York Times*, November 16, 1930; *New York Herald Tribune*, October 12, 1930; *New Republic*, December 24, 1930. Other reviews: *Bookman*, November 1930; *Boston Evening Transcript*, November 5, 1930.

The quotation beginning "It's too bad I'm always confiding in you" is taken from the so-called "Woggs" diary that Powell kept in the summer of 1915.

Quotations from *Come Back to Sorrento / The Tenth Moon*: "He wandered around the deck . . ." (page 279); "She was fond of him . . ." (page 7); "Her casual references . . ." (page 9); "The loveliest child . . ." (page 12); "The God-like ruthlessness . . ." (page 54); "I've gone over the whole thing . . ." (page 25); "You cannot talk about real things . . ." (page 82).

Quoted reviews: *New York Herald Tribune*, September 4, 1920; *New York Times*, November 20, 1932; *Saturday Review of Literature*, September 17, 1932. Other review: *Boston Evening Transcript*, September 7, 1932.

Chapter Five: Movies, the Theater, and Literary Philosophies

The chapter epigram comes from an entry in Powell's diary dated January 25, 1933. Other diary entries in this chapter: "Can't imagine they will do it . . ." (July 8, 1930); "[The Theatre Guild] bawled . . ." (June 16, 1932); *Big Night* not played "nervously enough" (December 9, 1932); "The Group has put on . . ." (January 13, 1933); "The accumulation of stupidity . . ." (January 25, 1933); "[She] studies her own role . . . (April 26, 1934); "Now impossible to sleep . . ." (January 8, 1932); "Disappointed in the page proofs . . ." (February 9, 1934); "The new Ohio must be the keynote . . ." (September 9, 1932); "Jack is talking and thinking so much . . ." (August 20, 1932); "Flying along as it should . . ." (July 17, 1933); "It isn't as good a book . . ." (February 2, 1934); "I want this new novel to be delicate and cutting . . ." (February 12, 1934); "Dr. Witt examined me with X-rays . . ." (January 31, 1934); "Mrs. Trollope didn't attack America . . ." (November 1, 1957); Djuna Barnes's "sad, brilliant book" (January 17, 1938); "O Boston girls how about it . . ." (July 28, 1935); "My seeming sentimentality . . ." (July 14, 1956); "All right, we know we're dying . . ." (May 22, 1939).

Quotations from Powell letters: "He is, near as I can figure . . ." (DP to Joseph Gousha, January 1, 1932); "The sheer geographical excitement . . ." (ibid.); "I feel all my old Elk . . ." (DP to John Dos Passos, circa May 1935, collection University of Virginia); "They are really excellent . . ." (DP to John Dos Passos, circa May 1933, collection University of Virginia); "Yes, I used to have some good times . . ." (DP to Phyllis Powell Cook, April 11, 1963).

Powell's article on the creation of *Big Night* ran in the *New York Evening Post* on January 14, 1933.

Reviews of *Big Night*: *New York Evening Post*, January 18, 1933; *New York Herald Tribune*, January 19, 1933; *New York Times*, January 18, 1933; *The New Yorker*, January 28, 1933.

Reviews of *Jig-Saw* as a play: *New York Times*, *New York Herald Tribune*, *New York American*, all May 1, 1934; *Nation*, May 16, 1934. Reviews of book *Jig-Saw: A Comedy* (Farrar and Rinehart, 1934): *Commonweal*, May 18, 1934; *New York Herald Tribune*, July 15, 1934; *New York Times*, July 15, 1934; *Saturday Review of Literature*, July 7, 1934.

I am indebted to Richard Koszarski's fine article "Hello, Sister," published in the Autumn 1970 issue of *Sight and Sound*, for the history of the curious Powell/Stroheim collaboration that transformed *Walking down Broadway* into *Hello, Sister!* Additional assistance was provided by Charles Silver of the Museum of Modern Art. Quoted reviews of *Hello, Sister!*: *Variety*, May 9, 1933; *New York Times*, May 6, 1933.

Quoted reviews of *Man of Iron*: *New York Times*, December 7, 1935; *Variety*, December 11, 1935.

Quoted reviews of *The Story of a Country Boy*: *New York Times*, March 24, 1934; *New York Herald Tribune*, March 24, 1934; *Saturday Review*, March 31, 1934. Other reviews: *Christian Science Monitor*, April 24, 1934; *Commonweal*, June 22, 1934.

As noted in the "letters" section above, the two letters to John Dos Passos quoted in this chapter belong to the Dos Passos Collection at the University of Virginia. I am grateful to Lucy Dos Passos Coggin for permitting me to copy these documents.

Chapter Six: The Escape into Satire

The chapter epigram is taken from a diary entry marked February 26, 1936. Other diary entries cited in this chapter: "If I could get away . . ." (May 12, 1931); "New novel must be burningly contemporary . . ." (December 1, 1934); "Since I can write so fluidly . . ." (January 29, 1935); "I never felt better . . ." (February 1, 1935); "Believe, in spite of unusual facility . . ." (February 19, 1935); "I think this is much my best book . . ." (April 2, 1935); "Fear is such an utterly disrupting force . . ." (April 12, 1935); "John wrote 'Better put aside' . . ." (February 18, 1954); Farrar calls *Turn, Magic Wheel* a "fine" novel (December 2, 1935); "In my satire . . ." (February 26, 1936); "Hanging over the hospital can . . ." (September 17, 1937); "He requires the most intense control . . ." (February 3, 1936); "In the morning Joe came in . . ." (March 22, 1939); "A worthless woman . . ." (December 24, 1936); "Fairies as an oasis . . ." (May 23, 1935); "The bachelors of New York . . ." (March 2, 1936); "There is no fighting mediocrity . . ." (January 28, 1940); "Obsessed this time with Ann De Silver . . ." (January 24, 1940); "Say what you will . . ." (February 7, 1940); "Fear is a primary factor . . ." (September 29, 1940); "There are, I have now learned, rigorous rules . . ." (October 8, 1940).

Quotations from letters: "I do what I like . . ." (DP to Joseph Gousha, circa September 1936); "DEFINITELY REFUSED . . ." (DP to Joseph Gousha, October 15, 1936); "Je souffle pour vous . . ." (DP to Edmund Wilson, August 16, 1962); "There are no portraits in *The Happy Island* . . ." (DP to Michael Sadleir, September 23, 1938); "I named him before I found out her arrogant nature . . ." (DP to Max Perkins, circa

August 1940); "I wanted to convey the sense of speed . . ." (DP to Max Perkins, August 4, 1940).

Quotations from *Turn, Magic Wheel*: "Some fine day I'll have to pay . . ." (page 3); "Past youth the sweet creature lies about her age . . ." (page 12); "How clever I was . . ." (page 16); "Monument to Hollandaise . . ." (page 93); "Magically the five o'clock people . . ." (page 10); "Clouds as white . . ." (page 188).

Quoted reviews: *New Republic*, May 27, 1936; *New York Herald Tribune*, February 16, 1936; *New York Times*, February 27, 1936; *Los Angeles Examiner* (undated clipping in Powell's collection). Other reviews: *New Statesman* and *Nation*, July 18, 1936; *Spectator*, July 10, 1936; *Times Literary Supplement*, July 18, 1936; *Yale Review*, Summer 1936.

The anecdote about Professor Haldane comes from Josephson, "Dawn Powell: A Woman of *Esprit*."

Quoted reviews of *The Happy Island*: *New York Herald Tribune*, September 11, 1938; *New York Times*, September 4, 1938; *The New Yorker*, September 10, 1938. Other reviews: *Saturday Review*, September 24, 1938; *Time*, September 19, 1938.

Vidal's comparison of the final lines of *The Happy Island* to the work of Thackeray may be found in his article "Dawn Powell: The American Writer." Powell's letter to Michael Sadleir is reproduced courtesy of the Temple University Library. I am grateful to *Max Perkins: Editor of Genius*, by A. Scott Berg, for providing much of my information about Perkins and his working methods.

Quoted reviews of *Angels on Toast*: *New York Times*, October 20, 1940; *New York Herald Tribune*, October 6, 1940. Other reviews: *Booklist*, December 15, 1940; *Springfield* [Mass.] *Republican*, October 27, 1940.

Chapter Seven: Wars—at Home and Abroad

The chapter epigram comes from page 3 of *A Time to Be Born*. Diary entries in this chapter: "From the appalling lack of progress . . ." (December 31, 1940); "Talented but shrewd users pursued him always . . ." (August 7, 1956); "The Brooklyn Widow . . ." (July 20, 1934); "If these things happened at a time . . ." (January 26, 1942); "I swear it is based on five or six girls . . ." (March 11, 1956); "After Clare Luce made such evil use . . ." (February 13, 1943); "This usual but new business of people I know . . ." (December 21, 1942); "Carol called to say she liked the first part . . ." (December 16, 1943); "If Bunny's review had been offset . . ." (November 28, 1944); "Strange combination of gland, appetite and Benzedrine . . ." (July 18, 1945); "Max was an admirable institution . . ." (November 4, 1947); "A lawn bloomed on this gray lovely day . . ." (September 21, 1947); "Evidently life gets incredibly more terrifying . . ." (November 28, 1947); "Stunned and frightened . . ." (December 5, 1947); "My veins flat, my reactions bad . . ." (December 7, 1947).

Quotations from Powell letters: "I hope the jacket for my book . . ." (DP to Max Perkins, July 6, 1942—possibly never sent); "Shy, wistful, little smile . . ." (DP to Orpha May Steinbrueck, circa January 1923); "Both my sisters met me —" (DP to Max Perkins, June 20, 1945); "I was glad to get my background into a fluid state again . . ." (DP to Max Perkins, June 20, 1945); "Expensive due to five overnights . . ." (DP to Joseph Gousha, November 14, 1945); "Offhand, I would say . . ." (DP to Max Perkins, July 10, 1946); "This is a wonderful place . . ." (DP to Max Perkins, September 29, 1946); "Millions of other people's tribulations . . ." (DP to Irma Wyckoff, June 17, 1947); "a perfect cesspool . . ." (DP to Max Perkins, December 20, 1946); "I am thinking about you constantly . . ." (DP to John Dos Passos, September 17, 1947).

The description of Powell at the Hotel Lafayette is from Josephson, "Dawn Powell: A Woman of *Esprit*."

Powell's article in the *Boston Post* about *The Lady Comes Across* was published on December 14, 1941. Quoted reviews of the production: *Variety*, January 14, 1942; *New York World-Telegram*, January 10, 1942; *New York Times*, January 10, 1942; *New York Post*, January 10, 1942. Other reviews, all of them published on January 10, 1942, include the *New York Sun*, *New York News*, *Brooklyn Daily Eagle*, *Brooklyn Citizen*, *New York Journal-American*, and *Christian Science Monitor*.

Quotation from *A Time to Be Born*: "This was no time . . ." (page 3). Powell's synopsis of the novel is to be found in the Powell Collection at Columbia University, as is the letter to Max Perkins.

Quoted reviews: *New York Herald Tribune*, September 6, 1942; *New York Times*, September 6, 1942; *Nation*, September 19, 1942; *Time*, September 7, 1942. Other reviews: *Boston Globe*, September 23, 1942; *The New Yorker*, September 5, 1942; *Pratt*, December 1942.

Information about the family portrayals in *My Home Is Far Away* comes from Powell's own papers, supplemented by the memories of Carol Warstler, Phyllis Poccia, and Dorothy Chapman.

Quotation from *My Home Is Far Away*: "She was still scared . . ." (page 311). Terry Teachout's article appeared in the *New York Times Book Review* on November 26, 1995.

Quoted reviews: *New York Times*, November 19, 1944; *New York Herald Tribune*, November 19, 1944; *The New Yorker*, November 11, 1944. Other reviews: *Booklist*, January 15, 1945; *Boston Globe*, November 8, 1944; *Kirkus*, September 15, 1944; *New Republic*, January 1, 1945; *Springfield* [Mass.] *Republican*, December 24, 1944.

Powell's description of her early plan for *The Locusts Have No King* is reprinted courtesy of the Scribner's Collection at the Princeton University Library. Powell's letter to Sara Murphy about John Dos Passos is reprinted courtesy of Honoria Murphy Donnelly.

Chapter Eight: Dreams and Destroyers

The chapter epigram is taken from *The Happy Island*, page 85.

Diary entries quoted in this chapter: "They have perverted their rather infantile ambitions . . ." (January 5, 1943); "Hogarthian record of the follies . . ." (April 12, 1947); "The moral of the story . . ." (November 11, 1947); "First awe and ecstasy of Nature . . ." (January 10, 1953); "Sweetly . . . gay in five o'clock . . ." (July 20, 1948); "Unable to have haircut . . ." (August 1, 1948); "Mabel died at 9:30 . . ." (October 26, 1949); "Odd thing about a death . . ." (November 17, 1949); "When I look over this novel . . ." (January 16, 1950); discovery of *The Creevey Papers* (January 29, 1950); "Delighted with new novel, . . ." (February 6, 1950); "Lunch with Dos . . ." (January 11, 1950); "What I wish to do . . ." (July 30, 1950); "Get in touch with someone . . ." (August 10, 1950); "The reason friends in late middle age . . ." (October 14, 1950); "You can live very cheaply . . ." (November 12, 1950); "French frown on Pernod . . ." (November 16, 1950); "His best period so far . . ." (March 26, 1951); "Novel began in January 1950 . . ." (July 11, 1951); "My feeling is that I need the confidence . . ." (July 11, 1951); "In their masquerade as wide-eyed youth . . ." (September 10, 1963); "An excellent real treatment . . ." (May 9, 1934); "The Secret of My Failure . . ." (March 8, 1956); "Each new day's labor . . ." (September 18, 1951); "I am New York . . ." (October 24, 1949); "Never forget geography . . ." (October 26, 1951); "Thinking of Josie Herbst . . ." (October 19, 1953); Vidal a "genuine novelist . . ." (May 9, 1954); "Delicate, sweet little thing . . ." (October 11, 1951); "Niles died . . ." (May 1, 1952); "I am exhausted by another night with the dead . . ." (May 23, 1953); "I feel there is a sudden rush . . ." (February 17, 1953).

Quotations from Powell's letters: "The theme, as you so perspicaciously gathered . . ." (DP to Michael Sadleir, December 30, 1947); "Beer bad and very high . . ." (DP to Joseph Gousha, March 11, 1948); "Can we get a Hollywood divorce . . ." (DP to Carl Brandt, October 1, 1948); "Here is the family scandal . . ." (DP to Mabel Powell Pocock and Phyllis Powell Cook, April 15, 1949); "The trip seems like a bad dream . . ." (DP to Phyllis Powell Cook, November 7, 1949); "The sheer shock of three or four miles . . ." (DP to Joseph Gousha, circa June 10, 1949); "There was a cocktail party . . ." (ibid.); "Did you know MacDowell was off his rocker . . ." (DP to Joseph Gousha, circa June 29, 1949); "A sock in the face . . ." (DP to Edmund Wilson, June 5, 1950); gossip about Edmund Wilson, Jacques LeClercq, Mary Grand, and Louise Lee all taken from a letter from DP to Margaret De Silver, Summer 1950; "I have a great deal to thank you for . . ." (DP to Margaret De Silver, Summer 1950); "Reading the gossipy letters of French ladies . . ." (DP to John Hall Wheelock, September 18, 1950); "The sequel to *My Home Is Far Away* . . ." (ibid.); "Boston spinster roommate . . . splendid filet mignons . . ." (DP to Joseph Gousha, October 15, 1950); "I have seen nobody and have not tried to . . ." (DP to Joseph

Gousha, October 24, 1950); "Very distinguished and faunish . . ." (ibid.); "God what terrifying women . . ." (DP to Margaret De Silver, late 1950); comments on Sartre and de Beauvoir (DP to Edmund Wilson, November 11, 1950); "Neuro, thinking everything I say . . ." (DP to Joseph Gousha, circa November 1950); "Xmas spirit was comparatively quiet . . ." (DP to Phyllis Powell Cook, December 9, 1950); "French elated at our Korean defeats . . ." (DP to Joseph Gousha, December 11, 1950).

Quotation from *The Locusts Have No King*: "The real night does not begin . . ." (page 57). The letters about *The Locusts Have No King* from Edmund Wilson and Michael Sadleir are part of the Scribner's Collection at Princeton University Library and are used by permission.

Quoted reviews of *The Locusts Have No King*: *New York Times*, May 9, 1948; *New York Herald Tribune*, May 2, 1948; *Nation*, May 29, 1948. Other reviews: *Kirkus*, February 1, 1948; *Library Journal*, April 15, 1948; *The New Yorker*, May 1, 1948; *Saturday Review*, May 15, 1948; *San Francisco Chronicle*, June 13, 1948.

Will Lee Doyle's letter about working with Joseph Gousha is reprinted with the author's permission.

Powell's letter to Edmund Wilson about Sue Lawson is part of the Edmund Wilson Collection at the Beinecke Rare Book and Manuscript Library at Yale University.

Quoted reviews of *Sunday, Monday and Always*: *New York Times*, July 28, 1952; *New York Post*, July 27, 1952; *Saturday Review*, July 26, 1952; *New York Times Book Review*, June 29, 1952. Other reviews: *Chicago Sunday Tribune*, July 27, 1952; *Kirkus*, April 1, 1952; *Nation*, August 2, 1952; *The New Yorker*, June 28, 1952.

Chapter Nine: The Collapse

The chapter epigram is taken from a diary entry dated June 20, 1959. Other diary entries in this chapter: "Adversity has its advantages . . ." (July 7, 1954); "The lostness of having no treasure chest . . ." (November 25, 1954); visit to Louise Lee (February 27, 1955); "This push-button sex . . ." (June 11, 1965); "'Marcia' was much better book . . ." (July 5, 1955); "There is no wit or humor . . ." (April 1, 1957); "Still convinced that it is a delicate, skillful dissection . . ." (August 12, 1957); "I regard *Cage for Lovers* . . ." (March 29, 1957); "Bobby Lewis's wonderful party . . ." (December 1, 1957); "That night, as we drank gin and ate hamburgers . . ." (September 3, 1959); "He finds me a combination . . ." (July 8, 1956); "Saw him and really was shattered . . ." (December 24, 1957); "The halls reek of old people . . ." (January 27, 1959); "Discovery that the only things I have . . ." (July 31, 1960); "Don't care if they turn it down completely . . ." (July 30, 1960). "Joe gasping and getting intravenous . . ." (August 21, 1960); "Joe improved mightily . . ." (September 22, 1960); "In afternoon he was 'floating on air' . . ." (November 10, 1960);

"Bunny and I, determined to be less than our sleepy age . . ." (February 15, 1961); "Typical of that loving golden Leo lad . . ." (February 14, 1965); "Every girl should know that in her wedding vows . . ." (February 15, 1962); the "reality" of the situation (February 18, 1962); "Must guard against the curious form death takes . . ." (February 22, 1962); "Someone asked me about the long marriage to Joe . . ." (March 8, 1962).

Quotations from Powell letters: "He got slowly worked up . . ." (DP to Phyllis Powell Cook, August 9, 1954); "We noticed a new advance . . ." (DP to Dr. Howard Zucker, February 9, 1957); "She has been living other people's lives . . ." (DP to Rosalind Baker Wilson, late 1956); "The dowdy and soppy aspects of Dickens . . ." (DP to Monroe Stearns, September 21, 1959); "A wing chopped off . . ." (DP to Phyllis Powell Cook, February 1960); "'I'd just love to, Aunt Dawn' . . ." (DP to Margaret De Silver, July 7, 1959); "More so than in my day . . ." (DP to Jack Sherman, March 22, 1961); "The difference between the boy and girl sex writers . . ." (DP to Edmund Wilson, August 15, 1962); "Would you say off-hand . . ." (DP to Phyllis Powell Cook, December 13, 1960); "Joe goes out once or twice a day . . ." (DP to Phyllis Powell Cook, November 3, 1961); "Get up, cook, wash dishes . . ." (ibid.).

Quotations from *The Wicked Pavilion*: "There was nothing unusual . . ." (page 4); "Philippe gave this question some judicious thought . . ." (page 9); "It was the first time he'd ever been in New York . . ." (page 11).

Quoted reviews of *The Wicked Pavilion*: *New York Times*, September 9, 1954; *New York Times*, September 12, 1954; *New York Herald Tribune*, September 12, 1954; *London Sunday Times*, November 18, 1954; *The New Yorker*, October 16, 1954. Other reviews: *Atlantic Monthly*, November 1954; *Kirkus*, July 1, 1954; *Library Journal*, September 1, 1954; *Saturday Review*, October 2, 1954.

Powell's own *Post* reviews include: Feiffer: *Sick Sick Sick* (July 6, 1958); *Short Stories of Russia Today*, edited by Yvonne Kapp (January 11, 1959); Holmes: *The Sheppard Murder Case* (August 13, 1961); Radin: *Lizzie Borden: The Untold Story;* Kronenberger: *A Month of Sundays* (April 16, 1961); Churchill: *The Improper Bohemians* (May 10, 1959); Hicks: *The Living Novel* (November 10, 1957); O'Hara: *Ourselves to Know* (February 28, 1960); McCarthy: *The Oasis* (August 14, 1949); Benchley: *Robert Benchley: A Biography* (November 13, 1955); Brinnin: *Dylan Thomas in America* (November 20, 1955); Graham: *Beloved Infidel* (January 4, 1959); Sagan: *A Certain Smile* (August 19, 1956); de Beauvoir: *America Day by Day* (December 20, 1953); Norman: *The Magic Maker: E. E. Cummings* (November 9, 1958); Norman: *Ezra Pound* (October 30, 1960); Gorey: *The Fatal Lozenge* and *The Hapless Child* (January 8, 1961); Jarrell: *Pictures from an Institution* (May 2, 1954); Swados: *Nights in the Gardens of Brooklyn* (January 29, 1961); Ingle: *Waters of the Edge* (January 17, 1954); Gaddis: *The Recognitions* (March 13, 1955).

Quoted reviews of *A Cage for Lovers*: *New York Times*, November 10, 1957; *New York Post*, October 19, 1957; *New York Herald Tribune*, October 20, 1957. Other reviews: *Booklist*, December 1, 1957; *Kirkus*, August 15, 1957; *Library Journal*, September 15, 1957; *San Francisco Chronicle*, November 24, 1957.

Powell's letter to Monroe Stearns was provided by his son Michael Stearns and is reprinted by his permission.

Chapter Ten: The End

The chapter epigram is taken from a diary entry made July 3, 1965. Other diary entries in this chapter: "Very vivid and shaking . . ." (June 24, 1962); "He wanted me to be sure . . ." (June 23, 1962); "Beautiful East River view . . ." (June 1, 1962); "In looking over Malcolm's comments . . ." (June 20, 1959); "Who was that lady . . ." (February 22, 1962); "Does she think we writers . . ." (January 12, 1963); "I have no equipment for prize-winning . . ." (March 8, 1963); description of Lake Erie College visit (May 26, 1964); tentative will (November 4, 1964); "He was in sarcastic Gousha dig mood . . ." (March 14, 1965); "Seven pages through two Ritalins . . ." (March 1, 1965); "To American Academy . . ." (May 19, 1965); "How wonderful if I had excitement . . ." (June 24, 1965); "How heavenly if I could get to work. . . ." (July 11, 1965); "God how wonderful if I could get some writing done . . ." (July 18, 1965); "Must try to Coué myself . . ." (July 18, 1965); "How alone we all are . . ." (July 3, 1965); "Most exhausting but worth it . . ." (July 29, 1965).

Quotations from Powell letters: "I am really fascinated by the aging process . . ." (DP to Phyllis Powell Cook, March 14, 1964); "Last year, a radium or X-ray job . . ." (DP to Alice Cook Hoover and Carol Cook Warstler, December 5, 1962); "She has a Murphy marvelous trait . . ." (DP to Gerald and Sara Murphy, March 5, 1963); "Exhausted by three years . . ." (DP to Malcolm Cowley, April 9, 1962); "The only place where people with nothing behind them . . ." (DP to Jack Sherman, circa June 1931); "Here is important *New Yorker* piece . . ." (DP to Phyllis Powell Cook, November 16, 1962); "I should have [the royalty statement] framed . . ." (DP to John Dos Passos, March 19, 1963); "It is terribly disheartening . . ." (DP to Alice Cook Hoover, January 10, 1963); "You will not be surprised to learn . . ." (DP to Phyllis Powell Cook, November 16, 1962); "The photograph was in fact a scream . . ." (DP to John Dos Passos, March 19, 1963); "How do you like me being that old flapper . . ." (DP to Jack Sherman, April 15, 1965); "Both are such efficient, willing girls . . ." (DP to Jack Sherman, October 7, 1965); "I adore the baby Hilary Dawn . . ." (DP to Jack Sherman, July 17, 1965); "Next thing I knew Sara had chuckles . . ." (DP to John Dos Passos, June 16, 1965); "I am sick of Civil Rights . . ." (ibid.); "Wildly irritated. . . . The author seems motivated . . ." (DP to Edmund Wilson, July 20, 1965); "I am a great Chaucerian . . ." (DP to Jack Sherman, October 7, 1965); "I am overwhelmed with admiration . . ." (DP to Phyllis Powell Cook, September 28, 1965); "Get started on novel . . ." (DP to Jack Sherman, May 13, 1965); "Surgeon said okay—my right . . ." (DP to Phyllis Powell Cook, late September or early October 1965); comments on Henry Fielding, Robert Ruark, and Dr. Robert Solley (DP to Jack Sherman, October 22, 1965).

Quotations from *The Golden Spur*: "A benign, white-haired old gentleman . . ." (page 7); "Can you tell me if there's something special . . ." (page 10).

Quoted reviews of *The Golden Spur*: *New York Times*, October 14, 1962; *New York Herald Tribune*, November 4, 1962; *Saturday Review*, January 12, 1963; *The New Yorker*, November 17, 1962. Other reviews: *New Statesman* (June 21, 1963); *Library Journal*, September 15, 1962; *Virginia Quarterly Review*, Spring 1963.

William Peterson's as-yet-unpublished "Dawn Powell Returns to Lake Erie College" is excerpted by kind permission of the author. The interview by W. M. H. van Okker appeared in *The Villager* on April 15, 1965.

The letter to Gerald and Sara Murphy is reprinted by permission of their daughter, Honoria Donnelly.

The quotation from Edmund Wilson is taken from his volume *The Sixties.*

Powell's poem about her treatment with barium is in the collection of Jack Sherman. The letter to Gerald Murphy about Dr. Solley is from the collection of Honoria Donnelly and is reprinted with her kind permission.

The excerpts and adaptations from Hannah Green's diary are published with the permission of her widower, John Wesley.

Excerpts from Robert H. Hethmon's taped interview with Dawn Powell are quoted with his permission.

Jack Sherman's letter about the death of Dawn Powell (written to Phyllis Powell Cook on November 15, 1965) is reprinted with his permission.

Epilogue: Afterward

Description of Jojo's reaction to his mother's death is from a letter by Jack Sherman, written on November 15, 1965, and addressed to Phyllis Powell Cook.

The bulk of the epilogue is based on interviews with Michelle Borsack, Jack Sherman, Rita Sherman, Jacqueline Miller Rice, the late Hannah Green, Carol Warstler, Dorothy Chapman, Phyllis Poccia, Rosalind Baker Wilson, Judith Faye Pett, Mark Chimsky, Michael Miller, and Anne Yarowsky.

The letter authorizing Dawn Powell's burial on Hart Island, written on May 4, 1970, by Jacqueline Rice, is in the archives of the Cornell Medical Center, New York.

❧ WORKS BY AND ABOUT
DAWN POWELL: AN
ABBREVIATED BIBLIOGRAPHY ❧

Novels

Whither. Boston: Small, Maynard, 1925.

She Walks in Beauty. New York: Brentano's, 1928.

The Bride's House. New York: Brentano's, 1929.

Dance Night. New York: Farrar and Rinehart, 1930.

The Tenth Moon. New York: Farrar and Rinehart, 1932; (reprinted, under Powell's original title, *Come Back to Sorrento*, South Royalton, Vt.: Steerforth, 1997).

The Story of a Country Boy. New York: Farrar and Rinehart, 1934.

Turn, Magic Wheel. New York: Farrar and Rinehart, 1936.

The Happy Island. New York: Farrar and Rinehart, 1938.

Angels on Toast. New York: Charles Scribner's Sons, 1940.

A Time to Be Born. New York: Charles Scribner's Sons, 1942.

My Home Is Far Away. New York: Charles Scribner's Sons, 1944.

The Locusts Have No King. New York: Charles Scribner's Sons, 1948.

The Wicked Pavilion. Boston: Houghton Mifflin, 1954.

A Man's Affair [abridged and rewritten version of *Angels on Toast*]. New York: Fawcett, 1956.

A Cage for Lovers. Boston: Houghton Mifflin, 1957.

The Golden Spur. New York: Viking Press, 1962.

Most of these books are now available from Steerforth Press, South Royalton, Vt.

Plays

Women at Four O'Clock. Written 1927; unpublished. Columbia University Library, Dawn Powell Collection.

Walking down Broadway. Written 1931; unpublished. Columbia University Library, Dawn Powell Collection.

Big Night. Written 1928 and revised through 1932; unpublished. With early drafts called *The Party*, Columbia University Library, Dawn Powell Collection.

Jig-Saw: A Comedy. New York: Farrar and Rinehart, 1934.

The Lion and the Lizard. Written 1934; unpublished. Columbia University Library, Dawn Powell Collection.

Every Other Day. Written 1939; unpublished. Columbia University Library, Dawn Powell Collection.

Red Dress. Setting of *She Walks in Beauty*, written 1937; unpublished. Columbia University Library, Dawn Powell Collection.

I'll Marry You Sunday. Musical adaptation of Shakespeare's *Taming of the Shrew*, written 1943; unpublished. Library of Congress.

You Should Have Brought Your Mink: A Teleplay. Written 1956; unpublished. Columbia University Library, Dawn Powell Collection.

The Golden Spur: A Musical Comedy. Written 1962–64; unfinished and unpublished. Columbia University Library, Dawn Powell Collection.

Short Stories

Although Powell wrote well over a hundred stories during her lifetime, only a few dozen have been identified to date. *Sunday, Monday and Always*, Powell's own selection of her best work in this genre, was published in Boston by Houghton Mifflin in 1952.

Selected Nonfiction

"Impressions of a First-Time Voter." *New York Sun*, November 8, 1919.

"What Are You Doing in My Dreams?" *Vogue*, October 1963.

"Staten Island, I Love You!" *Esquire*, October 1965.

Critical and Biographical Summaries
of Powell and Her Works

Feingold, Michael. "New York Stories." *Village Voice*, June 12, 1990.

Josephson, Matthew. "Dawn Powell: A Woman of *Esprit*." *Southern Review* 9 (1973).

Pett, Judith Faye. "Dawn Powell: Her Life and Her Fiction." Ph.D. diss., University of Iowa, 1981.

Vidal, Gore. "Dawn Powell: The American Writer." *New York Review of Books*, November 5, 1987.

Wilson, Edmund. "Dawn Powell: Greenwich Village in the Fifties." *The New Yorker*, November 17, 1962.

❧ SUPPLEMENTARY BIBLIOGRAPHY ✍

Over the course of the seven-year gestation of this book, I read extensively about people and places that were in one way or another associated with Dawn Powell. In some cases, I may not have taken anything specific from a text listed herein; still, because I read all of these volumes during the time I was working on my biography, I cannot imagine that each did not affect my thinking.

Aaron, Daniel. *Writers on the Left.* New York: Harcourt, Brace and World, 1961.

Baker, Carlos. *Ernest Hemingway: A Life Story.* New York: Charles Scribner's Sons, 1969.

Berg, A. Scott. *Max Perkins: Editor of Genius.* New York: E. P. Dutton, 1978.

Berman, Avis. *Rebels on Eighth Street: Juliana Force and the Whitney Museum of American Art.* New York: Atheneum, 1990.

Bishop, Elizabeth. *One Art: Letters.* Selected and edited by Robert Giroux. New York: Farrar, Straus and Giroux, 1994.

Bloch, Beverle Rochelle. *John Howard Lawson's* Processional: *Modernism in American Theatre in the Twenties.* Ann Arbor: University of Michigan Dissertation Services, 1988.

Botsford, Harry. *New York's 100 Best Restaurants.* Portland: Bond Wheelwright, 1955.

Brenman-Gibson, Margaret. *Clifford Odets: American Playwright*. New York: Atheneum, 1981.

Brightman, Carol. *Writing Dangerously: Mary McCarthy and Her World*. New York: Clarkson Potter, 1992.

Brooks, Paul. *Two Park Street: A Publishing Memoir*. Boston: Houghton Mifflin, 1986.

Cheney, Anne. *Millay in Greenwich Village*. Tuscaloosa: University of Alabama Press, 1975.

Cheyney, E. Ralph, ed. *The Independent Poetry Anthology 1925*. New York: Burke Printing Company, 1925.

Churchill, Allen. *The Improper Bohemians: Greenwich Village in Its Heyday*. New York: E. P. Dutton, 1959.

Clayton, Douglas. *Floyd Dell: The Life and Times of an American Rebel*. Chicago: Ivan R. Dee, 1994.

Clurman, Harold. *The Fervent Years: The Group Theatre and the '30s*. New York: Harcourt Brace Jovanovich, 1975.

Crawford, Cheryl. *One Naked Individual: My Fifty Years in the Theatre*. Indianapolis and New York: Bobbs-Merrill, 1977.

Donnelly, Honoria Murphy, with Richard N. Billings. *Sara and Gerald: Villa America and After*. New York: Times Books, 1982.

Dos Passos, John. *The Best Times*. New York: New American Library, 1966.

————. *The Fourteenth Chronicle: Letters and Diaries of John Dos Passos*. Edited by Townsend Ludington. Boston: Gambit, 1973.

Douglas, Ann. *Terrible Honesty: Mongrel Manhattan in the 1920s*. New York: Farrar, Straus and Giroux, 1995.

Drake, William. *The First Wave: Women Poets in America 1915–1945*. New York: Macmillan, 1987.

Drutman, Irving. *Good Company: A Memoir, Mostly Theatrical*. Boston: Little, Brown, 1976.

Eaton, Walter Prichard. *The Theatre Guild: The First Ten Years*. New York: Brentano's, 1929.

Fariello, Griffin. *Red Scare: Memories of the American Inquisition*. New York: Norton, 1995.

Field, Andrew. *Djuna: The Life and Times of Djuna Barnes*. New York: G. P. Putnam's Sons, 1983.

Fiske, Dwight. *Without Music*. New York: The Chatham Press, 1933.

————. *Why Should Penguins Fly?* New York: Robert McBride and Company, 1936.

Gallagher, Dorothy. *All the Right Enemies: The Life and Murder of Carlo Tresca*. New Brunswick, N.J.: Rutgers University Press, 1988.

Gelderman, Carol. *Mary McCarthy: A Life*. New York: St. Martin's Press, 1988.

Gorelik, Mordecai. *New Theatres for Old*. New York: Samuel French, 1940.

Green, Jack. *Fire the Bastards!* Normal, Ks.: Dalkey Archive Press, 1992.

Gross, Margaret Geissman. *Dancing on the Table: A History of Lake Erie College*. Burnsville, Ohio: Cedo Valley Books, 1993.

Gruen, John. *The Party's Over Now*. New York: Viking, 1972.

Hall, Lee. *Elaine and Bill: Portrait of a Marriage*. New York: Harper-Collins, 1993.

Hart, Henry, ed. *American Writers' Congress*. New York: International Publishers, 1935.

Hatcher, Harland, ed. *The Ohio Guide: Ohio Writers Project*. New York: Oxford University Press, 1940.

Hawk, Dorothy. *Shelby, Ohio Sesquicentennial, 1984*. Shelby, Ohio: Shelby Ohio Sesquicentennial Committee, 1984.

Hemingway, Ernest. *A Movable Feast*. New York: Charles Scribner's Sons, 1964.

Hertell, E. Sinclair. *New York City Guide and Almanac 1957–1958*. New York: New York University Press, 1958.

Hicks, Granville. *The Great Tradition*. New York: Macmillan, 1935.

Himelstein, Morgan. *Drama Was a Weapon*. New Brunswick, N.J.: Rutgers University Press, 1963.

Honan, William H., ed. *The Greenwich Village Guide*. New York: Bryan Publications, 1959.

Howe, Irving. *Sherwood Anderson*. New York: William Sloane Associates, 1951.

Jackson, Kenneth T., ed. *The Encyclopedia of New York City*. New Haven, Conn.: Yale University Press, 1995.

James, Rian. *Dining in New York: An Intimate Guide* ["repeal edition"]. New York: John Day, 1934.

Josephson, Matthew. *Life among the Surrealists*. New York: Holt, Rinehart and Winston, 1962.

————. *Infidel in the Temple*. New York: Alfred A. Knopf, 1967.

Kazin, Alfred. *On Native Grounds*. New York: Alfred A. Knopf, 1942.

Kreymbourg, Alfred. *Our Singing Strength: An Outline of American Poetry 1620–1930*. New York: Coward-McCann, 1929.

Lawson, John Howard. *The Hidden Heritage*. New York: Citadel Press. 1950.

LeClercq, Jacques. *Show Cases*. New York: Macy-Masius, 1928.

Levine, Ira A. *Left-Wing Dramatic Theory in the American Theatre*. Ann Arbor: University of Michigan Research Press, 1985.

Lewis, Joseph. *Ingersoll the Magnificent*. New York: Freethought Press, 1957.

Ludington, Townsend. *John Dos Passos: A Twentieth-Century Odyssey*. New York: E. P. Dutton, 1980.

Lynn, Kenneth S. *Hemingway*. New York: Simon & Schuster, 1987.

McAuliffe, Kevin Michael. *The Great American Newspaper: The Rise and Fall of the* Village Voice. New York: Charles Scribner's Sons, 1978.

Mellow, James R. *Hemingway: A Life without Consequences*. Boston: Houghton Mifflin, 1992.

Meyers, Jeffrey. *Edmund Wilson: A Biography*. Boston, Houghton Mifflin, 1995.

Miller, Linda Patterson. *Letters from the Lost Generation: Gerald and Sara Murphy and Friends.* New Brunswick, N.J.: Rutgers University Press, 1991.

Porter, Philip W. *Cleveland: Confused City on a See-Saw.* Columbus: Ohio State University Press, 1976.

Randrianarivony-Koziol, Liliane. *Techniques of Commitment in the Thirties: A Study of the Selected Plays of John Howard Lawson.* Ann Arbor: University of Michigan Dissertation Services, 1982.

Rideout, Walter. *The Radical Novel in the United States 1900–1954.* New York: Hill and Wang, 1956.

Rider, Freemont. *Rider's New York City.* New York: Macmillan, 1924.

Santmyer, Helen Hooven. *Ohio Town.* Columbus: Ohio State University Press, 1962.

Shaw, Archer H. *The Plain Dealer: One Hundred Years in Cleveland.* New York: Alfred A. Knopf, 1942.

Smith, Wendy. *Real Life Drama: The Group Theatre and America, 1931–1940.* New York: Alfred A. Knopf, 1990.

Smith, William Jay. *The Spectra Hoax.* Middletown, Conn.: Wesleyan University Press, 1961.

Spoto, Donald. *Lenya: A Life.* Boston: Little, Brown, 1989.

Trollope, Frances. *Domestic Manners of the Americans.* Reprint, New York: Alfred A. Knopf, 1949.

Van Gelder, Robert. *Writers and Writing.* New York: Charles Scribner's Sons, 1947.

Van Tassel, David D., with John J. Grabowski. *The Encyclopedia of Cleveland History.* Bloomington: Indiana University Press, 1987.

Walsh, Richard J. *Zanesville and Thirty-six Other American Communities.* New York: Literary Digest, 1927.

Ware, Caroline F. *Greenwich Village 1920–1930.* Boston: Houghton Mifflin, 1935.

Warfel, Harry D. *American Novelists of Today.* New York: American Book Company, 1951.

Williams, Jay. *Stage Left*. New York: Charles Scribner's Sons, 1974.

Wilson, Edmund. *Letters on Literature and Politics*. Selected and edited by Elena Wilson. New York: Farrar, Straus and Giroux, 1977.

————. *The Twenties*. Edited with an introduction by Leon Edel. New York: Farrar, Straus and Giroux, 1975.

————. *The Thirties*. Edited with an introduction by Leon Edel. New York: Farrar, Straus and Giroux, 1980.

————. *The Forties*. Edited with an introduction by Leon Edel. New York: Farrar, Straus and Giroux, 1983.

————. *The Fifties*. Edited with an introduction by Leon Edel. New York: Farrar, Straus and Giroux, 1986.

————. *The Sixties*. Edited with an introduction by Lewis M. Dabney. New York: Farrar, Straus and Giroux, 1993.

Wilson, Rosalind Baker. *Near the Magician: A Memoir of My Father, Edmund Wilson*. New York: Grove Weidenfeld, 1989.

✤ ACKNOWLEDGMENTS ✤

This is the first full biography of Dawn Powell, and in many ways, it was started too late. Had I begun work in, say, 1981, instead of ten years later, I might have talked directly with Powell's sister Phyllis, several additional nieces and nephews, and a great number of classmates, colleagues, editors, and friends. But it simply wasn't to be. As Powell's supposed rival Dorothy Parker once put it, "How people die. Lord, how people die!"

Still, the release of Powell's papers in 1994 was of extraordinary help in the creation of this book. Here at last were Powell's diaries, appointment books, manuscripts, newspaper clippings—even some of the angry letters from creditors that Powell and her husband received during their periods of poverty. Instead of sketchy gossip and rumor, here, finally, were some original sources from which to trace a life.

I owe an incalculable debt of gratitude to the members of Dawn Powell's extended family for their honesty, courtesy, and spectacular generosity. Jack Sherman, one of the world's great gentlemen, supported and encouraged my efforts from the day we met, sitting for countless interviews, copying photographs and letters, and correcting errors of fact and fancy. In guiding me through this project, Jack has forever transformed my life; it is fitting that he should be not only this book's dedicatee but the namesake of our youngest son, John Sherman Page.

Rita Sherman, the sister with whom Jack Sherman has lived for half a century, has also been wonderfully hospitable, and we have spent many hours in conversation together over sweet rolls and pots of strong tea. Carol Warstler went so far as to endure a long ride through a January blizzard to talk about her Aunt Dawn; I was a stranger to her at the time, but we immediately became fast friends, and the letters Powell wrote to her mother, the late Phyllis Powell Cook, permit a unique vantage point from which to view the author's familial relations.

I should also like to thank Dorothy and John Chapman, Phyllis and Nicholas Poccia, Richard and Judy McLaughlin, Dwaine Warstler, Robin and Debra Warstler, Wendy Silver, Vicki Johnson, and Holly Hoover, all of whom relayed stories of the Powell and Sherman families for me.

Now in his late seventies, Joseph R. Gousha, Jr., retains a phenomenal memory for people, places, and dates; in 1993, at the suggestion of his devoted social worker Michelle Borsack, he assembled a notebook called "Memories of My Mother," a dazzlingly accurate document that has proved invaluable on numerous occasions. I have intended no slight by referring to him as Jojo throughout the book; it is the name to which he has answered all his life, and recurring references to Joe and Joe Jr. would have become both cumbersome and confusing.

My mother, Elizabeth Thaxton Page, indulged her son with a deeply appreciated loan that allowed the Powell Papers to be brought to the Rare Book and Manuscript Library of Columbia University, a hundred yards or so from the hospital where Jojo was born and where Dawn Powell died. It is only the latest manifestation of the unwavering support she has given me all of my life.

I am grateful to Peter Skolnik, legal representative of the Powell Estate, for his support and help on matters too numerous to mention, and for his initial, quixotic agreement to take on our case. My friends Bruce Brubaker, Hilary Dyson, and especially Paula McDonald proved highly resourceful in tracking down hundreds of names and dates in libraries and university archives.

My relationship with Jacqueline Miller Rice has necessarily been a tangled one, and there were several years during which we barely spoke or communicated. Thereafter, many different times were set aside for a full-fledged interview; none of these ever came to fruition, for a variety of reasons. I hope we have settled our differences and that I have treated her fairly in these pages. If so, it is due in large part to Rosalind Baker Wilson, who served as a go-between and trusted friend to both of us—and a terrific source of information herself.

David Kanzeg of WCPN-FM in Cleveland has taken me through most of Ohio in search of Powelliana, and we have had many intensive discussions of Powell's work. Daniel Rhodebeck not only was savvy enough to conduct the sole interview with Phyllis Powell Cook (in 1978) but has been enormously generous in searching out archival material about Mount Gilead and Morrow County for me. William Peterson has been generous with his research on (and firsthand knowledge of) Powell's association with Lake Erie College.

I deeply regret that Hannah Green did not live to see this book. She was a brave woman and a wonderful friend, eloquent and tireless on the subject of Dawn Powell. I am grateful to her husband, John Wesley, for permitting me access to her diaries from the early 1960s onward, which span her association with Powell.

Avis Berman has served as my unofficial artistic adviser on this book, putting into perspective the lives and work of Dawn's many painter and sculptor friends; any mistakes I made in this unfamiliar territory are mine alone. Robert H. Hethmon spent hours talking with me about Powell's relationship with John Howard Lawson and then put me in touch with Jeffrey Lawson, the playwright's son. Hethmon also made the only surviving recording of Powell's voice—a unique document that he has kindly shared with me.

Joan Schellenberg and Anita Sparrock of Cornell Medical Center were helpful in locating Powell's physical remains. Special thanks are due Commander Tom Antenten of the New York City Department of

Correction for the information he provided about the mysterious Hart Island. The staff of St. Michael's Cemetery and Crematory in Queens was helpful in confirming the final resting place of Joseph Gousha.

Hundreds of other people have also contributed to this book, whether in personal interviews, by phone, or through the mail, offering facts, comments, suggestions, and clarifications. I apologize to those whose names have been inadvertently left out and will attempt to repair all omissions in a later edition.

And so I am grateful to Lee Adams, Antoinette Akers, Felipe Alfau, David C. Barnett, Gary Bennett, Nellie Bly, Carl Brandt, David Brezovec, Rachel Brown, Arnold R. A. Browne, Margaret Carson, Lucy Dos Passos Coggin, William Cole, John Gregory Connor, Robert Cowley, Camilla Crossgrove, Roger L. Crossgrove, Hope Hale Davis, Peter Davis, Anna Lou Kapell Dehavenon, Thomas Dobell, the late Maurice Dolbier, Honoria Murphy Donnelly, Will Lee Doyle, Susan Elliott, Olive Ernst, Allan Evans, the late Eleanor Farnham, Johanna Fiedler, Chip Fleischer, Michael Flynn, Gwendolyn Haverstock Freed, Dorothy Gallagher, Sylviane Gold, Christopher Gray, Elise and Arnold Goodman, Margaret Geissman Gross, Gladys Haddad, Jim Halbe, Anna Strunsky Hamburger, Elizabeth W. Harries, Laura Harris, Carol and Patrick Hemingway, Jeffrey Herman, Christina Hinton, Polly Holliday, Susan Hood, Neill Hughes, Russia Hughes, Ben Janney, Karen Johnson, Marjorie Howard Johnson, Betsy Jolas, Fred Kaplan, the late Frances Keene, the late Murray Kempton, Dr. Ben Kightlinger, Susan Koscis, Allan Kozinn, Hildie Kraus, Miles Krueger, Jeffrey Lawson, H. David Leventhal, Sir Michael Levey, the late Robert Lewis, Hanna Loewy, Steve Logan, Gloria Loomis, Townsend Ludington, Ben McCommon, David McDonald, Heather McGahee, the late Loren MacIver, James Magruder, Sally Maier, Andrew Manshel, Dawn Mendelson, Katharine Meyer, Claire Lissfelt Myers, Michael Miller, Marguerite Mills, Donald Mineldi, Thomas Monsell, Michael Moore, the late Charles and Diana Norman, Patrick O'Connor, Dr. Ellis B. Page, Dr.

Richard L. Page and Jean Reynolds Page, Judith Faye Pett, Morris Philipson, Dr. Jordan M. Phillips and Mary Zoe Phillips, Gabriel Pilar, Robert Pound, Eva Resnikova, Daniel Rhodebeck, Marcelline Smith Rice, Pamela Rice, Bryan Robertson, Cliff Robertson, Molly J. Robinson, Douglas Rose, Dr. Morton Schwimmer, Michael Sexton, Gene Seymour, Charles and Elizabeth Sigman, Phyllis Singer, Alfred Slote, Michael Stearns, Mark Steuve, Roger Straus, Jane Bouche Strong, Charles Strouse, Anthony Tommasini, Cia Toscanini, Amanda Vaill, Gore Vidal, Thomas Vinciguerra, Amei Wallach, Robert Wallsten, the late Andrews Wanning, Esther Wanning, Thomas Wanning, Harriet Ward, Alan Weeks, Maggy Wendel, Patricia Bosworth Wilson, Rosalind Baker Wilson, Robert Wyatt, Francis Wyndham, Anne Yarowsky, and Michael Zubal—all of whom granted interviews, answered questions, or helped in some significant way in my research.

Thanks to John Stark Bellamy II, Sharon Hoskins, Susan Mann, and Sandy Stuart, who were of enormous help tracking down historical data in Ohio. Thanks also to the Western Reserve Historical Society, the Harry Ransom Humanities Research Center at the University of Texas, Princeton University Library, the Boston Public Library, the Newberry Library in Chicago, the Beinecke Rare Book and Manuscript Library at Yale University, the University of Virginia Library, and Temple University Library, all of which made copies of their holdings available to me.

Thanks to the staff of the Columbia University Rare Book and Manuscript Library, particularly Jean Ashton and Bernard Crystal, who have been patient beyond all reason in dealing with my numerous requests. Thanks to the research librarians at the lamented *New York Newsday* and at the *Washington Post;* to Barbara Emch, Amanda Byers, Carole Houk, and Christopher Bennett at Lake Erie College; to Charles Silver at the Museum of Modern Art; to Charles Roberts at the Library of Congress; and to Jeanne Somers at the Kent State University Archives.

All gratitude to my literary agent, Melanie Jackson, who believed in the Powell revival from the beginning and fought hard to make it happen. Melanie introduced me to Ray Roberts at Henry Holt, a patient, painstaking, and persuasive editor with whom I hope to work for many years. Ray, in turn, put the manuscript in the hands of Dorothy Straight, a marvelous copy editor. I am also thankful for my ongoing association with Steerforth Press—particularly with Michael Moore, Chip Fleischer, Alan Lelchuk, and Thomas Powers.

Three of my closest friends—Leonard Altman, Kevin Cawley, and G. Christopher Fish—died during my work on this book. I remember them all with profound affection. Christopher drove through Ohio with me on several occasions, and we shared two lost, lovely afternoons with Jack and Rita Sherman in Shelby.

My wife, Vanessa Weeks Page, read this manuscript several times and played an enormous part in shaping the final work. M. George Stevenson gave the manuscript a painfully thorough examination after it was supposedly finished and radically improved the quality of the finished book. Thanks also to my sons, William Dean, Robert Leonard, and John Sherman Page. My oldest boy, William, assisted me in some editorial duties, which he handled both easily and smoothly.

Most of *Dawn Powell: A Biography* was written in Lakewood, Ohio, during a much-appreciated sabbatical made possible by my employers at the *Washington Post*. I would like to thank my colleagues Peter Hayes, John Pancake, Deborah Heard, David Von Drehle, Robert Kaiser, Leonard Downie Jr., and Donald Graham for their patience and indulgence. Thanks also to *Post* music critic emeritus Joseph McLellan for stepping once more into the maelstrom of running the department in my absence.

Tim Page
May 20, 1998
New York City

Index

Italic page numbers indicate principal discussions of works by Dawn Powell.